MAINSTREAMING

Practical Ideas
for
Educating Hearing-Impaired Students

CUED SPEECH CENTER
P. O. BOX 31345
RALEIGH, N. C. 27612
(919) 781-1105

MAINSTREAMING

Practical Ideas
for
Educating Hearing-Impaired Students

For Secondary and Postsecondary
Teachers and Administrators

Edited By
Milo E. Bishop, Ph.D.

The Alexander Graham Bell Association for the Deaf, Inc.
3417 Volta Place, N.W., Washington, D.C. 20007, U.S.A.

Library of Congress Catalogue Number 79-53680
ISBN 0-88200-126-4

This Book Is Dedicated To
BETH DUFFIN WHITEHEAD

A beloved friend and talented colleague whose dedication to improving educational opportunities for hearing-impaired students was demonstrated for the last time when she left her sickbed to help present a short course on mainstreaming at the June 1978 Convention of the Alexander Graham Bell Association for the Deaf. No one in the audience suspected that Beth would die of cancer in less than one month. Her optimism and courage in facing this dreaded disease reflected the way she lived her life. Those who knew her well will never forget her. Those who did not will never know how much they missed.

Acknowledgments

I wish to express sincere gratitude to the many individuals who have worked so hard to make this book a reality. I am indebted to my colleagues at the National Technical Institute for the Deaf (NTID) who expended countless hours of personal time preparing chapters and reviewing the work of others. Many staff members in our word processing, media production and duplication departments were extremely responsive to our needs. Without the assistance of these dedicated people, the publishing date for this book would have been significantly delayed. A number of individuals not directly connected in writing this book were also very helpful in gathering information and resource materials. Rosyln Rosen from Gallaudet College greatly assisted in the preparation of Chapter 2. Phil Weinbach of NTID's Office of Public Information, and Linda Bardenstein of the Department of Media Services compiled a list of resources which readers can use to inform others about impaired hearing and its effects (Appendix A). Julie Purchase, my executive secretary, Barbara Williams and Jackie Blackburn, members of my office staff, were always ready and willing to do any task needing to be completed. Julie Goldstein and Monica Schwab were very helpful in serving as liaisons to the publisher. Ron Hein freely gave of his time and talents in editing the references. Clearly this book is the result of hard work and dedicated efforts of many people. Unfortunately, it's impossible to recognize them all. There is one person, however, who contributed so much to this book that I will never be able to adequately express my gratitude. My heartfelt appreciation is extended to Mary Dallas for her very able assistance in proofreading and making numerous helpful editorial suggestions. Without her help this book would never have been a reality.

Finally, I would like to express love and gratitude to my family for their patience, understanding, and encouragement during the preparation of this book.

—Milo E. Bishop, Editor

About the Authors

Milo E. Bishop is the Associate Dean of Career Development Programs at the National Technical Institute for the Deaf in Rochester, New York. Since joining NTID in 1972 he has played a major role in mainstreaming deaf students attending the Institute. Prior to this, Dr. Bishop taught preschool deaf children at Purdue University and in the middle and upper schools at the Utah School for the Deaf. He received a B.S. in education of the deaf at the University of Utah, an M.S. in speech science at the University of New Mexico, and a Ph.D. in speech and hearing science at Purdue University.

Dr. Bishop has written many presentations and publications dealing with education of the deaf, and is co-author with Ron Hein of a two-volume *Annotated Bibliography on Mainstreaming* (1978). He has conducted many workshops in schools for the deaf in the United States and in Europe, and as keynote speaker at the European Teachers Federation meeting in Bordeaux, France, in 1977, his topic was mainstreaming. He is also actively involved in public education in the Rochester, New York, area where he serves on the local school board.

William E. Castle joined the staff of NTID in 1968 as Assistant to the Vice President. He became Dean of the Institute in 1969 and in 1977 was named Dean and Director.

Prior to joining NTID, Dr. Castle was Associate Secretary for Research and Scientific Affairs for the American Speech, Language and Hearing Association, where he served as Project Director of all activities of the Joint Committee on Audiology and Education of the Deaf, as Executive Secretary for the Joint Committee on Dentistry and Speech Pathology-Audiology, and was instrumental in obtaining federal support for those committees. He also obtained a two-year grant from the Vocational Rehabilitation Administration for a study on manpower and manpower utilization in speech pathology and audiology.

He has also been on the faculty of St. Cloud (Minn.) State College, Central Washington State College, and the University of Virginia.

Dr. Castle is a graduate of Northern State Teachers College (B.S.), State University of Iowa (M.A.), and Stanford University (Ph.D.).

Barry R. Culhane is Chairperson of the Academic Department for General Education at NTID. This department is responsible for the educational support services provided to the approximately 250 students mainstreamed in general education courses at RIT each academic quarter. He received his B.A. in psychology from the University of Windsor, Canada, and his Ed.D. in development, learning, and instruction from the University of Rochester.

Prior to joining NTID, Dr. Culhane served as Clinical Director of the Psychodiagnostic Laboratory for Learning Disabled Children at the University of Rochester. He is a trustee for the New York Association for the Learning Disabled and Chairperson of the American Educational Research Association's Special Interest Group on Education of Deaf People.

Dr. Culhane has authored numerous articles and conducted many workshops related to the educational process for learning-disabled and hearing-impaired individuals. His teaching responsibilities include courses in the areas of psychology, child development, and parenting.

Loy E. Golladay lost his hearing at age 8 and, therefore, has a strong empathy for deaf students and their special problems. He has taught English literature and reading to deaf students at the high school and college levels for more than four decades. His experience includes the editing of school and professional publications; college-preparatory curriculum planning; captioning of recreational and educational films for the deaf; a variety of professional writing and speaking workshops, and other experience-sharing activities as a career teacher with the hearing impaired. He was readability and language editor of the Dictionary of Idioms for the Deaf (American School for the Deaf, 1966). He joined the NTID staff in 1969, and in 1976 he received the Rochester Institute of Technology Eisenhart Award for Outstanding Teacher of the Year.

Mr. Golladay holds a B.A. in liberal arts and an M.A. in English from Gallaudet College, Washington, D.C., and an M.Ed. in reading pedagogy and language arts from the University of Hartford, Connecticut. He is presently Associate Professor of English and General Education at NTID.

Ron Hein, a native of Colorado, completed his B.A. in special education (K-12) at the University of Northern Colorado in 1972. He is currently completing his dissertation at the Center for Development, Learning, and Instruction at the University of Rochester. Mr. Hein is a Research Assistant at NTID where he is researching learning strategies and techniques designed to improve deaf students' comprehension of prose materials. Along with Milo E. Bishop, he is co-author of the two-volume *Annotated Bibliography on Mainstreaming* (1978).

William Hinkle joined the staff of NTID in 1975 as Chairperson of the General Studies Education Support Team. He is presently serving as the Assistant Dean and Director of Technical and Professional Education Programs and has responsibility for all the degree-granting programs of NTID and the students enrolled therein. Dr. Hinkle has responsibility for the approximately 200 students mainstreamed in the other colleges of RIT. As such, he is very interested in the process of integrated education and in the delineation and delivery of special services to hearing-impaired students.

He has a B.S. (1965) from Bloomsburg (Pa.) State College, an M.S. (1969) and a Ph.D. (1971) in speech pathology from Purdue University.

T. Alan Hurwitz is Director of the Office of Support Services at NTID. This office is responsible for the training of interpreters, notetakers, and tutors and for providing interpreting services. The son of deaf parents, Alan was born profoundly deaf and was trained at Central Institute for the Deaf in St. Louis for 10 years before attending public schools in Sioux City, Iowa, as a mainstreamed student. Mr. Hurwitz received his B.S. in electrical engineering at Washington University and M.S. in electrical engineering at St. Louis University. He worked as Associate Electronics Engineer and Computer Specialist at McDonnell-Douglas Corporation for five years prior to coming to NTID in 1970. Presently Mr. Hurwitz is a doctoral candidate in curriculum at the University of Rochester and expects to complete his dissertation by 1980. Mr. Hurwitz has served as president of the Empire State Association of the Deaf since 1975 and is a member of the Executive Board of the National Association of the Deaf.

Mr. Hurwitz is familiar with mainstreaming, as he was a consumer of such services himself and now is a provider and manager of this type of support service. As the father of two deaf children, he is able to see some direct effects of current mainstreaming efforts on students.

Lawrence L. Mothersell received undergraduate and graduate degrees from the State University of New York at Geneseo in special education, general education, and English. He has studied curriculum development at the University of Rochester and is currently completing study in theology and Biblical studies at the Colgate Rochester Divinity School.

Since 1969 Mr. Mothersell has taught deaf students at NTID, where he received the Outstanding Teacher Award in 1971. He has taught numerous college-level, integrated classes in the humanities.

Mr. Mothersell holds memberships in the Conference of American Instructors of the Deaf, the Registry of Interpreters for the Deaf (both national and New York State units), the National Association of the Deaf, and the International Association of Parents of the Deaf. He has a deaf daughter and many friends in the field of deaf education.

Russell T. Osguthorpe is a research associate in the Department of Research and Development at NTID. He has directed the development of educational programs in the areas of tutoring and notetaking, leadership training, and career decision making. Dr. Osguthorpe is the author of numerous publications including journal articles and instructional materials, and has made presentations at educational conventions. Most of his research and development efforts have focused on assisting handicapped and other low-achieving students. He holds a Ph.D. in instructional psychology from Brigham Young University.

E. Ross Stuckless is presently a professor and Director of the Office for Integrative Research at NTID. He did his undergraduate work in honor psychology at the University of Toronto, obtained his master's degree in education of the deaf at Gallaudet College, and received his Ph.D. in special education and rehabilitation in 1963 at the University of Pittsburgh. Work experiences include being a houseparent, a psychologist, and a teacher in schools for the deaf.

Dr. Stuckless is the author of numerous papers on the education of the deaf. He brings both a personal and a professional interest to his work, as he has a deaf brother whose elementary and secondary education included a mix of mainstream and residential school experiences.

Karl R. White is Chairperson for the Department of Research and Development at NTID. He received his undergraduate degree at Brigham Young University, and his M.A. and Ph.D. in educational research and evaluation methodology from the University of Colorado, Boulder.

Dr. White has worked extensively in the areas of test development, program evaluation, and applied research. He is the author of numerous articles and presentations at educational conventions, and has conducted a variety of workshops at schools for the deaf around the country.

Beth Duffin Whitehead, to whom this book is dedicated, had experience in teaching deaf children in a residential situation, a private day school for the deaf, and in a public school where deaf children from self-contained classrooms were mainstreamed into classes with hearing children. She had also worked with children with various other handicaps who were being mainstreamed into public schools. At NTID, she assisted in developing the Tutor/Notetaking Program and served as Coordinator of the Tutor/Notetaking Training Services. She earned her M.S. in deaf education from the University of Oklahoma.

Anna B. Witter is Staff Chairperson of NTID's Interpreting Services Section. She served as coordinator of the Interpreting Services/Referral and Informational Center at the joint office of the Georgia Association of the Deaf and the Georgia Registry of Interpreters for the Deaf before coming to NTID. Ms. Witter has interpreted in a wide variety of settings, from educational situations to courtrooms. She holds a Comprehensive Skills Certificate from the National Registry of Interpreters for the Deaf, and is one of the few interpreters in the country to be certified as Legal Specialist Interpreter. Ms. Witter has coordinated interpreter training programs at NTID since 1976 and has been involved in interpreter workshops under the auspices of the National Interpreter Training Consortium.

Table of Contents

List of Tables

List of Figures

Introduction

Regular classes, the primary educational environment for normally hearing students, are one of several educational environments which can serve students with hearing impairments. In the literature, the process of integrating the deaf minority and the hearing mainstream is sometimes referred to as regular class placement, fusing, or "mainstreaming." Whatever the term, mainstreaming, when appropriately implemented, has proven to be an effective educational process for some youngsters. For others, it has been less than satisfactory.

The purpose of this book is not to debate the relative merits of mainstreaming as compared with other educational processes. Neither is it to debate whether or not mainstreaming should be implemented. The fact is, mainstreaming *is* being implemented all across the country. Teachers, administrators, and special educators suddenly, and without preparation, find themselves "caught up" in this movement to mainstream hearing-impaired individuals. Frequently they feel compelled by parents and the law to make decisions about how to best educate hearing-impaired students *in* a mainstreamed environment. They must develop an individualized education program (IEP) for each student describing what the student will accomplish. In the midst of this unfamiliar situation an interpreter is requested for one student, aural/oral rehabilitation for another, notetaking and/or tutor for still another. Then when one seeks assistance from professionals experienced with the deaf one may well be faced with conflicting counsel. Some professionals strongly advocate that students be taught using an "oral" approach. Others advocate use of "total communication." It is no wonder that one can become confused and frustrated when facing this challenge.

This book is written to help reduce the confusion and the frustration experienced by public school personnel suddenly faced with educating hearing-impaired students. Its preparation is sponsored by the National Technical Institute for the Deaf (NTID). NTID's experience in mainstreaming over 2,300 hearing-impaired students during the last 10 years places NTID in a unique position to be helpful to those embarking on this exciting but demanding challenge. This one-of-a-kind facility was created by an Act of Congress in 1965 and has as its primary mission the preparation of postsecondary deaf students for economic parity and personal satisfaction in the mainstream of the American society. It was no accident that Rochester Institute of Technology (RIT), located in Rochester, New York, was chosen over 30 other major universities as the host institution for this national center. RIT, with its internationally recognized programs in graphic arts, photography, and the crafts and with its equally excellent programs in science, technology, business, and human services, has been a quiet leader in educational innovation for 150 years. Cooperative work experience was one such innovation begun at RIT in 1912 and now being embraced by colleges and universities across the country.

Placing NTID on the RIT campus has provided deaf students full access to these excellent baccalaureate and master-level programs in addition to the technical level programs offered by NTID. These career programs combined with communications and personal social preparation have resulted in 97 percent of the graduates being placed in jobs upon entry into the work force.

With 10 years of successful experience NTID is now ready to share what it has learned about the educational mainstreaming of hearing-impaired students. This book is written specifically for those teachers, administrators, and supervisors who are uncertain as to how to appropriately meet the educational needs of hearing-impaired students. It should also prove useful as a text and/or resource book for those preparing to become teachers.

The focus of this book is on the adolescent and young adult age group. Nevertheless, most of the issues, principles, and strategies are applicable for younger students. The first six chapters should be especially helpful to those involved in deciding when and to what extent a hearing-impaired student will be mainstreamed. An introduction to impaired hearing and its implications for educating hearing-impaired students is provided for those unfamiliar with this handicap. Public Law 94-142 and Section 504 of the Rehabilitation Act of 1973 are reviewed in terms of the social, educational, and legal forces leading to these laws and their implications for educating hearing-impaired individuals. Critical issues needing consideration are discussed. For example, is mainstreaming a goal, or is mainstreaming an educational process which should not be confused with the goal of education? Models and processes commonly used in mainstreaming are reviewed and contrasted. Factors to be considered in selecting the appropriate process for a given student are discussed, and practical considerations are presented for assessing student strengths and weaknesses in order to decide the extent to which a student should be mainstreamed.

The last five chapters focus on specific strategies that teachers and program managers should use to better meet the needs of hearing-impaired students who are mainstreamed. Suggestions are provided for selecting, preparing, or modifying materials which are appropriate for use with hearing-impaired students. These suggestions focus on the physical characteristics of the classroom; on the various ways of communicating; and on the valuable manipulation of methods, materials, and media.

The last three chapters describe support services which have worked well at NTID, and have been adapted for use in secondary programs. Suggestions are made for selecting and training interpreters, tutors, and notetakers. A detailed and professional view is drawn of the educational interpreter (oral and manual), and equal attention is given to the principles of tutoring and notetaking. The options of organizing professionals, paraprofessionals, and volunteers are provided with final attention given to the management of a support team.

Conspicuously absent from this book are suggestions regarding important areas such as counseling, personal/social development, and communications development. These and other related topics are being included in a second volume planned for publication in 1980.

It is appropriate to point out that the contributors to this book are all members of NTID's professional staff who, while knowledgeable and experienced, have drawn extensively upon the experience and research of their colleagues at the National Technical Institute for the Deaf (NTID) and across the country.

In order to make this book more accessible the authors and NTID have waived all royalties. We have tried to avoid the use of jargon and the journal style of writing. Efforts were made to keep the book conversational in nature and straightforward in its presentation. We hope you will find it readable and informative. Your ideas and constructive suggestions for how such books could be improved will be welcomed.

—Milo E. Bishop
August 1979

CHAPTER I

Hearing Impairment: What It Is and What Its Implications Are

Milo E. Bishop

This chapter provides some basic information about hearing impairments, explaining conductive and sensorineural losses in lay terms. The writer points out that the implications of a hearing impairment depend upon: (a) the type of hearing loss, (b) the severity of the loss, and (c) the age at which the loss occurs.

These variables are discussed in terms of their effect on communications, personal/social development, and educational development. Some common myths associated with deafness are discussed, and one deaf person's perspectives on coping with deafness are shared.

The focus of this book is on mainstreaming hearing-impaired students into programs with normally hearing students. Because many of the intended readers may be unfamiliar with hearing and deafness, it is important to introduce some basic information about impaired hearing and its educational implications before discussing issues related to mainstreaming hearing-impaired students. In so doing I have taken the liberty of borrowing extensively from materials developed and published by the National Technical Institute for the Deaf (NTID).

An in-depth study of hearing impairment and its implications can become very technical and complicated. In the jargon of the audiologist, the educator of the deaf, or the speech pathologist, it can be, and frequently is, further complicated by divergent communication philosophies (e.g., oral vs. manual vs. total communications). The reader is cautioned that more important than understanding any single term about hearing impairment, is the understanding that hearing-impaired people are, first of all, people.

1

Schein and Delk (1974) reported that 13 million persons in the United States have some type of hearing impairment, ranging from a minor loss to profound deafness. Of this number, 1.8 million are considered "deaf," meaning they cannot hear well enough to understand speech. It is important to point out that hearing-impaired people are tall and short, thin and stout, black and white, brown and yellow, male and female, young and old. Some are intelligent, some are average. Some are athletic, some are clumsy. Some are personable, some are quiet. Some are high achievers, some are low achievers. They have families, hold jobs, attend churches, make installment payments, throw parties, watch television, and enjoy dancing.

The point is that hearing-impaired people are more like you than they are unlike you. Their deafness is only one dimension of their character. Each deaf person is unique, as you are. Nevertheless, all hearing-impaired people do have one thing in common: some physical impairment has caused a hearing disability, a condition where, without assistance, hearing is not *functional* for the ordinary purposes of life.

Many people believe impaired hearing is the loss of hearing, where sound is just not loud enough. It is not that simple. The real handicap of impaired hearing is being cut off from the normal means of acquiring and transmitting language. For young children, the loss of hearing means the absence of the language base needed for learning to speak, to read, and to write. Unable to communicate, these children experience no daily communication gain because they cannot hear a radio announcement, cannot understand a TV program, cannot catch a casual remark, cannot share the latest joke. All of this affects children's sophistication about the world and results in personal, social, educational, and occupational obstacles. It has been said that blindness separates people from things, whereas deafness separates people from people. It is through the efforts of dedicated families, concerned educators, and significant others that hearing-impaired individuals are able to break down the barriers that separate them from people. Education, carefully designed and consistently practiced, is the solution for eliminating such barriers.

Hearing Impairment: Some Basic Information

The term "hearing-impaired" is used to describe individuals who have hearing defects ranging from a very slight loss to a total loss of hearing. Hearing impairment affects more than 13 million persons, making it the single most prevalent chronic physical disability in the United States. Hearing can be impaired as the result of many different factors, including heredity and disease.

The hearing mechanism, as illustrated in Figure 1.1, is made up of the outer ear, the middle ear, the inner ear or cochlea, the VIII cranial nerve, known as the auditory nerve, and the brain. Sound, which results from air vibrating, enters the outer ear and travels through the auditory canal until the air vibrations strike the eardrum (tympanic membrane) and cause it to vibrate. These vibrations are conducted through the middle ear to the inner ear (cochlea) through three tiny interconnected bones called the ossicles. The cochlea, which contains approximately 50,000 sensory nerve endings, converts mechanical vibrations into electrical impulses which are transmitted to the brain through the VIII nerve. Anything which impedes the individual's ability to receive and conduct vibration to the cochlea is called a *conductive loss*. A disorder which interferes with the conversion of vibration to electrical impulses or with the transmission of the impulses through the VIII nerve is called a *sensorineural loss*.

FIGURE 1.1
A sectional illustration of the hearing mechanism.

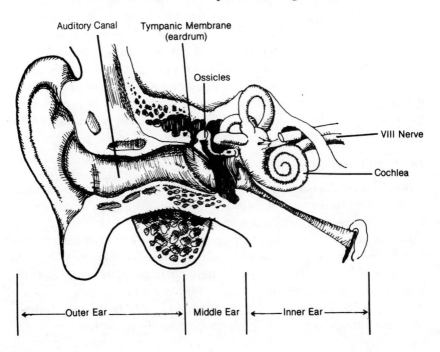

A conductive loss occurs when the ear canal is blocked or when the eardrum or the ossicles are damaged or their movement is restricted. Conductive losses can frequently be fully or partially corrected as a result of medical intervention. For example, the eardrum can be surgically repaired or replaced, with the result being only a minor reduction in hearing. As people grow older, the ossicles sometimes fuse together, or ossify, and their movement becomes increasingly stiff until there is no movement. This condition can be surgically treated by replacing the bone with a very small artificial device. Hearing does not return to normal, but it does significantly improve. Sensorineural hearing loss, on the other hand, cannot be medically improved at the present time.

To more fully understand the implication of either a conductive or sensorineural hearing impairment, knowledge of three things is essential: the *degree of loss*, the *configuration of the loss*, and the *age at which the loss occurred.*

Degree of Loss

Hearing loss is measured in decibels—dB. To make this more concrete, conversational speech at 3 feet is measured at about 60 dB; the noise from a vacuum cleaner is measured at about 70 dB; noise generated by a garbage disposal, 75 dB; noise from a power lawn mower, 95 dB; and music from a rock band, 110 dB. A person is considered to have normal hearing if the loss is between 0–25 dB. If a person has a loss between 30–40 dB, it is considered slight; 45–55 dB, mild; 60–70 dB, moderate; 75–90 dB, severe; and over 90 dB it is considered a profound loss. The term "deaf" is commonly used when the hearing impairment is diagnosed as *severe* or *profound.*

The Configuration of the Loss

Sound is an impression received from many different frequencies or pitches. The frequency of sound is determined by the number of vibratory cycles received in one second. Speech, for example, is made up of sound vibrations ranging from about 125 cycles per second (cps) to 3,500 cps (or, using more common notation, 3500 Hertz [Hz]). The human ear is sensitive to sounds ranging from 20 Hz to 20,000 Hz. When hearing is impaired, it may or may not affect all frequencies in the same way: a person may have normal hearing in the low frequencies and a moderate loss (65 dB) in the high frequencies.

The audiogram is a device used to display a person's ability to hear at specified frequencies. Examples of two audiograms are shown in Figure 1.2. The first audiogram, noted as (A) in the figure, is for a

FIGURE 1.2

Audiograms of two people, both having an average hearing loss of 55 dB in the better ear, but each having very different functional hearing.

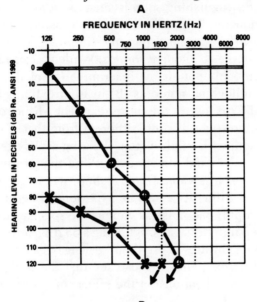

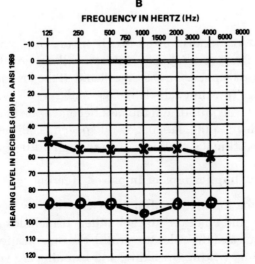

person who, in the right ear (represented by circles on the audiogram), has normal hearing at 125 Hz, a 25 dB loss at 250 Hz, 60 dB at 500 Hz, 80 dB at 1000 Hz, 100 dB at 1500 Hz, and no response (N/R) at 2000 Hz. In the left ear (represented by X's on the audiogram), the loss is more severe. This person is said to have a 55 dB loss in the better ear. This is derived by averaging the loss at 250 Hz, 500 Hz, and 1000 Hz. Such a person is generally able to distinguish among vowels but will have difficulty distinguishing sounds such as /s/ and /sh/ because of their high frequencies. This will result in confusions between words such as *sew* and *show* because the only difference in how these two words sound is in the /s/ and /sh/ sounds. While a hearing aid may be useful, it will probably not enable discrimination of all sounds.

The second audiogram, noted as (B) in Figure 1.2, is for a person who also has a 55 dB loss in the better ear. The shape, or configuration, of the loss, however, is quite different from that of the first person. Such a person, with amplification (hearing aid), is generally able to receive and understand almost everything that is said in a quiet situation. However, in a cafeteria or a shop, where there is a lot of background noise, difficulty could be experienced because the hearing aid would amplify the noise as well as the speech. It is important to realize that two individuals, both having a 55 dB hearing loss, might have very different abilities to use their hearing because the natures of the losses are different. Thus, we can see that the configuration of a loss has important implications on the effects of a hearing loss.

Age at Onset

This is important because if the loss is severe or profound and occurs before age 2 or 3 (prelingual), children will *not* develop language without special assistance. On the other hand, if the loss occurs at ages 4 and 5 or older (postlingual), language and speech will generally already have been acquired, and the task becomes one of maintaining, as opposed to developing, language and speech. The implications of prelingual vs. postlingual deafness are extremely different.

Implications of Impaired Hearing

Language is the foundation of the process whereby people convey ideas, concepts, and emotions to each other. It includes learning the meaning of words and the rules governing the organization and usage of words. Reading, writing, speaking, and listening are vehicles used to convey language. Most normally hearing children acquire language simply by being around people who speak a language. Of course, as children with normal hearing learn to speak a language, they also learn the meaning of its words and its rules.

When children are unable to hear the language being spoken, they are unable to learn its rules until special instruction is provided. The impact of this can be better appreciated when one considers that children with normal hearing usually have acquired all of the basic structure of their language and a vocabulary of several hundred words by the time they are 3 years old.

Until the mid-1960s, special instruction for hearing-impaired children generally did not even begin until the children were 5 years old. Since the sixties, educators and audiologists have realized the urgent need for early identification of hearing loss and for preschool educational programs. Now, fortunately, early identification and education are the rule, and hearing-impaired children are benefiting substantially from it. Nevertheless, the basic implications of impaired hearing for communication, personal/social development, and educational development remain with us and must be given careful consideration.

Implications for Communication Development

As previously stated, language is the foundation of the communication process. Although speech and language are different, they normally develop together, usually without formal instruction. In fact, the developmental process is so robust that it is impaired only when the ability to think and reason is severely limited, or when hearing is seriously disrupted.

Reading and writing are quite another matter because their development depends upon a satisfactory language foundation and is facilitated by a reasonable speech vocabulary. Speech vocabulary is important for normally hearing children to acquire because, while learning to read, they are able to correctly associate the written form of a word with a word already in their speech vocabulary. Once the association is made and the meaning of the word is comprehended, they remember the printed symbols representing the word. For words not in their repertoire, they have their knowledge of language to help them derive meaning from contextual clues or from explanations provided through the use of language.

The young, severely hearing-impaired child, on the other hand, usually has neither the vocabulary nor the language structure upon which to draw. As a result, every new word is a lesson in itself. It is no wonder, then, that such youngsters usually lag behind their normally hearing peers as much as two to four years in reading and writing ability by the time they reach junior high school age.

Implications for Personal/Social Development

Deafness separates people from people, consequently separating individuals from the means of learning the social rules of the culture in which they live. They are deficient in values and interests shaped by linguistic interactions with others. When communication is severely reduced, it is not surprising to find that personal values remain undefined, interests are different, and abilities go unrecognized or are inappropriately assessed.

In discussing personal and social development, Emerton, Hurwitz, and Bishop (1979) cited reports suggesting that a substantial number of hearing-impaired individuals (children, adolescents, and adults) had appeared to be socially naive or immature and had encountered personal and social difficulties in daily life. For example, McHughes (1975) found frequent reports from employment counselors that hearing-impaired clients had been fired from jobs for personal/social reasons. Deaf writers Jacobs (1974) and Stewart (1972) related anecdotes about many socially difficult encounters deaf persons experience with society at large.

Also, there have been numerous studies of the psychosocial aspects of profound hearing impairment. These studies have frequently found "abnormal" personality characteristics and/or less than adequate adjustment among deaf subjects as compared with normally hearing subjects. These characteristics include emotional instability, egocentricity, impulsiveness, poor self-concept, and tactlessness. However, recent work by Garrison, Tesch, and DeCaro (1978) raised serious questions about the validity of instruments such as those used to derive these findings. There is general agreement among educators, nevertheless, that additional attention should be given to the personal and social development needs of hearing-impaired individuals.

NTID, working with teachers of the hearing impaired from six schools across the country representing a variety of educational settings, identified six competency areas in urgent need of improvement. These six competencies were derived through a process developed to extract, from a list of 24 competency areas, those areas most in need of urgent attention. A total of 281 educators and counselors of the deaf participated. The results are listed in Table 1.A. Accepting responsibility for one's own actions was selected by all of the schools as one of the six most urgent areas. Being aware of one's own values, strengths, weaknesses, interests, and goals, and making sound decisions were considered to be in urgent need of attention by five out of the six schools participating. Dependability, initiative, and self-confidence were selected by four of the six schools. None of the other competencies considered was selected by more than one school.

TABLE 1.A
Personal/social competencies selected by six schools as being in urgent need of attention.

	Total Votes (n = 251)	Number of Schools (n = 6)
Accepts responsibility for own actions	161	6
Aware of own values, strengths, weaknesses, interests, and goals	139	5
Makes sound decisions	118	5
Dependability	110	4
Initiative	84	4
Self confidence	76	4

It is important to again point out that this does not mean that *all* hearing-impaired individuals are deficient in these areas. What it does mean is that these areas are considered to be important with respect to hearing-impaired students and should be given special attention.

Implications for Educational Development

Given that language and communication development is delayed by severe hearing loss, it is not surprising to find that educational attainment is also adversely affected. DeFrancesca (1972) reported achievement test data which placed profoundly hearing-impaired persons several years behind their peers with normal hearing. This does not mean that the ability to learn is any less; rather, it suggests that instructional methods have probably not been effective in overcoming the communication problems experienced by hearing-impaired students. It is also important to point out that not all profoundly hearing-impaired individuals are underachievers. Many deaf individuals have excelled academically in spite of the adversities which they faced. Generally, however, hearing-impaired youngsters are academically behind their peers with normal hearing. Teachers working with hearing-impaired individuals need to be prepared to modify the way in which they organize and present instructional material if they are to meet the needs of these students.

Facts from Myths

The purpose in addressing some of the commonly held myths is to clarify misconceptions about hearing-impaired individuals. In preparing this section, materials have been borrowed extensively from a pamphlet prepared by NTID's Office of Public Information entitled *Setting the Record Straight.*

A quiz on concepts about deafness is provided in Table 1.B. We suggest you check your answers against those at the end of this chapter (Table 1.C) before reading further.

Misconceptions about deafness, often myths with no basis, in fact, need clarification because of their historically negative influence on attitudes toward the education of hearing-impaired persons.

Intelligence Potential or IQ

Derogative references such as "deaf and dumb" or "deaf-mute" are both outmoded and uninformed. The basic intelligence of hearing-impaired individuals is comparable to that of the normal distribution of a normally hearing population.

Speech Capabilities

Voice use. Hearing-impaired persons have normal vocal organs. Some hearing-impaired persons choose not to use their voices if they think their speech is difficult to understand or if they feel they have inappropriate pitch or volume control. However, a large number of hearing-impaired individuals do choose to use their voices in communicative interactions.

Speech intelligibility. The understandability of a hearing-impaired person's speech varies greatly depending on the degree of hearing loss and the age at which it occurred, as well as on skills and abilities. As previously stated, there will generally be marked differences between the understandability of "hard of hearing" and "profoundly deaf" individuals. The same is true for prelingually and postlingually

TABLE 1.B
*Fact or myth quiz to test one's knowledge
about hearing-impaired people.*
(Answers are provided in Table 1.C at the end of the chapter.)

True	False	
_____	_____	Hearing-impaired people have better eyesight than people with normal hearing.
_____	_____	Profoundly hearing-impaired people cannot think in abstractions.
_____	_____	Hearing-impaired people do not use Braille to help them communicate.
_____	_____	Most profoundly hearing-impaired deaf people have *some* hearing.
_____	_____	Profoundly hearing-impaired people cannot talk.
_____	_____	Many severely to profoundly hearing-impaired people hold bachelor's or master's degrees.
_____	_____	Hearing-impaired people can hold competitive positions in a wide range of professional and technical fields.
_____	_____	Hearing-impaired people are individuals with unique personalities and skills.
_____	_____	Hearing aids cannot restore hearing, they only amplify sound.
_____	_____	Everyone can use a hearing aid.
_____	_____	Deaf people cannot become lawyers or doctors.
_____	_____	Hearing-impaired people cannot enjoy music.
_____	_____	Loud noises do not bother people with impaired hearing.
_____	_____	Profoundly hearing-impaired people are all underachievers.
_____	_____	Profoundly hearing-impaired people have lower IQs than people with normal hearing.
_____	_____	Hearing-impaired people learn to read lips as well as people with normal hearing can hear.

deaf persons. There is absolutely no correlation between a hearing-impaired person's speech abilities and intelligence.

The speech of many hearing-impaired persons seems difficult to understand at first: most normally hearing people have found that such speech becomes easier to understand after being around the person for awhile. It is similar to becoming accustomed to someone who speaks rapidly with a strong foreign accent.

Hearing Capabilities

Residual hearing. The limited amount of hearing that most hearing-impaired persons have is called *residual hearing.* Its usefulness for listening and understanding speech varies with the individual.

Hearing aid use. A hearing aid amplifies sound; however, not all deaf people benefit alike by wearing one. The hearing aid's usefulness for speech communication depends on the wearer's ability to discriminate among speech sounds and environmental sounds. But even with a confusion of sounds, an aid may help reduce the feeling of isolation from the environment. So, a hearing aid that may not be conducive to speech communication may still provide important psychological support.

Telephone use. Some severely and profoundly hearing-impaired persons may have enough residual hearing or may have developed techniques to allow them to use the telephone. In addition, special telephone equipment has been developed for use with the standard telephone. One of these aids, an amplifier, can be easily installed in a telephone receiver for a minimal charge.

Speechreading Capabilities

It is often thought that hearing-impaired people can "speechread" as well as normally hearing people can "hear." However, speechreading (or lipreading) is a skill in which only *some* hearing-impaired persons are proficient, while others have difficulty mastering it. While good speechreading skills can help in communication, only 26 percent of all speech is visible on the lips. Even the best speechreaders cannot "see" everything that is said. However, a good speechreader can identify about 70–80 percent of a message since speechreading is aided when words, phrases, and sentences are used in context.

Work Performance

Potential. While hearing-impaired persons vary greatly in their ability to cope with hearing loss, they are generally capable of performing almost any job if they are given realistic opportunities and adequate training.

Safety records. Hearing-impaired workers have above-average safety records, and most jobs do not involve safety risks for them. In several studies, including one done by the DuPont Company (1974), hearing-impaired people have demonstrated that they are usually more visually alert to hazards than are hearing persons because they do not rely solely on sounds to warn them of danger.

Noise on the job. Some hearing-impaired persons can handle noisy jobs which normally hearing persons cannot tolerate. It is inaccurate, however, to think that "any" deaf person can work in such a situation. For some, depending on the type of hearing loss, working in a noisy environment can be quite uncomfortable and can impair whatever residual hearing they may have.

Coping with Deafness

The degree to which a person is able to cope with language and communication handicaps is dependent upon many variables: native intelligence, personality, family environment, age at onset of deafness, degree and type of deafness, language background, residual hearing, listening skills, speechreading, speech abilities, and educational preparation. Each adds to the unique way each individual deals with deafness. Loy Golladay, an associate professor at NTID and one of the contributors to this book, recently reflected on his own experiences of deafness:

> I am sometimes asked how it feels to be deaf. My answer is that most people have to adjust to a handicap of some sort, even if it's only being nearsighted or freckle-faced, or weak in math, or unable to bowl ten strikes in a row. As a friend of mine once said, "There are 215 million handicapped Americans."
>
> Although deafness involves far greater consequences than these other *handicaps*, it feels perfectly normal to me now because I've had it so long, and I've had to adjust to it. A reasonable sense of proportion and the ability to laugh at one's self have been important assets, too.
>
> Deaf people will never fully overcome their handicaps. But, generally,

they will do their best to deal with their deafness and develop themselves to the fullest potential within their capabilities.

Deaf people ask just one thing of their hearing counterparts: to be provided the dignity of being openly and willingly approached as individuals with unique qualities and skills. □

TABLE 1.C
Answers for Table 1.B fact or myth quiz of knowledge about hearing-impaired people.

True	False	
	X	Hearing-impaired people have better eyesight than people with normal hearing.
	X	Profoundly hearing-impaired people cannot think in abstractions.
X		Hearing-impaired people do *not* use Braille to help them communicate.
X		Most profoundly hearing-impaired deaf people have *some* hearing.
	X	Profoundly hearing-impaired people cannot talk.
X		Many severely to profoundly hearing-impaired people hold bachelor's or master's degrees.
X		Hearing-impaired people can hold competitive positions in a wide range of professional and technical fields.
X		Hearing-impaired people are individuals with unique personalities and skills.
X		Hearing aids cannot restore hearing, they only amplify sound.
	X	Everyone can use a hearing aid.
	X	Deaf people cannot become lawyers or doctors.
	X	Hearing-impaired people cannot enjoy music.
	X	Loud noises do not bother people with impaired hearing.
	X	Profoundly hearing-impaired people are all underachievers.
	X	Profoundly hearing-impaired people have lower IQs than people with normal hearing.
	X	Hearing-impaired people learn to read lips as well as people with normal hearing can hear.

CHAPTER II

The Law and Its Implications for Mainstreaming

E. Ross Stuckless and William E. Castle

This chapter focuses on some of the social, educational, and legal forces which converged to produce Public Law 94-142 and Section 504 of the Rehabilitation Act of 1973. Selected excerpts of these two federal laws are identified and discussed with particular reference to their implications for the mainstreaming of hearing-impaired students primarily at the secondary and postsecondary levels.

It is the purpose of this Act to assure that all handicapped children have available to them . . . . a free appropriate public education which emphasizes special education and related services designed to meet their unique needs, to assure that the rights of handicapped children and their parents or guardians are protected, to assist States and localities to provide for the education of all handicapped children, and to assess and assure the effectiveness of efforts to educate handicapped children.

> The United States Congress:
> The Education for All Handicapped
> Children Act of 1975. P.L. 94-142

No otherwise qualified handicapped individual in the United States . . . shall, solely by reason of his handicap, be excluded from the participation in, be denied the benefits of, or be subjected to discrimination under any program of activity receiving federal financial assistance.

> The United States Congress:
> Section 504 of the Rehabilitation
> Act of 1973. P.L. 93-112[1]

---

[1]In its original version, Section 504 defined "handicapped individual" only with respect to employment. This was subsequently amended under the Rehabilitation Act Amendments of 1974 (P.L. 93-516) to include education.

I mportant social and educational legislation does not just happen. To grasp its significance we must understand its origins and its implications.

This chapter is concerned with two federal laws which have been described by some as the declaration of civil rights for all handicapped children and adults. The laws to which we refer are Public Law 94-142, the Education for All Handicapped Children Act of 1975, and Public Law 93-112, the Rehabilitation Act of 1973.

We caution the reader against regarding this chapter as a summary or legal interpretation of these two laws, for that is not its intent. In this regard, a number of excellent references are cited, including an annotated bibliography of references to legal considerations in the education of the handicapped (Berry, 1978). Because this book focuses on the mainstreaming of hearing-impaired students, these laws and their companion regulations are discussed within that context.

Both in anticipation and as a consequence of these two federal laws, many states have enacted legislation and adopted regulations with similar purpose. Also, virtually all states have developed and submitted state plans in compliance with these two laws' regulations. The responsiveness of these states to the rights of their handicapped children and adults should not be overlooked but is beyond the scope of this chapter to describe.

It should be stated at the outset that the mainstreaming of hearing-impaired students did not originate with this legislation. Most mildly and moderately hearing-impaired children, traditionally classified as hard of hearing,[2] have generally been educated in the regular public schools, sometimes within special classes and often with only the support of itinerant teachers and speech therapists. Most severely and profoundly hearing-impaired students, traditionally classified as deaf, have been taught in special schools by teachers who are specifically trained and certified to work with deaf students. Mainstreaming has become increasingly common among these deaf students, also. For example, 43 percent of the students who entered NTID directly from high school in 1969 were graduates of public high schools. Many had

---

[2]P.L. 94-142 defines "deaf" as a hearing impairment which is so severe that the child is impaired in processing linguistic information through hearing, with or without amplification, which adversely affects educational performance. "Hard of hearing" is defined as a hearing impairment, whether permanent or fluctuating, which adversely affects a child's educational performance but which is not included under the definition of "deaf." (Sec. 121a.5)

experienced a combination of special and regular school and class placement at different points in their school histories.

Selected Factors Leading to the Legislation

Many forces converged to produce this legislation, some of which are more closely associated with hearing-impaired students than others. Cruickshank (1975) has stated that the historical development of services to the handicapped has been related to social change, including changing attitudes toward handicapped persons. While our focus is on hearing-impaired students, it should be remembered that the legislation is intended to benefit all handicapped people. Most of the factors which led to the legislation were common to the needs of all. While we have grouped some of these factors as social, some as educational, and some as legal, obviously they overlap.

Social Factors

The history of deaf people in this country and elsewhere is a history of denial and struggle for full human rights (Bender, 1971; Breunig & Nix, 1977). Although deaf children were the first among all severely handicapped groups to be educated at public expense, their education was long neglected because they were considered uneducable. Even today there are those who unwittingly persist in using the demeaning expression "deaf and dumb."

Records of the *American Annals of the Deaf* suggest that at the turn of the century, 90 percent of all deaf children were being educated in public residential schools for the deaf (Brill, 1971).[3] Beginning in 1817, and extending into the early years of this century, residential schools for the deaf were established in virtually every state. At the time, the total population of each state was much smaller than it is today, and the incidence of deafness among children was low—as it is today—relative to the total school-age population. Additionally, society was much more rural, and the homes of deaf children were more scattered.

It was not uncommon, until distances were reduced by modern transportation, for students to return home only at vacation time. The residential school for the deaf took on many of the responsibilities normally assumed by the family and the local community and was central to both the educational and social development of the child. In

---

[3]By 1961, this percentage had dropped to 50 percent, while close to 50 percent were being educated in public day schools. The percentage of deaf students enrolled in residential schools has continued to decline since that time.

recent years, residential schools have adopted policies which encourage students to return home regularly. Many schools now require that all their students return home each weekend, and in urban-based residential schools, most local students commute daily. This has come about for a number of reasons, including improved transportation and the costs associated with full-time residential care for the student.

Most important, educators and parents have come to attach greater value to the role of the family and the local community in the child's development. Over the past decade or two, parents have become more sophisticated and assertive in expressing their rights in managing the development of their hearing-impaired child. They have sought more social options for their child, including the right of their child to become a "full-time" member of the family and the local community while retaining the benefits of a special education as needed.

Social factors are encapsulated in the concept of mainstreaming itself. When we speak of educational mainstreaming, we are implicitly speaking of social mainstreaming, or a more "normal" social environment for handicapped people. The expression "deaf people must learn to live in the hearing world" has often been used in this regard. Like many such expressions this statement contains elements of both truth and myth. Most people who have been deaf throughout most of their lives have close ties with other deaf people through friendships, marriage, social and civic activities, and indeed language, i.e., the language of signs. Most deaf people do not, need not, and wish not to live exclusively in a "hearing world."

Nevertheless, society entertained too long the principle of "separate but equal" when the intent of "separate" was to keep handicapped people at a distance. The concepts of "least restrictive environment" and "accessibility," imbedded in the laws, emphasize what is considered best by and for the handicapped person, rather than what is socially most comfortable and least costly to the community and its institutions.

Educational Factors

P.L. 94-142 calls for the education of *all* handicapped children. In large measure, because of the presence of residential and day schools for the deaf, most hearing-impaired children have had special educational services available to them for many years. This is not to say, however, that all hearing-impaired children have been served.

There are better statistics on hearing-impaired students who have participated in special education programs, particularly in schools for the deaf, than on those who have been fully or partially mainstreamed in local public schools, simply because the educationally integrated child *ipso facto* has been more difficult to identify.

The incidence of additional handicaps, e.g., mental retardation, learning disabilities, and visual disorders, is quite high among hearing-impaired children. Historically, few schools for the deaf perceived their role as providing services to children with severe additional handicaps. These children, unless accepted elsewhere, were often denied an education.

Secondary handicaps were probably much less prevalent among deaf children 35 years ago than they are today. Brill (1971) has indicated that the advent of antibiotics in 1942 was largely responsible for changes in the deaf population, saving the lives of many infants, but adding appreciably to their educational needs. For the most part, schools for the deaf and teacher-training programs were slow in adapting to a new population which included many children with multiple handicaps. But today virtually all schools for the deaf have added programs to provide services to these students, and most teacher-training programs for the deaf have modified their curricula to train teachers to work with such children. One can look increasingly to the schools for the deaf to meet the educational needs of hearing-impaired students with additional handicaps because of the compelling needs they present and because of the extensive resources of these schools.

P.L. 94-142 calls for *appropriate* education for handicapped children. No one is satisfied with the present level of academic and communicative skills among most deaf students. But neither are we resigned to the view that this is a "natural" consequence of hearing impairment. We should, and indeed we must, seek more appropriate strategies to provide an education of quality to all hearing-impaired students. This dissatisfaction with the educational progress of many handicapped students and the imperative for additional alternatives was clearly a major force behind P.L. 94-142 and its doctrine of "appropriate" education.

What is appropriate for one child may be inappropriate for another. This is recognized in the law when it calls for an "individualized education program" for each child. It is not an intent of the law to remove the existing education options offered by special schools and classes for the deaf. Indeed, the law preserves these options. Rather, it is to extend the options to assure that every student is educated, with appropriate services, in the environment which is least restrictive to his or her development. Some people predict that P.L. 94-142 will lead to the demise of schools for the deaf. Although this is most unlikely, should it occur it would be a gross disservice to many deaf students because it would mean the withdrawal of a major educational option for them. Schools for the deaf will continue to provide services for the same fundamental reasons they were first established: (a) because deaf children present unique communications deficits and educational needs, and (b) because resources can be readily brought together to bear on the education of deaf children when they are educated together (Brill, Merrill, & Frisina, 1973).

At the same time, most authorities agree that the role of the school for the deaf, and particularly that of the residential school, is in transition (Griffing, 1977). Reynolds and Birch (1977) have suggested that its new position is emerging as a "regional resource, a research agency, a training promulgator, and a school specializing in work with hearing-impaired pupils with the kinds of complex educational problems which defy solution in the mainstream [p. 537]."

We mentioned earlier the increasing assertiveness of parents in seeking more social options for their hearing-impaired child and their insistence on a stronger voice in selecting from among these options. Social and educational options are closely linked.

In the past, many professionals "spared" the parents of young hearing-impaired children many of the uncertainties and possible trade-offs which accompany the selection of a particular educational path for the child. Most parents tended to defer to the judgments of those who were professionally qualified. But we know that professionals even today do not always stand in full agreement as to the most appropriate education for a particular hearing-impaired student. This is perhaps best illustrated by the continuing issue over the role of the language of signs in the education of the hearing-impaired student.

Parents today have much better access to information than a few years ago. Numerous books have been written to answer questions raised by parents (Katz, Mathis, & Merrill, 1974). Excellent parent education films and other materials are available from the A.G. Bell Association. Numerous schools for the deaf have established lending libraries—often through the mail—for parents in their states. More parent groups have been organized at local, state, and national levels, enabling the parents of young hearing-impaired children to profit from the experiences of parents of older children.

In short, there is now ample opportunity for the parent to acquire the information needed to play a major role in educational planning for his or her hearing-impaired child. Needless to say, some parents will seek out more information than others, and some will insist on a more active role than will others in the construction of an individualized education plan.

Legal Factors

The legislative and judicial antecedents of the current legislation have been brought together elsewhere (Abeson, Bolick, & Hass, 1975; Vlahos, 1977; Weintraub, Abeson, Ballard, & LaVor, 1976). It is the intent of this section merely to touch on a few of the highlights. The roots of this legislation lie in the 14th Amendment to the Constitution, which guarantees equal protection under the law. This Amendment is the basis for insistence upon equal educational opportunity for handicapped children.

In 1971, the Pennsylvania Association for Retarded Children brought action against the Commonwealth of Pennsylvania for the state's failure to provide access to a free public education for all retarded children (PARC v. Commonwealth, 1971). A U.S. District Court ruled that the state could not delay, terminate, or deny mentally retarded children access to a publicly supported education. The decree asserted that it was highly desirable to educate these children in an environment most like that offered to nonhandicapped children.

In the same year, parents brought action against the Board of Education in Washington, D.C. (Mills v. Board of Education, 1971), charging failure to provide all children with a publicly supported education. A U.S. District Court reaffirmed the constitutional right of all children, regardless of any exceptional condition or handicap, to a publicly supported education and indicated that any policies or practices which excluded children without provisions for adequate and immediate alternative services and without prior hearing and review of placement procedures are in violation of the rights of due process and equal protection of the law. The Court further added that the District of Columbia's interest in educating the excluded children must outweigh its interest in preserving its financial resources. Legislation and new regulations responsive to these rulings soon followed in a number of states, e.g., Massachusetts and Tennessee in 1972.

The Courts also began to speak of appropriate and least restrictive educational environments. In one ruling (Lebanks v. Spears, 1973) it was specified that (see following page):

all evaluations and educational plans, hearings, and determinations of appropriate programs of education and training . . . shall be made in the context of a presumption that among alternative programs and plans, placement in a regular public school class with the appropriate support services is preferable to placement in special public school classes.

P.L. 94-142, the Education for All Handicapped Children Act, is an extension of P.L. 93-380, the Educational Amendments of 1974. We will not linger on the earlier act except to point out its emphasis on "due process." Among its provisions was the insistence that states receiving federal support for the education of their handicapped students develop and submit a plan which includes procedures for ensuring "prior notice to parents or guardians of the child when the local or state educational agency proposes to change the educational placement of the child" and "an opportunity for the parents or guardians to obtain an impartial due process hearing, examine all relevant records with respect to the classification or educational placement of the child, and obtain an independent educational evaluation of the child."

Little has been said up to this point about Section 504 of the Rehabilitation Act of 1973. It is not coincidental that Section 504 contains language quite similar to the language of Title VI of the Civil Rights Act of 1964 and to Title IX of the Education Amendments of 1972 which applied to racial discrimination and to discrimination in education on the basis of sex. The *Federal Register,* in presenting rules and regulations concerning this law, states: "Section 504 thus represents the first federal civil rights law protecting the rights of handicapped persons and reflects a national commitment to end discrimination on the basis of handicap. . . . It establishes a mandate to end discrimination and to bring handicapped persons into the mainstream of American life" (Vol. 42, No. 86).

When this law was passed in 1973, Section 504 was directed essentially against discrimination in employment. The following year, Congress extended the focus beyond employment so that the amended Section 504 now pertains to a broad range of civil rights, including education at all levels.

So these laws and regulations did not "just happen"; they are a culmination of many forces. And just as they were a long time in the shaping, they will undoubtedly continue to be reshaped and reinterpreted through litigation; through the experience of parents, educators, and others who implement the law; and through the experiences of those for whom the law was created—hearing-impaired and other handicapped people themselves.

The Federal Legislation and Regulations

A number of excellent references are available describing and interpreting the two laws and their regulations.[4] This chapter will highlight only those sections which have particular bearing on the mainstreaming of hearing-impaired students.

The Education for All Handicapped Children Act of 1975

The purpose of this act was stated early in the chapter. It is not surprising that legislation as fundamental as this won the overwhelming support of Congress; in fact, it was passed by a 404 to 7 vote in the House, and an 87 to 7 vote in the Senate.

This law sets forth a number of basic rights of all handicapped children, including the right to a free and appropriate public school education, the right to be educated in an environment which is least restrictive to the child, and the right to be educated in a private school at no cost to the parents—if such placement is necessary to provide appropriate special education and related services (National Education Association, 1978; Rosen, Skinski, & Pimental, 1977).

Other aspects of the law are intended to further assure that the rights of the handicapped child and his or her parents are preserved. These provisions include the requirement that an individualized education program (IEP) be developed for each child on an annual basis (a) with both teacher and parental involvement in the process; (b) the establishment of procedures to assure that the evaluation and testing of students are nondiscriminatory; (c) the right of due process on the part of parents, including meaningful involvement in decisions affecting their child; and (d) the removal of various kinds of barriers which threaten to limit educational opportunities (DuBow, 1977).

Still other aspects of the law relate to priorities and a timetable to meet the goals of the law: (a) basic responsibilities of state and local agencies, (b) provision of services, (c) inservice training of teachers and other educational personnel, and (d) responsibilities for financing the additional costs likely to be incurred at the local level. It is a complex law befitting a complex, albeit a fundamental, need.

A free appropriate education. The law states, "Each state shall ensure that free appropriate public education is available to all handicapped children aged 3 through 18 within the state not later than

---

[4]The regulations for P.L. 94-142 may be found in Vol. 42, No. 163 (August 23, 1977) of the *Federal Register*. Regulations concerning Section 504 of the Rehabilitation Act of 1973 are contained in Vol. 42, No. 86 (May 4, 1977).

September 1, 1978, and to all handicapped children aged 3 to 21 within the state not later than September 1, 1980." The lower- and upper-range requirements are qualified by some conditions with which parents and educational authorities should become familiar.

The question has been asked whether this legislation extends to postsecondary education up to age 21. Since in general a free public education is guaranteed nonhandicapped students only through the secondary level, this provision of P.L. 94-142 does not apply to the handicapped student in college. Section 504 of the Rehabilitation Act of 1973 speaks more directly to postsecondary education.

Free appropriate public education applies also to residential placement. P.L. 94-142 stipulates that, "If placement in a public or private residential program is necessary to provide special education and related services to a handicapped child; the program, including nonmedical care and room and board, must be at no cost to the parents of the child."

The law highlights particular services which must be available to the child. For example, it is stated that "Each public agency shall ensure that the hearing aids worn by deaf and hard-of-hearing children are functioning properly."

The law requires that the range of educational services available to nonhandicapped children in the area also be available to handicapped children. Art, music, industrial arts, consumer and homemaking education, and vocational education are mentioned by way of illustration. It is noted in the federal regulations as a specific point that "Vocational education programs must be specifically designed if necessary to enable a handicapped student to benefit fully from those programs."

Nonacademic and extracurricular services must be provided "in such a manner as is necessary to afford handicapped children an equal opportunity for participation in those services and activities." Such services "may include counseling services, athletics, transportation, health services, recreational activities, special interest groups or clubs sponsored by the public agency; referrals to agencies which provide assistance to handicapped persons, and employment of students, including both employment by the public agency and assistance in making outside employment available."

Physical education receives prominent attention in the law. The general statement is made that "Physical education services, specially designed if necessary, must be made available to every handicapped child receiving a free appropriate public education."

Least restrictive environment. The concept of least restrictive environment has come to be associated with mainstreaming. In a general statement about the least restrictive environment for handicapped children, P.L. 94-142 states:

> Each public agency shall ensure (1) that to the maximum extent appropriate, handicapped children, including children in public or private institutions or other care facilities, are educated with children who are not handicapped; and (2) that special classes, separate schooling or other removal of handicapped children from the regular educational environment occurs only when the nature of severity of the handicap is such that education in regular classes with the use of supplementary aids and services cannot be achieved satisfactorily.

While the above statement does not hold least restrictive environment to be synonymous with mainstreaming, the implication is that the education of handicapped children with children who are not handicapped should be the *first* of *several alternatives* considered.

The law specifies that there be a continuum of alternative placements. This continuum must be inclusive of a range of placements such as "instruction in regular classes, special classes, special schools, home instruction, and instruction in hospitals and institutions." The law also specifies that this continuum "make provision for supplementary services [such as resource room or itinerant instruction] to be provided in conjunction with regular class placement."

Each child's placement must be based on the child's individualized education program, must be redetermined at least annually, and must be as close as possible to the child's home. It is further stipulated that "unless a handicapped child's individualized education program requires some other arrangement, the child is educated in the school which he or she would attend if not handicapped." Also, the law stipulates that in selecting the least restrictive environment, consideration be given to "any potential harmful effect on the child or on the quality of services which he or she needs."

It is very clear that convenience on the part of a local educational agency may not enter into the determination of educational placement of the handicapped child. Disruptive activity on the part of the handicapped child may or may not enter into a placement decision. P.L. 94-142 does not deal directly with this question, but draws upon an analysis of Section 504 of the Rehabilitation Act of 1973. This analysis states, "It should be stressed that, where a handicapped child is so disruptive in a regular classroom that the education of other students is significantly impaired, the needs of the handicapped child cannot be met in that environment. Therefore, regular placement would not be appropriate to his or her needs" (National Association of State Directors of Special Education, undated a).

Special class or special school placement need not preclude contact with nonhandicapped students outside the classroom itself. An analysis of Section 504 regulations specifies that "handicapped children must also be provided nonacademic services in as integrated a setting as possible. This requirement is especially important for children whose educational needs necessitate their being solely with other handicapped children during most of each day. To the maximum extent appropriate, children in residential settings are also to be provided opportunities for participation with other children."

It is clear that many teachers of nonhandicapped children will feel poorly equipped to meet the needs of hearing-impaired students. Under the law, "Each state educational agency shall carry out activities to ensure that teachers and administrators in all public agencies (a) are fully informed about their responsibilities for implementing Section 121a.550 (pertaining to Least Restrictive Environment), and (b) are provided with technical assistance and training necessary to assist them in this effort." Provisions for in-service training are also contained in the law.

Individualized education program. A major aspect of P.L. 94-142, and the heart of its implementation, rests with the development and action upon an individualized education program for each handicapped child. This must be done at least once a year. Torres (1977) has edited an excellent basic guide for the development of an individualized education program (IEP).

The law states, "On October 1, 1977, and at the beginning of each school year thereafter, each public agency shall have in effect an individualized education program for every handicapped child who is receiving special education from that agency." The law is quite specific in describing how the IEP will be developed and reviewed and who will participate in its development. It includes provisions for a strong voice on the part of parents (Walker, 1976).

The program's content must include "(a) a statement of the child's present levels of educational performance; (b) a statement of annual goals, including short-term instructional objectives; (c) a statement of the specific special education and related services to be provided to the child, and the extent to which the child will be able to participate in regular educational programs; (d) the projected dates for initiation of services and the anticipated duration of the services; and (e) appropriate objective criteria and evaluation procedures and schedules for determining, on at least an annual basis, whether the short-term instructional objectives are being achieved."

It should be noted that the annual goals and objectives set forth in the IEP do not constitute guarantees on the part of the educational agency that these will be met. However, if an effort is not made in good faith to meet these goals and objectives, parents have the right to invoke due process procedures.

Evaluation procedures. Student assessment/evaluation at best is less than totally reliable. With handicapped students, error can be even greater. The law says:

> State and local educational agencies shall ensure, at a minimum, that: (1) tests and other evaluation materials: (a) are provided and administered in the child's native language or other mode of communication, unless it is clearly not feasible to do so; (b) have been validated for the specific purpose for which they are used, and (c) are administered by trained personnel in conformance with the instructions provided by their producer; (2) tests and other evaluation materials include those tailored to assess specific areas of educational need and not merely those which are designed to provide a single general intelligence quotient; (3) tests are selected and administered so as best to ensure that; when a test is administered to a child with impaired sensory, manual, or speaking skills, the test results accurately reflect the child's aptitude or achievement level or whatever other factors the test purports to measure, rather than reflecting the child's impaired sensory, manual, or speaking skills (except where those skills are the factors which the test purports to measure); (4) no single procedure is used as the sole criterion for determining an appropriate educational program for a child; (5) the evaluation is made by a multidisciplinary team or group of persons, including at least one teacher or other specialist with knowledge in the area of suspected disability; (6) the child is assessed in all areas related to the suspected disability, including; where appropriate; health, vision, hearing, social and emotional status, general intelligence, academic performance, communication status, and motor abilities.

Due process. The law speaks of numerous rights of parents on behalf of their handicapped child. The reader is referred to an excellent reference written by Abeson, Bolick, and Hass (1975) in this regard.

Under P.L. 94-142, parents have the right to inspect and review all educational records pertaining to the identification, evaluation, and educational placement of their child—and more broadly with respect to the provision of a free appropriate education for their child. Parents have the right to obtain an independent evaluation of their child at public expense, subject to certain conditions.

Parents have the right to prior written notice when the educational agency proposes to—or refuses to—initiate or change the identification, evaluation, or educational placement of the child or the provision of a free appropriate public education to the child. This written notice must include an explanation of procedural safeguards available to the parents and a description of reasons for the agency's proposal or refusal. The law also contains provisions for hearings and appeals.

P.L. 94-142 and its rules and regulations extend considerably beyond the provisions suggested in this chapter. Once again, the reader interested in the full scope of the law is referred to other sources, including the *Federal Register* (Vol. 42, No. 163).

Section 504 of the Rehabilitation Act of 1973

Less will be said about this law than about P.L. 94-142 because in many respects they are parallel. A preliminary comparison of some of the provisions of the regulations accompanying the two laws has been described elsewhere (National Association of State Directors of Special Education, undated b).

We will highlight some of the provisions of Section 504 which extend beyond those of P.L. 94-142, and particularly those which have implications for the mainstreaming of hearing-impaired children and adults. Rules and regulations pertaining to Section 504 are to be found in Vol. 42, No. 86, of the *Federal Register*. Highlights of this law are available in a *Fact Sheet* (1977) prepared by the Office of the Secretary and the Office for Civil Rights of the Department of Health, Education and Welfare.

Subpart E of this law applies to all *postsecondary* education programs and activities, including vocational education programs and activities that receive or benefit from federal financial assistance.

Admissions. The law contains a general statement prohibiting denial of admission or discrimination in admission or recruitment of qualified handicapped persons. With respect to postsecondary education, a "qualified" handicapped person is one who meets the academic and technical standards requisite to admission or participation in the program or activity.

In its admissions policies, the institution may not (1) apply limitations upon the number or proportion of handicapped persons who may be admitted, (2) may not use any test or admission criterion that has a disproportional, adverse effect on handicapped persons or any class of handicapped persons unless (a) the test or criterion has been validated as a predictor of success in the educational program, and (b) alternate tests which have a less adverse effect are not available. The law also speaks of test validation.

Further, the institution should:

assure itself that (1) admissions tests are selected and administered so as best to ensure that, when a test is administered to an applicant who has a handicap that impairs sensory, manual, or speaking skills, the test results accurately reflect the applicant's aptitude or achievement level or whatever other factor the test purports to measure; (2) admissions tests that are designed for persons with impaired sensory, manual, or speaking skills are offered as often and in as timely a manner as are other admissions tests; and (3) admissions tests are administered in facilities that, on the whole, are accessible to handicapped persons.

The institution may invite applicants for admission to indicate whether—and to what extent—they are handicapped, provided that it is made clear to the applicant that the information is intended for use solely in connection with the institution's immediate action obligations or its voluntary action efforts, that it is being requested on a voluntary basis, that it will be kept confidential, that refusal to provide it will not subject the applicant to adverse treatment, and that it will be used only in accordance with the law. Pre-admission inquiries as to whether an applicant is handicapped may not be made except as provided above. Following admission, however, inquiries as to handicaps that may require accommodation may be made on a confidential basis.

General Participation of Students

Section 504 states:

No qualified handicapped student shall, on the basis of handicap, be excluded from participation and be denied the benefits of, or otherwise be subject to discrimination under any academic, research, occupational training, housing, health, insurance, counseling, financial aid, physical education, athletics, recreation, transportation, other extracurricular, or other postsecondary education program or activity . . . Qualified handicapped students may not, on the basis of handicap, be excluded from any course, course of study, or other part of the education program or activity. Programs and activities offered the handicapped student should be in the most integrated setting appropriate.

Academic adjustments. The postsecondary institution shall make such modifications to its academic requirements as are necessary to ensure that such requirements do not discriminate—or have the effect of discriminating—on the basis of handicap, against a qualified applicant or student. Academic requirements that the recipient (institution) can demonstrate are essential to the program of instruction being pursued by such student or to any directly related licensing requirement will not be regarded as discriminatory within the meaning of this section. Modifications may include changes in the length of time permitted for the completion of degree requirements, substitution of specific courses required for the completion of degree requirements, and adaptation of the manner in which specific courses are conducted.

Course examinations and other procedures for evaluating the students' performance must be such that "the results of the evaluation represent the students' achievement in the course, rather than reflecting the students' impaired sensory, manual, or speaking skills (except where such skills are the factors that the test purports to measure)."

Auxiliary aids. The law states that an institution must take the steps necessary to ensure that no handicapped student is denied the benefits of, excluded from participation in, or otherwise subjected to discrimination because of the absence of educational auxiliary aids for students with impaired sensory, manual, or speaking skills. Examples of auxiliary aids are presented, and include "interpreters or other effective methods for making orally delivered materials available to students with hearing impairments."

This stipulation has caused some concern to colleges and universities about the cost of compliance with this requirement. We quote a portion of the analysis of this requirement as contained in the regulations for Section 504. "The Department emphasizes that recipients (institutions) can usually meet this obligation by assisting students in using existing resources for auxiliary aids such as state vocational rehabilitation agencies and private charitable organizations. Indeed, the Department anticipates that the bulk of auxiliary aids will be paid for by state and private agencies, not by colleges and universities. In those circumstances, where the recipient institution must provide the educational auxiliary aid, the institution has flexibility in choosing the methods by which the aids will be supplied."

In the subpart of Section 504 specific to postsecondary education, reference is also made to provisions for housing, financial and employment assistance to students, and nonacademic services including physical education and athletics, counseling and placement services, and social organizations.

Program accessibility. The law specifies that educational institutions and agencies which provide health, welfare, or other social services must be physically accessible to handicapped persons. Accessibility may be achieved in a number of ways, such as the redesign of equipment, rescheduling of classes including handicapped students to accessible buildings, and providing aides. Structural changes in existing facilities are required only if there is no other way to make the program accessible. A postsecondary handicapped student may not be denied a specific requested course because it is not presently being offered in an accessible location. All new construction must be so designed as to make the facility accessible to and usable by handicapped persons.

Since these regulations pertain particularly to accessibility by persons with mobility problems, they have particular relevance to hearing-impaired persons with additional physical handicaps.

Employment practices. One general outcome of education is, of course, employment. Section 504 states that no qualified handicapped person shall, on the basis of handicap, be subjected to discrimination in employment. Nor may handicapped applicants or employees be limited, classified, or segregated in any way that adversely affects their opportunities or status.

The regulations make reference to many employment activities to which the law applies, including recruitment, promotion, pay rates, job assignments, benefits, selection and financial support for training, and participation in professional meetings.

The employer must make reasonable accommodation to the special needs of the handicapped employee, including accessible facilities, job restructuring, and provision of interpreters as needed. The regulations provide for certain exceptions if the employer can demonstrate that the accommodation would impose an undue hardship on the operation of the program.

As stated earlier, it is beyond the scope of this chapter to describe all aspects of P.L. 94-142 and Section 504 of P.L. 93-112. The above is intended merely to suggest some of their highlights, particularly as these pertain to the mainstreaming of hearing-impaired students at the elementary, secondary, and postsecondary levels.

Conclusion

An eminent special educator has reflected some of the uncertainty about the shape that special education will take in the future in his statement, "Clearly, special education for handicapped children is in the throes of transition. Any pronouncement at this point . . . , is likely to be viewed in retrospect as less than completely accurate" (Dunn,

1973b). What he has said is undoubtedly true. Certainly it is safe to say that, although our nation has demonstrated an interest in equal educational and employment opportunities for its citizens through the years, the fulfillment of that interest has not been something easily effected. This is due primarily to the diverse makeup of our citizenry and to the diverse nature of the educational programming of the states and local school districts.

The fulfillment process has been complicated throughout the past two centuries by our dealings with American Indians from the beginning of colonization; the uncertainty about the role of women as full citizens from the time the U.S. Constitution was written; the granting of citizenship to our Black population; the diversity of the nation's immigration program; and the recent influx of Spanish-speaking Americans from Puerto Rico, Cuba, Mexico, and other Latin American countries.

The history of these groups presents a sobering thought. Although women were assured the right to vote in 1920, they strive today for an Equal Rights Amendment to give fuller assurance of equal educational and employment opportunities. Although Blacks and other minority groups were assured the right to vote in 1870, they have needed civil rights legislation in recent years to foster equal educational, housing, and employment opportunities.

Clearly there is nothing in this nation's history to suggest that the mere presence of legislation designed to bring equal rights to the handicapped will make this suddenly happen. Nor is there evidence that it will happen in those modes that many now anticipate, including the mode of mainstreaming. □

CHAPTER III

Mainstreaming: A Goal or a Process?

Milo E. Bishop

In this chapter it is asserted that mainstreaming is an educational process and, as such, should not be confused with the goals of education. Nine assumptions are presented which provide the foundation for a framework to be used in delineating competencies students need to develop. Issues are discussed relative to deciding whether or not a student should be mainstreamed. For example, to what degree is the school prepared to meet a student's needs in the areas of communications, personal/social development, and academic development?

Experiences as a preschool, secondary, and postsecondary teacher of the deaf, as a researcher, and as an administrator have enabled me to view education of hearing-impaired students from a variety of perspectives. These perspectives have significantly shaped my thinking and have resulted in the following postulates which provide the foundation for what is presented in this chapter:

1. The purpose of education is to prepare individuals for the many roles they will have in society. For example, it is important that individuals appreciate the value of work and be prepared to earn a living. They need to be able to wisely use what time is not spent in earning a living. They need to develop an appreciation for beauty and quality. In other words, the goal of education is to prepare individuals to function in school, at work, at home, and in the community.

2. If education is to be successful, it must be concerned with a group of *individuals* and not with the *group*.

3. Nothing in education is all good or all bad.

4. The passing of a law or a court decision does not change the quality of education in the school. Quality cannot be legislated, it must be developed. By the same token, the declaration by a school that it has programs and services for the hearing impaired does not mean it has quality programs and services.

33

5. Quality education begins with quality teaching, and quality teaching requires a skilled teacher. Not even the most sophisticated educational processes or resources can compensate for an inadequate teacher. The most such processes or resources can do is make a good teacher better.

6. Each school (and its associated programs) must be evaluated individually by what it does, not by what method or philosophy it uses or by what it says it does.

7. It is important to maintain the distinction between educational goals and the processes for achieving those goals. Educational mainstreaming is a process, not a goal; it is a means, not an end. And while mainstreaming is a very important process, it may or may not be appropriate for assisting a given student in achieving the needed competencies.

8. It is important that one clearly understands why what is being done *is* being done and what effect it has. It is expected that students will change over time. It should also be expected that the educational setting may need to change.

9. The home and the school must cooperate in selecting, implementing, and following through on the various educational processes available for assisting children to develop needed academic, personal/social, and communication competencies.

I have seen and do now see many exciting and positive advances being made in the education of hearing-impaired students. Unfortunately, I also see a lack of clarity in the purposes of some programs serving the hearing impaired. I see confusion between the goals of programs and the processes being used to achieve those goals. Without clearly defined goals and a system of monitoring progress toward their attainment, it is easy for the *process* to become the *goal.*

Issues which have been with us for a long time can be used to help us focus on this confusion and clarify the difference between processes and goals. For example, a goal of education is to prepare hearing-impaired students to function in society as adults. Oral and manual educational programs are processes for achieving this goal. In using the illustration of oral vs. manual communication, it is important to recognize that, to the credit of some educators, the goal and the process are kept separate. Nevertheless, to many of their disciples, oral or manual education become the goal. In the absence of conclusive data, the issue of which process (oral or manual) should be used has been debated at the philosophical and emotional levels. As a result, many of us have become so concerned with ensuring that our personally favored process is adopted, that it has become the "goal." There is danger of the same thing occurring with mainstreaming.

That education in America moves in cycles from one-room schools to separate classrooms and back to one-room schools has been pointed out by Osguthorpe, Whitehead, and Bishop (1978). As reference to "one-room schools," however, does not connote a change (hence, progress), they are now called "open classrooms" or "open schools." Another cyclical movement in full swing is in the area of special education. Here new terms—"integration" or "mainstreaming"—have been invented to connote change and/or progress. When Binet began his work more than half a century ago, his aim was to correct the "injustice" of leaving handicapped learners in the regular classroom. Now, after years of separating children who learn differently, America has decided it must correct that injustice and "integrate" them with "normal" learners. As educators we should keep in mind, however, that while there are some data to suggest that present special education practices have not succeeded (Gordon, 1970; Hoeltke, 1969; Mercer, 1972), there is little *definitive data* to suggest that integration or mainstreaming is better. What is it that mainstreaming is expected to accomplish, and how will we know if mainstreaming has accomplished it?

While conducting a comprehensive review of the literature on mainstreaming (including over 900 references), my colleague Ron Hein and I observed a rather strong tendency in the literature toward treating educational mainstreaming as the goal rather than as a process for achieving a goal. Without clearly defined goals, success cannot be monitored. It is critical, therefore, that what is to be accomplished is set in a framework so that the contribution of mainstreaming toward the desired ends may be assessed.

A Framework for Determining Educational Goals

The postulates stated above form the foundation for a conceptual framework to be used in delineating the attributes people need to function in society. This framework, which was developed at NTID through the interactions of many professionals, is shown in Figure 3.1 as a matrix (Bishop & Clarcq, 1977). The columns represent the environments in which people function: namely, the home, school, work, and community. The rows represent educational components considered to be important in preparing hearing-impaired people to function in society. These components are: (1) academic and technical prepara-

FIGURE 3.1

A framework for determining educational goals.

	Home	School	Work	Community
Academic Development				
Personal/Social Development				
Communications Development				

tion, (2) personal and social preparation, and (3) communication preparation. The academic/technical component, as shown in Table 3.A, refers to such subjects as mathematics, science, drafting, biology, electronics, office practice, data processing, humanities, social sciences, history, etc. The personal/social component has been defined to include the ability to manage oneself, interact with others, and manage one's environment (Emerton & Bishop, 1977). Communication relates broadly to expressive and receptive skills including reading, writing, oral and manual expression, and oral and manual reception. To ignore any one of the three components is to ignore an important educational need of hearing-impaired students.

It is the parents of the young child who have stewardship for ensuring that the child is prepared to function in the society in which he or she will live as an adult. It is true that schools and the staffs which run them have a legal responsibility to provide each student with an education. However, teachers and administrators come and go, no matter how dedicated and competent, and in the end it is the child and the parents who are left to live with their decisions and the results. Wise parents use the school and the church to prepare the child to develop and assess his or her own values, interests, strengths, and weaknesses; parents ensure that the child is exposed to careers and their requirements; and they participate with the school and involve the child in deciding on which courses should be studied and why. Care must be taken to ensure that career doors are not prematurely closed because

TABLE 3.A

A framework outlining the areas to be considered in assessing the strength of students as compared to the expectations of programs in making placement decisions.

Components	Student Performance	Program's Expectations
Academic/Technical - Math - Science - History - Social Studies - etc.		
Communication Skills - Reading - Writing - Oral Receptive - Manual Receptive - Oral Expressive - Manual Expressive		
Personal/Social - Manage Self - Interact with Others - Manage Environment		

of inadequate academic preparation. At the same time, equal care must be given in establishing academic expectations which realistically consider the child's ability. Wise parents also carefully and systematically shift the role of decision maker, with respect to the child's future, from themselves to the child.

The framework described above is intended to serve as a guide for parents, schools, and mature students in defining minimum attributes considered to be important for the child's preparation to function as an adult in society. Once the desired academic, personal/social, and communication competencies are identified, student strengths and weaknesses can be assessed relative to each of these competencies. Once the assessment is completed, it is possible for the parents and student, in consultation with professionals, to develop a plan of action for the student. The plan of action I am referring to is *not* the IEP described in Chapter 2. Rather, it is a plan addressed to the broad question as to which of the educational processes available is best for the student, given the desired outcome. In developing this plan, it is essential that the processes are not confused with the goals. If the options include both a special school for the deaf and a local community school with a resource room, then a decision must be made as to which is best for the student, given his/her needs.

Good decision making requires criteria. Such criteria become critical not only in making the placement decision, but also in the ongoing assessment of the student's progress. The IEP, when appropriately developed and successfully carried out, should ensure the progress needed to achieve the overall goal. Hence, progress relative to outcomes, defined in the IEP, can serve as an indicator of the appropriateness of the placement decision. This means that the method of evaluating student progress needs to be understood and accepted by teachers, by parents, and, to the degree possible, by students.

Consider the Gap

Parents and professionals alike would benefit from a comprehensive, longitudinal, objective evaluation of the merits of mainstreaming. Unfortunately, such an evaluation, to my knowledge, does not exist. To conduct one requires time, and time is not available to the student awaiting a decision. Fortunately, there are factors which can be used in selecting the alternative which is best for the student. One very important factor is the nature and the extent of the *gaps* between the student's performance and the program's expectations of how students will perform. For instance, any time a course or a curriculum is developed, its organization and content should be based on what the student is expected to be able to do upon entering the program, and what the student is expected to be able to do when leaving the program. Expectations related to where students are assumed to be when they begin the program are critical in deciding whether or not a given student should be mainstreamed.

In considering the placement of hearing-impaired youngsters, it is useful to refer back to the components of the conceptual framework. The first set of questions as shown in Table 3.A relates to the entrance expectations of the available educational program relative to components of the framework. For example, what are the program's expectations in the areas of science, mathematics, history, social studies, etc.? What are the communications expectations regarding reading, writing, oral and/or manual reception, and oral and/or manual expression? What are the personal/social expectations of individuals in terms of their ability to manage self, interact with others, and manage different environments?

Information about the expectations of programs being considered combined with information on the student's performance is critical to defining the nature and the extent of the *gaps* between the student's performance and the expectations of alternative programs. This is an essential step in the decision-making process. The next step in evaluating the merits of different programs—where gaps exist—is to determine the extent to which the program is prepared to *deal with those gaps.* At NTID we have identified three basic approaches to narrowing and/or compensating for the negative effects of the *gaps.* They are (a) working with a student to upgrade performance prior to a program, (b) working with faculty members to help them understand the educational needs associated with the particular hearing impairment and to modify their courses and/or methods of presentation accordingly, and (c) providing support services such as notetaking, tutoring, and interpreting in an effort to compensate for the negative effect of the gaps. Only (b) and (c) are within the scope of this book.

In evaluating the appropriateness of placing deaf students in a class with normally hearing students, one needs to ascertain what *evidence* there is that the organization and delivery of content in the course or courses will be modified so as to reduce the gaps, and that support services will be provided which will compensate for negative effects of the gaps. As such modifications and support services are described in later chapters, only a few examples will be cited here. Are instructional strategies oriented visually as well as auditorily? Is the instruction well organized? Are examples provided to illustrate points and concepts? Are relationships between connecting concepts clearly established? Do students have the opportunity to apply principles discussed in class? In other words, are instructional techniques which will help deaf students learn (or, internalize) the content employed?

What evidence is there that the school will be able to help bridge the communications gap in the classroom? Will an interpreter be provided if needed? If so, what will be done to enable students to watch the teacher and/or interpreter and still obtain a written record of important points in the class? Will handouts be provided, or will a notetaker be available? Will students be instructed on how to take notes for themselves?

Communications Development

What evidence is there that the school can and will provide programs and services which will enable students to become proficient in communicating with both hearing and hearing-impaired people? Before discussing this issue it is important to provide readers with additional background information.

There is no single, agreed-upon mode for the hearing impaired to communicate with normally hearing people: for some, it is speech and listening and/or speechreading; for others, it is reading and writing; and for still others, it is through the use of an interpreter. For the most fortunate, who can choose the mode of communication best suited to the occasion, it is any of the three.

Similarly, there is no single, agreed-upon mode for the hearing impaired to communicate with other hearing impaired: for some, it is speech and listening and/or speechreading; for others, it is signs and fingerspelling; and for still others, it is through the use of an interpreter. Again, the most fortunate can make a choice best suited to the occasion. For young adult and older persons who are prelingually deaf, the mode of communication will, in general, depend upon the attitudes and efforts of their parents, the attitudes and competencies of school personnel, the pressure exerted by peers and adult role models and, finally, by the motivations, efforts, and aptitudes of the individuals themselves.

The early years are, by far, the most critical years for developing language and the associated communications skills. The literature is full of assertions, arguments, and philosophical statements regarding how to capitalize on these early years (Hein & Bishop, 1978). There are those who argue that the use of signs and fingerspelling will seriously impede the development of oral communications. There are others who argue with equal vigor that an early emphasis on oral communications will result in an irreparable delay in language development and that signs should be used with young children in order to make language available to them. This argument is frequently countered by a reminder that the linguistic structure of sign language is different from that of English and that textbooks are written in English. And so the arguments go. Unfortunately, there is little definitive data with which to evaluate the merits of the arguments.

For the purposes of this book, it will suffice to say that such issues exist. Caution should be used against jumping to conclusions which in the end may influence teachers against accepting students who at age 14 and older are generally set in their communication performance. The implications for those who teach adolescent and young adult hearing-impaired individuals are much different than for those who teach preschool and elementary grades. The latter are involved in formulating the communication attitudes and skills of young children as they begin the process. Those who teach older children need to accept students as they are and work with them to build upon whatever communicative foundation they have acquired.

It is well beyond the purpose of this chapter to review and discuss merits of the various methods used with young children. Rather, its purpose is to raise critical issues which should be considered in the placement of hearing-impaired adolescent and young adult individuals. With this background we are now prepared to explore issues related to communications development that are important in selecting a school.

Language Development

As pointed out in the introductory chapter, the primary problem associated with impaired hearing is language development. For a school to even be worthy of consideration, the school's teachers and administrators must realize the importance of this statement and its implications. They must understand that speech and language are different and be prepared to act accordingly. They must know that speech therapy which focuses on articulation or even on vocabulary enhancement will not aid language development. It is essential that special language development programs be available to students needing such assistance. If language is not given the necessary attention, efforts to improve reading, writing, and speaking will be minimized, and academic growth will be significantly impaired.

Reading and Writing

It is highly desirable that reading and writing programs be offered in conjunction with programs for language development. Such programs should allow for individual attention and for practice with immediate feedback to the student. Chapter 8, relating to selection and preparation of materials, offers more on this topic. It is important to understand at this point that the need for and availability of services to improve reading and writing is a basic consideration in choosing a school in which to place a hearing-impaired student.

Speech and Residual Hearing

Any educational program for hearing-impaired students must have access to a certified audiologist and be prepared to encourage and assist students in learning how to use their residual hearing effectively and to use amplification. Over the past 10 years NTID has learned that, even though the average hearing loss for its students is between a 90 and 100 dB in the better ear, 85 to 95 percent of the students can effectively use amplification. Amplification helps some students to monitor their own speech as well as to understand the speech of others. For others, amplification simply serves as a means of alerting them to danger. Still others may find amplification enables them to use a telephone.

Determining if a hearing aid can be beneficial and selecting the appropriate hearing aid for a given student are critical matters best done by a certified audiologist. The student must be taught how the aid works, how to use it, and how to care for it, for the aid itself and the battery require regular checking. When proper orientation and follow-up are *not* provided, an aid may be worn with a dead battery or a broken cord, or it may simply end up in a drawer.

Programs claiming suitability for hearing-impaired individuals also must be prepared to assist students in enhancing their ability to speak and to speechread. In analyzing the suitability of a school in terms of speech development, a great deal depends on the particular student. With the adolescent and young adult, one must put things into perspective. What is the likelihood that the student will develop speech which is understandable? What will be sacrificed in the pursuit of that speech? In considering these points, it is important to remember that this discussion is focused on the adolescent and young adult student and not on the young child.

By far the most important variable in developing understandable speech is the student's ability to use his residual hearing. By the time students reach high school age, they have usually received extensive speech training and have experienced some degree of success (or the

TABLE 3.B

A framework showing the relationship between a student's speech ability and motivation for speech training. Used in deciding if speech development should be a major factor in selecting a program.

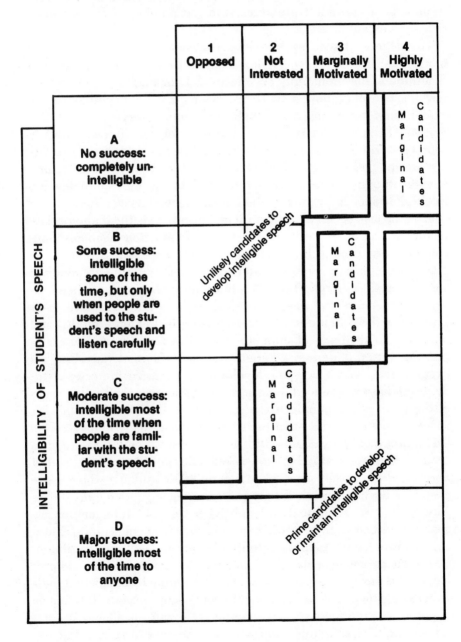

lack of it). The critical variable now is motivation. At this stage of development it is not unusual to find students who are either "turned on" or "turned off" regarding speech. Their attitude has been shaped by many factors: parental involvement, teacher attitudes and techniques, peer and adult pressures, and the number of successful or defeating experiences.

The degree of success experienced is not only a factor affecting motivation; it is in its own right a separate factor to be considered in determining the probability of "success." I am suggesting, therefore, that the two most important factors which can be attributed to the student in determining the probability of future success are (a) how motivated the student is, and (b) the level of development already achieved. Different levels and the interactive nature of these two factors are shown in Table 3.B. This table is intended to serve as a guide in estimating how likely it is that the student will be able to develop intelligible speech by the time he finishes school. As age increases, of course, the task becomes more difficult because existing inappropriate motor patterns associated with the speech production mechanism become more and more firmly stabilized, and there is less time to replace inappropriate patterns with correct ones. With this in mind we are prepared to discuss Table 3.B more fully. Letters have been assigned to each of the rows of the matrix, and numbers have been assigned to the columns to enable us to describe the intelligibility and motivational attributes of students in an abbreviated form. For example, D4 is used to denote a student who is highly motivated and has experienced major success in developing speech. B3 indicates a student who has experienced some success in that he is intelligible some of the time (when people listen carefully and are familiar with his speech), and it indicates that the student is marginally motivated.

I submit that any student with a level 4 motivation has the right to try and develop intelligible speech regardless of his current level of intelligibility. By the same token, young adult students who are opposed to further speech training should, in my judgment, not be "forced" to take it. Students at levels B4 or C3 and C4, in general, are prime candidates for continued speech improvement with a reasonable chance of developing intelligible speech without sacrificing other educational aspects. This, of course, assumes that they are provided with the appropriate kind of speech training by competent individuals. A student who has experienced major success (D1) but is opposed to continued speech training (D1) will, in all probability, remain highly intelligible simply through the use of speech in communicating with others. Students characterized as B3 or C2 could be considered marginal candidates for continued speech training. Similarly, students with attributes denoted by A4 could also be considered marginal candidates, providing that a quality intensive training program is available.

The point here is that if a student is a "marginal" or a "prime" candidate to develop intelligible speech without sacrificing educational development, then the quality of the speech program becomes an important consideration in selecting a school. Otherwise, there is no need to be concerned about it.

Signing and Fingerspelling

For students who need and desire to develop the ability to communicate with other hearing-impaired persons through the use of signs and fingerspelling, the availability of instruction in these communication modes will be an important consideration in selecting a school. As previously stated, American Sign Language (Ameslan or ASL) has a different linguistic structure than does English. Some deaf individuals rely completely on Ameslan. Others will use English as their basic language and will convey that language through the use of hand signs which represent words and/or by using different finger shapes to spell out words.

Combining signs and fingerspelling in the syntax of English is known as "signed English." There are several additional variations which make use of signs and fingerspelling to convey language.

In deciding where to place a student, it is important to consider what the student needs and desires to learn, the method of communication the student uses, and methods used in the school. If the student wants to learn Ameslan and that desire is to be satisfied, special instruction in that language is required. Simply because a student picks up a few signs does not mean the student knows sign language.

For students who rely primarily on Ameslan, the school will need to provide teachers competent in Ameslan or a qualified interpreter for use in the classroom; otherwise, communications will generally be very poor or will not occur. It is important to point out, however, that although P.L. 94-142 and Section 504 of the Rehabilitation Act recognize that interpreters may need to be provided, qualified interpreters will not necessarily be available. The issue of educational interpreting is discussed in depth in Chapter 9.

Another consideration should be how the normally hearing students communicate with their hearing-impaired peers. Does the school offer sign language instruction to hearing students desiring it? If not, what steps will be taken to facilitate communications between hearing-impaired students who rely on sign language, and other students who are not aware of it?

Personal/Social Development

While the final area to be considered in this chapter is personal and social development, it is by no means the least important.

Social development is the result of interactions with others. Such interactions shape one's social knowledge, social attitudes, and social skills. These in turn determine one's social behavior. Bishop, White, and Emerton (1977) pointed out that while one can focus on improving a student's knowledge, attitudes, and/or skills through curricular activities, perhaps the most powerful resource for integrating these into social behavior which is "acceptable" to society is the environment in which the student resides. Knowledge of how to make decisions will never be internalized in an environment in which there is no opportunity for making meaningful decisions.

One must consider, therefore, the nature of the environment provided by the schools under consideration. Is it an environment that provides opportunity? What are the attitudes of the other students, of the administration, and of the teachers? Are they enthusiastic about the prospects of interacting with hearing-impaired students, or are they reticent? If reticent, are they open about it? Are they reticent because they lack knowledge or because they don't want the "extra work" and the "hassle"?

Finally, and perhaps most important, how does the student feel about the alternatives? Have the various schools been visited? Has he had an opportunity to observe and to meet with teachers and students? How large is the "gap" in social behavior between the student's performance and the school's expectations, and the expectations of peers? What evidence is there that the school (teachers, administrators, peers) will provide appropriate opportunities for developing needed personal/social competencies?

Summary

Mainstreaming is one alternative process for educating hearing-impaired students. It is a process, not a goal. Physical integration can be accomplished by placing separate schools for deaf and hearing on the same campus, by placing a class or classes for the deaf in a school for the hearing, or by placing individual deaf students in classes with normally hearing children. Of course, reverse integration (normally hearing students in programs for the hearing impaired) is also possible. It should be remembered, however, that physical integration does not necessarily mean that there will be academic or social integration. The amount of academic or social integration will depend upon the nature and the extent of the gap between the student's performance and expectations in the classroom. Such gaps are most likely to occur in the areas of communication, academic, and personal/social development. Where the size of the gap adversely affects academic and social integration, the following alternatives are available:

1. Reduce and/or adequately compensate for the gap
2. Don't mainstream the students

When mainstreaming is the course of action chosen, the following areas will need to be considered:

1. Class size (proportion of hearing to deaf and student-teacher ratio)
2. Preparation of regular classroom teachers
3. Support services for students
4. Support services for parents
5. Support services for teachers

History attests to the fact that for most hearing-impaired students it is not sufficient to simply place them in a class with normal-hearing students and expect that all will be well. Special attention is required. The central issue in deciding whether or not to mainstream a given student focuses on how well the school can and will deal with the gap between student performance and classroom expectations. □

CHAPTER IV

Reflections of a Mainstreamed Deaf Person

T. Alan Hurwitz

Editor's note: In setting the stage for the remaining chapters of this book, I thought it would be beneficial to share with you the personal reflections of one who has successfully coped with the challenges associated with educational mainstreaming. For that purpose, I asked Alan Hurwitz, a contributor to this book, to reflect on his experiences as a deaf person attending public schools.

Before you go on to Alan's story, test your understanding of key points previously made about deafness by asking yourself, what three basic facts about Alan's hearing loss are necessary in order to appropriately consider his reflections? To check your answer, turn to the footnote at the end of this chapter.

I was not aware of the frustrations I had in the regular classroom until much later, when I first started to have access to interpreting services at NTID and in my doctoral studies at the University of Rochester, New York.

After completing my 10-year elementary education at Central Institute for the Deaf (CID) in St. Louis, I entered eighth grade at a regular junior high school in Sioux City, Iowa, at the age of 13 in 1955. Originally, I was prepared for entry into ninth grade as most of my classmates at CID were; but my mother, who happens to be deaf herself, felt that I should repeat eighth grade. She knew that my going to a hearing school for the first time would be a totally new experience for me. Having had the experience herself, she tried to convince me that it would be a good idea to stay in the same grade for another year. My father, who graduated from the Iowa School for the Deaf, never had the experience of being mainstreamed himself.

I did not have any brothers or sisters, much less any hearing friends, who could assist me in my new endeavor. Interpreting in those days was voluntary and normally limited to religious and social services activities; no one ever had thought of trying out an interpreter in educational settings. Hearing-impaired students in those days either had to make it on their own or resort to residential schools for the deaf. Naturally, I was very upset at the thought of having to repeat the eighth grade, but my mother was adamant. I realized much later that she was wise in making this decision, since I did have a difficult time getting adjusted to the regular classroom setting without any supporting services. It was a trauma for me and a very lonely experience since, in my hometown, I had no one with whom I could share my experiences. My mother had a limited experience, but she had faith in me and kept encouraging me all the time. At one point during the first few weeks, when I was very depressed, my mother did ask me if I wanted to transfer to the Iowa School for the Deaf. I think that this made me more determined than ever before to persevere.

My first semester was awful. I even got D's in physical education, which was one of my favorite subjects. There were too many new things I had to learn, but not being able to read the lips of my teachers in any typical class, I missed out on much crucial information.

What kept me going is still a miracle to me. I do, however, recall that all of my teachers and classmates were great to me. There were a few students who ridiculed me; one pushed my head down when I was drinking from a water fountain in the hall. I did not lose my temper; strangely enough, I laughed with him. We became friends thereafter.

I also remember another incident where I was very embarrassed with myself. In one of my first classes in history, a teacher asked the class to recite with her the Gettysburg Address. The entire class except myself went along with the teacher. I was bored, so, eventually, I decided to join the class recital. I became fascinated with the Gettysburg Address and was absorbed with using my voice. Moments later, the teacher told the class to stop and discuss a point. Not knowing that the class had stopped, I kept on reciting for awhile. Suddenly I became aware that the entire class was waiting for me to stop. I wanted to die at that moment or find a hole in the floor so I could disappear. The teacher smiled at me and told me to keep on going. I was too speechless to do anything.

Another embarrassing incident occurred in the same class. The teacher had written a lot of historical information on the blackboard, and I thought she had written something wrong, so I mentioned this to her in front of the class. She did not understand me. After repeating it about four or five times, I finally walked up to the blackboard to make the change. As I came closer to the blackboard, I realized that I was wrong in the first place; the teacher had written the information correctly. I stood there for a moment, gazing at the blackboard and trying to find a way out of the jam. I walked back to my seat red-faced and wished to myself that I had kept my mouth shut. To this day the teacher does not know what I was doing. Thereafter, I turned into a very passive student during the rest of my academic schooling. I was afraid to make myself look silly again.

A third incident, in another class, was the turning point in my determination to become a better student. I had the habit of going to my teacher to check every problem I did during the work sessions. Finally, the teacher asked me if I wanted to be "spoonfed" all the time. I did not really understand the meaning of this expression, but it did teach me that I should not depend on the teacher too much.

From then on I was an independent student, working by myself. I did not understand anything any of my teachers said in the classrooms. It was impossible for me to read their lips. I learned a trick which probably carried me throughout the high school. Since the teachers usually followed their textbooks very closely, I was able to use my books as the main source of learning. Notes written on blackboards by teachers served as reference points for me in these class sessions. Sometimes I would ask my classmates where we were in the text. I did my homework on time and went to the library often to seek additional information to supplement my learning.

I survived high school academically, but my social/extracurricular activities at the school were limited. I was very shy and bypassed all school social functions except sports. I enjoyed watching my peers socializing with each other; I was more like a goldfish swimming in a bowl watching the outside action. Luckily for me, my social development was not a total bust, as I was able to socialize with deaf friends of my parents. Each day at home was a retreat away from mainstreaming for me.

I was accepted into Morningside College, a four-year liberal arts college in my hometown, under the condition that I work out a satisfactory means of acquiring support services (e.g., notetaking and tutoring). Naturally, I was upset and tried to talk the registrar out of it. He argued that college education would not be the same as in high school, since professors hardly used textbooks as a main source of instruction. He was concerned that I would miss out on a lot of information from lectures. My pride was shattered, of course. I had no recourse but to yield to his wishes.

The only solution was to work out an arrangement whereby one of my classmates, registered in the same courses, would take notes with carbon copy in every class. He would give me the copies, and I would rework them as necessary and ask him questions if I did not understand his notes. The registrar could not find an academically strong student to work with me, so we settled for a weak-C student who happened to be enrolled in all of my classes. He agreed to help me, since he needed the money which was financed by the Office of Vocational Rehabilitation. At first, he would use carbon copy papers, and I would sit next to him to read his notes. It did not work out well because I was bored. The teacher's lecture was often not relevant to the textbooks I had before me on my desk. My notetaker would take the kind of notes he felt would be useful for me and himself. So we agreed to eliminate the carbon papers and I would copy his notes in the class as he took them. I would try to analyze the notes with my textbooks. Whenever I needed to ask a question, I would write it down on a scratch paper and give it to my notetaker to ask the teacher for me. It worked out well. At the end of the academic year my notetaker became an honor student! I did well myself, too. The support services program worked out well not only for myself but also for my notetaker. It enabled him to take better notes for himself, too.

The following year my notetaker had to leave Morningside College for family and financial reasons. I could not find another classmate who would be enrolled in all of my classes. Hence, I decided to try out another approach. I did not want to make it too obvious that I needed support services. Basically, I was still a shy person. I did not feel it was necessary to inform my teachers that I was deaf or needed any help. What I did was to look around the class for someone who appeared to be taking a lot of notes. I would sit next to that person, offering no explanation about my special needs, and copy his notes. I learned quickly that the student would become suspicious of what I was doing, and he'd turn his shoulder down to block my line of view at his notes. I felt sheepish, and then I'd explain to the student that I was deaf and needed help with notes. I found that every student would be understanding and willing to share his notes with me. I was able to form close friendships with these wonderful people and we would help each other in our homework. I also learned quickly that teachers needed to know about my deafness, because some of them would throw questions at me without any warning or ask me to make oral presentations to the class. Thereafter, I would introduce myself to new teachers and prospective volunteer notetakers in subsequent classes. Oftentimes, a teacher would be shocked to learn that a deaf student was in his class and would say that I couldn't make it in his class. I would then assure him that I would do fine and tell a "white lie"—that I could read his lips very well. This was enough to make teachers leave me alone in their classes. This continued throughout the remainder of my undergraduate studies at Morningside College and Washington University. I did the same at St. Louis University where I did my graduate work in engineering.

Coming to NTID in 1970, to assume my new job as Educational Specialist for deaf students majoring in engineering and computer science, was my first exposure to a comprehensive model of support services. Never before in my life had I had access to an interpreter in staff meetings. I realized that the five years I worked as engineer at McDonnell-Douglas Corporation, before coming to NTID, were truly a time of isolation. The staff meetings at McDonnell were useless to me; all of my work was done on an individual basis with very little team effort with other engineers. At NTID it was just great being able to understand, through interpreters, what my colleagues and/or other hearing people were talking about in staff meetings. The first time I had an interpreter in a staff meeting I felt as if I were on Cloud 9; I had a chill in my spine and goose pimples all over myself. It was a total explosion for me after all those years.

Presently, as a doctoral student working on my dissertation at the University of Rochester, I have full use of interpreting services in all of my classes. Now all of my frustrations for the past years in schools have come to the conscious level. I am amazed at the wealth of information being delivered through interpreters. Oftentimes I am amused at the irrelevancy of a teacher's lecture to the subject matter. By having an interpreter in my classes, I have been transformed from a totally passive student to an active learner in the classroom for the first time since I left CID. I have learned to use interpreters to my advantage so that I can participate in class discussions, ask questions, and make oral presentations. My confidence as a scholar has blossomed . . . a late bloomer I may be.

As I reflect over my 22 years as a mainstreamed student, it is frightening for me to realize the full implications of Public Law 94-142 as it impacts on some of the hearing-impaired students who may need

---

Basic facts about T. Alan Hurwitz's deafness:
1. Age of onset of hearing loss—prelingual
2. type of loss—flat sensorineural
3. degree of loss—103 dB in the better ear.

more assistance than just support services in regular classrooms. Some may have the capacity to succeed in mainstreaming; others will require continuous cultivation to become successful mainstreamed students. Still others might benefit more from alternative schooling in special education classes or in residential schools for the deaf.

Editor's Note: Alan's experiences clearly point out the struggle that even a bright, motivated, self-disciplined deaf person faces in a mainstreamed situation. Alan speaks of frustration, determination, embarrassment, and love. He also speaks of the benefits derived from educational support services. However, his primary message to us as teachers and administrators should be that mainstreaming affects the lives of students. We must care and extend ourselves to ensure that we understand the strengths and weaknesses of the options for mainstreaming and that we can communicate well enough with the students to determine if the selected option is meeting their needs.

The following chapters are written to help you understand options for mainstreaming and how to make them responsive to student needs. Interested teachers and administrators will search out ways to develop the needed communication skills. □

CHAPTER V

Models and Processes of Mainstreaming

Ron Hein and Milo E. Bishop

This chapter reviews various models and processes of mainstreaming. It builds on the distinction between the goals of education and the processes (including mainstreaming) used in reaching these goals. The chapter suggests that mainstreaming should not be considered the same as regular class placement—regular class placement is only one process of many. Mainstreaming, dependent upon the process used, can lead to many degrees and several types of educational integration (i.e., academic, social, and/or physical). There are many different models and processes; however, they are interrelated in that they all address the physical settings, the degrees of and types of integration, and the support services offered. These categories provide a framework for evaluating the potential usefulness of the process. Finally, this chapter suggests that not every process will work for every student, and, based upon local variables and the individual student's needs, each process will need to be evaluated regarding its appropriateness for any given student.

With the passage of P.L. 94-142 (discussed by Stuckless and Castle in Chapter 2), boards of education, district administrators, building principals, and teachers and parents alike find themselves searching for "the best way" to implement this new law in their particular school district.

School boards and administrators must determine which processes will be made available for educating hearing-impaired students in their district. If mainstreaming is among the processes chosen, then teachers and support personnel will need to be prepared to meet the new challenges mainstreaming will present. Cautious parents, who have long been searching for better ways to meet the educational needs of their child, will need to analyze the strengths and weaknesses of the available options in order to avoid leaping on a bandwagon which conceivably could lead to yet another disappointment. While each of these groups approaches this issue from a different perspective, all are faced with the problem of sorting through a literature filled with assertions, arguments, statements of belief, and definitions which are frequently in conflict.

In this chapter we have attempted to synthesize the major models and processes found in the literature. In doing so, it is hoped that the full range of options available for mainstreaming hearing-impaired students will become evident. Emphases are placed on describing the characteristics, the strengths, and the weaknesses of the options as opposed to prescribing a "best process." Where there is disagreement in the literature regarding a particular process, the alternative views are presented. Principles are described for assessing the appropriateness of the different processes relative to the needs of the students in a given school district.

You will recall in Chapter 3, Bishop notes the critical importance of maintaining a distinction between the goals and the processes of education. He points out that education has two primary goals: to prepare a student to earn a living and to live a life. In contrast, mainstreaming is not a goal, but a means by which these goals may be reached by some students. In considering the literature relative to the "means," it is helpful to understand the differences between the models of education and the processes. In a recently completed literature search, Hein and Bishop (1978) found that this distinction is not always clear and that mainstreaming is often equated only with regular class placement. However, this is not its only meaning. Mainstreaming is used to describe both regular class placement and other general processes of educating handicapped students with nonhandicapped students.

For our purposes, educational processes (such as resource rooms, regular class placements, special schools, etc.) are descriptions of the various physical settings, the different degrees of and types of integration, and the range of support services which can be provided. Models have been developed in order to describe the relationships among the processes in terms of how and under what conditions the various processes should be used.

Common Models

Historically, the number of educational alternatives available to deaf students has been limited. Since 1960 there have been many changes in the models and processes used within the field of education. These changes have significantly expanded the available alternatives. Education is no longer restricted to a system of regular classes, special classes, or special/residential schools. A wider variety of processes, such as those formalized by the Hierarchy of Services (Reynolds, 1962) and the Inverted Pyramid (Dunn, 1973a), are becoming commonplace. These models, and the processes they incorporate, promote varying degrees of physical, social, and academic integration. A basic understanding of the major models is helpful in evaluating the strengths and weaknesses of a given school district's program.

There are at least four major models of educational processes in the literature: (a) the Hierarchy of Services Model by Reynolds (1962), (b) the Cascade Model of Deno (1970), (c) the Inverted Pyramid Model of Dunn (1973a), and (d) the early and secondary education models of the Advisory Council for the Deaf of Massachusetts (1975). Others with a process orientation include Anderson (1973), Lilly (1971), and the new "Cascade" of Reynolds and Birch (1977).

Of the four major models, the earliest is Reynolds' (1962) Hierarchy Model. As can be seen in Figure 5.1, this hierarchical model includes 10 different processes arranged in the order of preference, starting with regular class placement. The model suggests initially placing the more severely handicapped students in one of the less integrated settings, but as soon and as rapidly as feasible, returning these students to the regular classroom.

A very similar model is the Cascade of Services by Deno (1970), represented in Figure 5.2. This model has been adopted by the Council for Exceptional Children since 1973. In contrast to the Reynolds Model with 10 processes, this model specifies seven categories of processes ranging from regular classes with or without supportive services to homebound, hospital, or residential settings with total exclusion. This model, like Reynolds' (1962), advocates placing most students in regular classes, and, if alternative settings are necessary, returning the students to the regular classroom as rapidly as is feasible. The Cascade Model makes a distinction about how students are assigned to settings. At the more exclusionary levels (residential, hospital), the assignment is by agencies other than schools, whereas above the homebound level the assignment is by the school system.

Dunn's (1973a) Inverted Pyramid Model, illustrated in Figure 5.3, is related to those models, but has four major levels (day schools, residential schools, hospital instruction, and homebound instruction). This plan, as in the Reynolds Model and the Cascade Model, advocates varied degrees of integration. Dunn recognizes 11 alternative processes ranging from only materials and equipment changes in a

FIGURE 5.1
Reynolds' (1962) Hierarchy Model which includes 10 different processes arranged in the order of preference, starting with regular class placement.

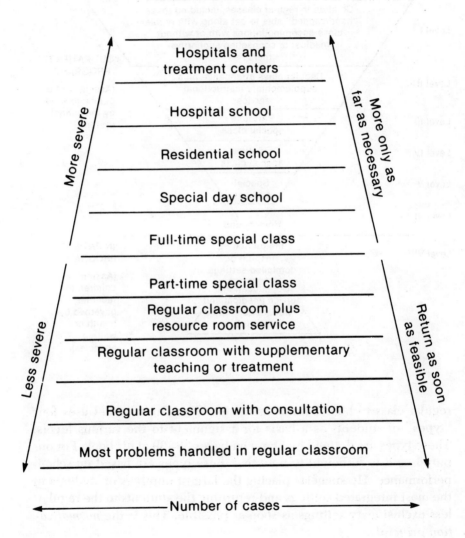

FIGURE 5.2
Deno's (1970) Cascade Model of Services specifies seven categories of processes.

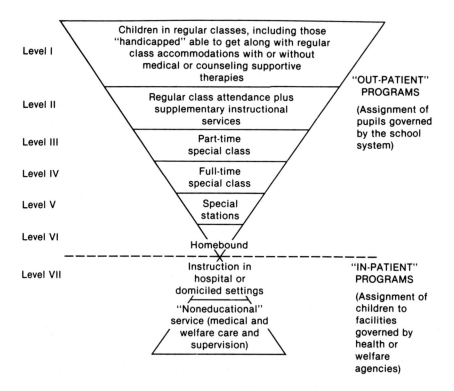

regular class to homebound instruction. The Dunn model uses four "types" of students as a basis for assignment to the various levels. These types are defined by Dunn on pages 38–39 of his book. For our purposes it is sufficient to note that these types are based on school performance. He suggests placing the largest numbers of students in the most integrated settings and returning the students to the regular/ less exclusionary settings as soon as possible. This is the *normalization principle.*

It is important to stress the similarities of the Reynolds, Deno, and Dunn models. They are similar in that they say the same things in different ways. They are all hierarchical. Each *assumes* that the regular class placement is the best setting for educating the majority of handicapped students. The reader should understand, however, that

FIGURE 5.3
*Dunn's (1973) Inverted Pyramid Model contains four major levels
with 11 plans or processes.*

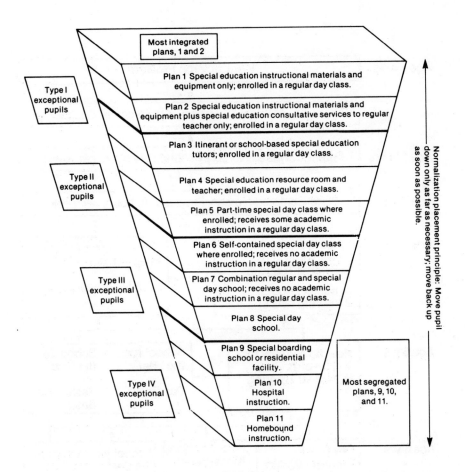

there does not appear to be data in the literature which either support or deny this assumption. Third, the models are based on the premise that no one process can work for all, and that a spectrum of complementary processes should be available. Fourth, there is no assumption that one process should be sequential to another (i.e., that you should place the student in perhaps a special class, then a resource room, and only then in a regular class). Fifth, there is no agreement as to which processes or combinations of processes should be made available. Finally, all of these models were developed for groups of special students other than hearing impaired.

FIGURE 5.4

Illustration of the Massachusetts early education model reflects a series of alternatives as the child increases in age up to 6 years.

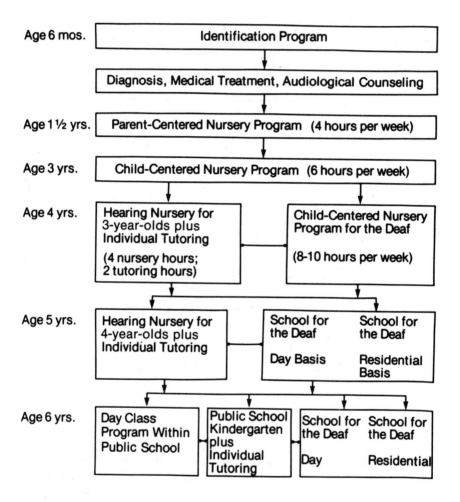

Massachusetts' models for early and secondary education, unlike the models described above, have been designed specifically for deaf children. An illustration of Massachusetts' early education model as designed by Dr. David Luterman is shown as Figure 5.4. This illustration outlines a series of alternatives to be available as the child moves from the identification stage (age 6 months) to the elementary school stage beginning at about age 6. The secondary model describes six alternatives which can be available for educating deaf students in the state of Massachusetts. These alternatives are:

1. Full-time integration in regular schools without support services,
2. Specialized supportive services in regular schools with resource classes or self-contained classes in regular buildings,
3. A four-year regional vocational-technical school with integrated classes or self-contained classes,
4. A two-year short-term vocational training program in a regional vocational-technical high school,
5. A special high school for the deaf,
6. A work-study program in a high school for the deaf.

In an effort to facilitate the understanding of Massachusetts' secondary model, we have graphically displayed its relationships in Figure 5.5. It is important to contrast this model with those discussed earlier. This model is not illustrated as a hierarchy of alternatives, but rather as a listing of available alternatives, each of which has important contributions to make in educating deaf students. The choice of an alternative is based on the needs of the youngster, not on a predetermined assumption about the inherent goodness or badness of the alternatives. These models advocate a smaller number of processes than the other models. Additionally, these models were developed and implemented to serve a population of deaf students. The most important point about these models is that they do *not* assume that regular classes have an inherent irrevocable superiority to all other processes. Processes are judged according to whether or not they meet a student's needs. This is especially important when one recognizes that there are multiple processes available, and that these should be evaluated on sound criteria, not on predetermined biases.

Educational Processes

Processes are the component parts of models. The models presented above, and others in the literature, reveal that there are 11 common processes. They are:

1. Regular class placement only
2. The consultant process
3. The itinerant teacher process
4. The resource room
5. Both regular class placement and special *class* placement

6. Both regular class placement and special *school* placement
7. Special class placement only
8. Special school placement only
9. Residential school placement only
10. Homebound instruction
11. Exclusion

Other processes which are occasionally used include reverse residential school placement (placing normally hearing students into classes at the residential school), residential school placement and regular class placement, and special class placement and resource room placement. Various authors—Adamson (1972), Adamson and Van Etten (1972), Berry (1972), Bitter and Johnston (1973), Cruickshank and DeYoung (1975), Dunn (1973a), Kirk (1972), and Kolstoe (1972a, 1972b)—discuss these and other processes in some detail. Some common citations and the key points of various processes are reviewed below.

Definitions of the Processes

It would be helpful if we could provide a universally accepted definition of each process. However, when reviewing the literature, it is readily apparent that universally agreed-upon definitions of the processes are not available. Even the most widely known introductory texts on special education (Cruickshank & Johnson, 1975; Dunn, 1973a; and Kirk, 1972) have points of significant difference. This disagreement is equally true when their definitions are compared to those in Good's *Dictionary of Education* (1973). In the absence of a single definition, we have chosen to provide the most common definitions for each process in the hope that it will serve to broaden the reader's understanding of the meaning behind the "labels."

Regular class placement. Although there are points of similarity in the definitions of a "regular class," there are differences on whether or not special equipment and materials are used depending on the composition of the student population, on the provision of special teachers, and on the amount of time exceptional students can spend with a special teacher if one is provided. For example:

1. Good (1973) indicates that a regular class is a general class, such as most classes other than those comprised of exceptional students.

2. Dunn (1973a) states that for exceptional students regular class placement involves special materials and equipment modification only.

FIGURE 5.5

Illustration of the Massachusetts secondary model reflecting educational alternatives available for older students.

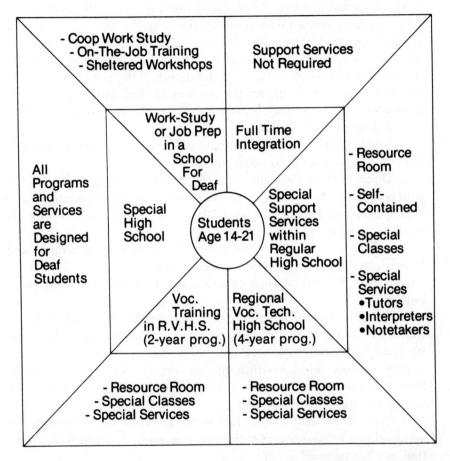

3. Massachusetts (1974) also considers a time variable. Its model states that for exceptional students this placement involves only a regular class assignment and that no more than 10 percent of students' weekly class time is to be set aside for work with special teachers.

The consultant process. When the definitions of a consultant process are contrasted with those of a regular class placement, it is apparent that there are overlaps, in that the consultant primarily serves the teacher of the regular classroom.

1. Good's (1973) definition states that the consultant is a specialist who serves as an adviser to curriculum and teaching problems for the regular class teacher.

2. Dunn (1973a) states that a consultant is a central office staff member who gives indirect service to students by working directly with the regular class teacher.

The itinerant process. When the definitions given for a consultant process are contrasted with those for the itinerant process, an overlap is again apparent. Within the definitions of the itinerant process, differences are apparent, for example, on the location of the itinerant; on the number of schools served; on the nature of the population served (teacher versus student); on the amount of time spent serving one population versus another; and on the size of the groups served. Illustrative definitions include:

1. Good (1973) defines an itinerant teacher as a teacher who travels to two schools/settings to teach pupils.

2. Dunn (1973a) indicates that the primary responsibility of the itinerant is to the classroom teachers and that the itinerant is also school-based and spends at least 50 percent of his/her time directly serving students.

3. Kirk (1972) notes that the itinerant serves several schools and travels considerable distances. He also states that the student is removed from the regular class as he/she needs help and for only short periods.

4. Cruickshank and DeYoung (1975) state that the student is enrolled in the regular class but is cooperatively served by both the itinerant and regular teachers.

The resource room. Within the definitions on resource rooms, there is again overlap with the previous definitions and disagreements among the specific definitions:

1. Good (1973) emphasizes that in the resource room students are assigned to a regular teacher, and that a resource room provides part-time service to small groups.

2. Dunn (1973a) states that the resource room provides more specialized help to larger groups than that of the itinerant process. He notes that both instructional services to students and consultant services to staff are provided.

3. Cruickshank and DeYoung (1975) note that the resource room provides a more coherent, fully integrated experience than the special class and that, additionally, the resource room teacher serves as a consultant on materials and methods.

4. Massachusetts (1974) references two educational processes which are resource-room related: (a) a regular program with not more than 25 percent time out, wherein the special leader does not serve

the student for more than 25 percent of a day and wherein the ratio is not more than eight students to one teacher, and (b) a regular program with not more than 60 percent time out of the regular class.

Within these five definitions, time is an important variable, but one upon which there is disagreement. While most cited definitions advocate the use of the resource room teacher as a consultant for methods, materials, etc., this is not always true in definition or reality. Sabatino (1972a, 1972b) discusses many such points.

Regular and special classes and/or regular and special schools. Most definitions of these combinations of processes are merely composites of other definitions. Most authors, including Dunn (1973a), indicate that the utilization of these processes varies, dependent upon the local districts. One common point is in the definitions of the regular/special class combination, where the homeroom assignment is often the special class.

Special class placement. Definitions of special class placement emphasize location of the student for instruction, curriculum differences, and often methodological/teaching differences from those used in a regular class. Some illustrative definitions are:

1. Good (1973), who notes that it is a class with a curriculum differing from that of a regular class in content, method of instruction, and rate of progress.

2. Dunn (1973a), who states that it is usually a segregated categorical plan with the instruction occurring in a special physical plant.

3. Cruickshank and DeYoung (1975), who note that it is physically located in a regular elementary or secondary school and that it provides proximity along with a special program.

4. Massachusetts (1974) calls the special class program a substantially separate program. Its model indicates that all the students of the class are special, but with comparable needs. The student-teacher ratio is eight to one, and the age spread is a maximum of 36 months. A special curriculum is provided.

From these definitions, it is apparent that many major definitional distinctions exist between special classes and other types of processes. This is true relative to the characteristics of the primary teacher (i.e., trained in special education methods and materials) and the characteristics of teachers in other settings. However, equally true is the fact that among the special class definitions there are differences on whether or not special methods, materials, settings, curriculums, etc. are provided. Also it is apparent that some operational definitions (e.g., Massachusetts) are more specific and detailed.

Special schools. There is a good deal of commonality among the five definitions of special schools cited below. There are, however, major differences, especially with the Massachusetts definition which classifies a special school as a nonpublic school facility. The common theme of the definitions is that these are day schools, wherein the students return home in the evening.

1. Good (1973) defines it as a school serving the educational needs of students either in a single *or* several classifications.

2. Dunn (1973a), in contrast, states that such schools usually serve only one type of student in a specialized physical plant. He also notes that such a school offers the services of a variety of special educators and thus numerous services.

3. Kirk (1972) equates special schools with day schools.

4. Cruickshank and DeYoung (1975) emphasize that special schools are community-based, and they define them much as does Good (1973). But they note that such schools serve students who either can't function in regular schools or who need costly equipment or sheltered environments.

5. The Massachusetts (1974) definition states that a special school is a nonpublic school facility that operates for at least five hours per day each day the public school meets, and that the students return home at night.

Residential schools. In contrast to special schools, whose students return home at night, are residential schools, whose students live at the school. Five illustrative definitions are:

1. Good (1973), who notes that these are boarding schools with a public school-like curriculum, but that the teachers use special methods and materials.

2. Dunn (1973a), whose definition differentiates between two types of residential schools: (a) one for the deaf or blind, which provides potentially comprehensive services including diagnostic, counseling, and disability-trained specialists, and (b) schools for the retarded and emotionally disturbed, which are often run for the protection of the society, as well as for the corrective treatment and care of the students.

3. Kirk (1972), who makes many of the same points noted above but provides an additional point: the schools are sometimes private and sometimes state-operated.

4. Cruickshank and DeYoung (1975), who also state that differences between various types of residential schools exist, and that these are related to the category of students served.

5. Massachusetts' (1974) operational definition is that the facility

will be a nonpublic school with a special 24-hour course of education and treatment. It also states that the school will meet daily, and that appropriate personnel will be available.

Homebound. In terms of personal-social restrictiveness, the homebound instructional process is more restrictive than the process defined above. This type of process denies the student almost all contact with appropriate peers and/or role models. Four definitions of the homebound process are:

1. Good (1973) states that it is education in the home which is directed by the school.

2. Dunn (1973a) notes that homebound instruction is typically for the chronically ill or the convalescing. He also notes that the student is served by either a full-time itinerant teacher or by the regular teacher after school.

3. Kirk (1972) indicates that the process uses itinerant teachers. He further notes that for some students phone connections to the regular classroom are provided. This allows the student access to the regular curriculum and to his/her peers.

4. Massachusetts (1974) defines two types of homebound instruction which differ along a time variable. Type A is for students who will be out of school for less than 60 days, whereas Type B is for students who will miss more than 60 days of class. Both offer the curriculum which would be offered in the class the student would normally attend and instruction from either his regular or special teacher, whichever would be typical.

Other processes. Beyond the processes we have noted, three others are commonly found: (a) hospitals, (b) a combination of special class and resource room, and (c) diagnostic and prescriptive centers. Within the definitions of each of these processes, there are again variations, both as to the intent of the process and on the time variable. Good (1973) and Dunn (1973a) point out that for hospital settings, there is a purpose beyond education—for example, shelter, physical care, and/or psychological care. For the diagnostic and prescriptive centers, Dunn (1973a) states that such centers are staffed by special educators and specialized ancillary personnel (medical/psychological) who use a team approach with special programs and materials. In contrast, Massachusetts (1974) states that such centers are for diagnosis, not primarily for instruction, and that such a placement should not last in excess of eight weeks.

Other authors, and often entire issues of journals (e.g., Volume 6, Number 4 of the *Journal of Special Education*), have devoted much effort to discussions of the pros and cons of various processes as well as to defining the processes. Resource rooms are critiqued in the journal cited, whereas for special classes, Kolstoe (1972a, 1972b) is an excellent source of information. Dunn (1973a) also discusses the advantages and disadvantages of most of these processes. Surprisingly, however, specific articles on models often do not define the individual processes, nor do the authors of various articles address the advantages and disadvantages of the various processes they incorporate. Dunn (1973a) is a notable exception.

The Educational Processes Evaluation Framework

In reviewing this literature, one's initial feeling is that of chaos and confusion. However, in looking more deeply, it can be seen that for the most part these processes vary only with respect to the following three dimensions:

1. physical setting
2. degree and type of integration
3. provision of direct or indirect support services, special methods, and/or special materials.

The processes cited above have been compared along these dimensions and are summarized in Table 5.A. This table provides the basis for considering the processes in terms of the needs of your students.

From this table it can be seen that, in theory and under optimal conditions, regular class placement leads to the highest degree of integration. However, this does not mean that such a setting is the best one for a given student. Nor does it mean that simply because there is physical proximity, there is interaction which is mutually beneficial to the participants. It is our professional judgment that alternative educational processes must be considered in terms of the needs of the child and not on a predetermined assessment of the inherent "goodness" or "badness" of the alternatives. Such an approach is essential if mainstreaming is to be viewed as a process and not as the goal, as a means and not as an end.

Student Characteristics

From the literature, it appears that the *needs* of certain types of students are better met using certain processes. It should be noted, however, that local variables within specific processes will ultimately control the appropriateness of the process; but, in general, we believe

Name of Process	Physical Setting	Degree and Type of Integration (Academic, Physical, Social)			Direct and (Indirect) Support Services		
		Full	Partial	None	Personnel	Special Materials	Special Methods
Regular Class Placement	Regular Class	Academic Physical Social			None Support Service (T.N.I.)	None	None Yes
Consultant	Regular Class	Physical Social	Academic		Consultant (T.N.I.)	Optional	Optional
Itinerant Teacher	Regular Class	Physical Social	Academic		Itinerant Teacher (T.N.I.)	Optional	Yes
Resource Room	Regular Class & Resource Class		Academic Physical Social		Resource Room Teacher (T.N.I.)	Yes	Yes
Regular Class & Special Class	Regular Class & Special Class		Academic Physical Social		Special Class Teacher (T.N.I.)	Yes	Yes
Regular Class & Special School	Regular Class & Special School		Academic Physical Social		Special School Teacher(s) (T.N.I.)	Yes	Yes
Special Class Placement	Special Class		Physical Social	Academic	Special Class Teacher	Yes	Yes
Special Schools	Special School			Academic Physical Social	Special School Teacher(s)	Yes	Yes
Residential School	Residential Schools			Academic Physical Social	Special School Teacher(s)	Yes	Yes
Home-bound	Hospital/ Institution/Home			Academic Physical Social	Home-bound Teacher	Optional	Optional

T = tutor,   N = notetaker,   I = interpreter

TABLE 5.A

A framework describing the characteristics of educational processes in terms of the physical setting, degree and type of integration, and the type of support service.

that the following characteristics represent students whose needs can be best met by a specific process:

1. Regular class placement appears to best serve students who: (a) are above average in intelligence, (b) are on grade level relative to language development, reading, writing, and math, (c) can communicate with teachers and peers, and (d) have the general ability to fully access the school programs.

2. Consultant or itinerant processes appear to best serve students with many of the same characteristics as those prepared for regular class placement, but who have some needs for which the regular class teachers must have assistance (e.g., regarding materials, equipment, methods, etc.).

3. Resource rooms appear best for students: (a) of average ability, (b) with communications skills which are, in general, adequate for the regular classroom, (c) with a grade level lag/gap relative to the regular classroom, and (d) who need additional help with one or more subjects or skills (language development, math, reading, speech, etc.).

4. Special classrooms or combinations of special and regular classrooms often meet the needs of students who have a need similar to or perhaps more profound than resource room students. The fundamental difference is that, for a special classroom to be feasible, there should be several students who share sufficiently common needs so as to allow for grouping.

5. Special or residential schools have the most flexibility in meeting student needs which can not be met in other settings. These needs often include extensive language and academic development as well as vocational training. This is not to say that a given special or residential school may not be best for more capable students. For example, the Texas School for the Deaf has implemented a special program for students who are gifted.

Missing from the literature is an assessment of the strengths and weaknesses of the various processes in terms of academic, personal/social, and communications development. Perhaps this is as it should be, given the extent to which the processes and the quality of their implementation vary from school to school. What is needed is for each educator to carefully assess each educational program available locally to determine its effects on the academic, personal/social, and communications development of deaf students. An analysis of local processes using the Career Development Framework and the Educational Processes Evaluation Framework should be useful in considering such information. When possible, it is wise to examine what has happened to students who have previously gone through the program.

Selecting an Appropriate Process

In the last sections, definitional and functional differences among various models and processes were described. For the local teacher, school psychologist, and administrator, these differences raise several important procedural points:

1. First, the staff must determine which of the previously described

TABLE 5.B

A framework outlining the areas to be considered in assessing the strength of students as compared to the expectations of programs in making placement decisions.

Components	Student Performance	Program's Expectations
Academic/Technical - Math - Science - History - Social Studies - etc.		
Communications Skills - Reading - Writing - Oral Receptive - Manual Receptive - Oral Expressive - Manual Expressive		
Personal/Social - Manage Self - Interact with Others - Manage Environment		

processes are available within the local school settings. If only one or a few options are available, there is little that parents can do short of lengthy due-process proceedings, unless the students' needs fit into those processes. The law and the associated regulations do not require that school districts provide any or all of the processes described, only that a free appropriate education is provided. What is appropriate for a given student is the central issue.

2. Second, the local definition of each process must be discovered. It can not be assumed that a resource room will always provide the same services either within or across districts. The local definition of a process can be determined by analyzing the program in terms of the Educational Processes Evaluation Framework shown in Table 5.A.

3. Third, these processes must be evaluated and matched to a specific student or group of students' needs. This can be done by filling out the component parts of the Career Education Framework as provided in Table 5.B.

In completing these frameworks, the key point to keep in mind is that it will be necessary to use common sense to help you arrive at certain decisions. Because there are no pat answers, and without access to assessment information such as that described in Chapter 6, we can not specify which process to use with a given student. This can be done only by looking at the needs of the individual student and determining the match of these needs with locally available processes. To help you determine the nature and extent of this match or mismatch, we have provided the frameworks in Tables 5.A and 5.B.

Summary

It is important to remember that the goal of academic, personal/social, and communications development is to prepare the individual to function in the home, the school, the community, and in the world of work. This chapter has not attempted to answer the question of which process is best. Rather, its purpose has been to clarify the alternatives and present two frameworks within which professionals using these systems can answer the question, given their situations and the characteristics of the students to be served.

Will educational integration be successful? The answer is yes, for some students. Can educational integration be successful for most students? That depends on several factors. One of the most important is whether or not it is viewed by educators and those controlling the purse strings as a goal or as one alternative educational process. Another factor in its success will be whether or not public school systems think of it as a more economical means of educating handicapped children. To take such a position is to ignore reality. Teachers will have to be prepared. They will need to be supervised. Adequate support services will need to be provided and supervised. To place a hearing-impaired child in a classroom without properly preparing the teacher and without providing *needed* support services is, in our professional judgment, tantamount to child abuse. □

Figure 5.1 reprinted from "A framework for considering some issues in special education," by Maynard C. Reynolds, ©*Exceptional Children*, March 1962, by permission of The Council for Exceptional Children; Figure 5.2 reprinted from "Special education as developmental capital," by Evelyn Deno, ©*Exceptional Children*, November 1970, by permission of The Council for Exceptional Children; Figure 5.3 reprinted from *Exceptional Children in the Schools*, Lloyd M. Dunn, Ed., © 1963, 1974, Holt, Rinehart & Winston, by permission of the publisher; Figures 5.4 and 5.5 reprinted from *A Comprehensive Plan for Education of Hearing Impaired Children and Youth in Massachusetts*, David Luterman, Boston, Massachusetts, by permission of the Department of Education, © 1975.

CHAPTER VI

Assessment and Educational Placement

William Hinkle and Karl R. White

This chapter discusses the assessment process and how it relates to making educational placement decisions for hearing-impaired people. The student variables and school variables, which should be simultaneously considered before the placement of students, are presented along with guidelines, recommendations, and cautions which should be considered in each case. The chapter shows that placement decisions are never without some risk, but that the degree of risk can be substantially reduced if the assessment and decision-making process is structured so that a balance is achieved between technical expertise and common sense. This balance can be achieved by involving people with different backgrounds and different points of view so that a variety of opinions may be wisely deliberated. We have proposed that considered assessment will dramatically increase the probability of placing each hearing-impaired student in an appropriate educational setting.

Introduction

This chapter is written for the many professionals and lay persons involved in making decisions about the educational placement of secondary and postsecondary hearing-impaired students. Placement decisions are by no means new, but recent pressures and trends in education have increased the complexity of such decisions by broadening the number of available options, emphasizing the educational rights of the handicapped, and properly expanding the role which parents and family have in making such decisions. Brill, Merrill, and Frisina (1973) point out that in 1900, 90 percent of the deaf children of this country were being educated in public residential schools. By 1961 this number had dropped to about 50 percent, and by 1973 only 43 percent of deaf students were still being educated in

74

residential schools. The remaining 57 percent were enrolled in day school and day class programs. Most recently the trend has been to place more and more students in educational programs where they can be mainstreamed to varying degrees with their hearing peers.

As this trend continues and choices are being made from among the increasing number of educational alternatives for more and more hearing-impaired students, the process of assessment for making placement decisions becomes increasingly important. The purpose of assessment is to provide reliable, valid, and useful information which will help in making a choice from among the available or readily organizable educational options.

As the term is used in this chapter, assessment implies not only the measurement of various student characteristics but also the evaluation of such measurements, using professional judgment in order to make relative judgments about the appropriateness of various options for a particular student.

When assessment activities are deliberately planned and then performed with an appropriate balance of technical expertise, experience, and common sense, the ultimate decision becomes an invaluable aid in placing each child in an educational setting where optimal learning is possible and success is most probable. It is useful to remember that the assessment process is much like fire. Properly understood and used, fire is an extremely useful tool in our society. It is through the appropriate use of fire that the wheels of industry are turned, homes are heated, electricity is generated, and rapid transportation is provided. But it is this same force, if not controlled or if used improperly, which can destroy property and cause massive injury and death. The way in which fire is controlled and applied determines whether it is helpful or destructive. So it is with the educational assessment of students.

People assured in their opinion that educational assessment can provide all of the information necessary to make accurate placement decisions are naive. We do not view present—and possibly future— assessment techniques as having the power to eliminate all uncertainty, risk, and error in educational placement decisions. The literature is full of examples of children who were incorrectly diagnosed and placed where long-term damages resulted, based on inappropriate assessments. However, comprehensive assessment information can dramatically increase the probability of correct decisions. Like fire, the utility of any assessment process depends on how well it is planned, implemented, and used. For assessment, the key to how it is used resides in how the assessment findings are interpreted.

This chapter does not offer a cookbook approach to assessment, where the reader need only plug the appropriate test scores of a given child into an "empirically derived and validated" formula to arrive at the "correct" placement decision. Unfortunately, the world of education—particularly when dealing with a handicapped population—is not so simple. Instead, this chapter (a) identifies what we consider to be the most critical variables to be considered in such assessments; (b) references, describes, and critiques some of the possible strategies and alternatives for gathering information about those variables; (c) details a number of guidelines which should be followed; and (d) discusses the limitations and cautions which must be kept in mind with such assessment activities.

What Variables Should Be Assessed?

The first step in the assessment process is to identify those variables that need to be included. Unless care is taken, it is easy to overinvest in the assessment of student variables to the exclusion of other equally important variables, such as those that involve the school. Obviously, the assessment process should lead to a decision which is in the best interests of the student and, as such, assessment activities should be student-centered. But, the student's best interests cannot be adequately served unless it is remembered that the individual student's probability of success depends on the ability of the selected program to meet his unique needs. The capability of various programs to "bridge the gap," referred to by Bishop in Chapter 3, must be a central consideration in gathering assessment information. Consequently, this chapter will discuss the assessment process as it relates to two sets of variables—student variables and school variables. In addition, procedures and guidelines for collecting specific information in each of the general areas will be presented.

Program Alternatives

Before data collection is begun, it is important to have a basic idea of the program options which are available or readily organizable in a given locality. In Chapter 5, Hein and Bishop describe a number of models which provide a basic understanding of the theoretical placement options. It is improbable, however, that any one of these models provides an accurate description of the options that are available or easy to develop in a given locality. While P.L. 94-142 requires that local educational agencies provide free appropriate education to handicapped students, the implementation of this law is subject to some local interpretation. Realistically, the options available to a particular student and family will probably consist of limited combinations and variations of the components or processes presented in the basic models outlined in Chapter 5. The initial identification of what basic options are available in a given locality is important when beginning to organize the school variables. If it is found that none of the available options is satisfactory, it may be necessary to develop an appropriate program. However, a firm understanding of the available options at the beginning of the assessment process facilitates making decisions more quickly and confidently. A simplified combination of the options presented in the various models discussed in Chapter 5 is presented in Table 6.A.

TABLE 6.A
Potentially available educational placement options.

1. Regular class placement with very little, if any, additional resources
2. Regular class placement with consultation
3. Regular class placement with supplementary teaching or treatment
4. Regular class placement with resource room
5. Part-time special class
6. Full-time special class
7. Special day school
8. Residential school

Underlying Principles of Assessment and Decision Making

Before collecting specific data about children and programs, it is important to be aware of some philosophical perspectives about how such data should be interpreted and applied in a decision-making framework.

Input From a Variety of Sources

First, input from a wide variety of people should be considered, for the careful consideration of a multiplicity of perspectives will result in better final decisions. Although it is not necessary for everyone to be present at one time, at least the following should be significant participants throughout the assessment and decision-making process: a previous classroom teacher, consulting and/or supervising specialists (e.g., audiologist, school psychologist, speech pathologist, supervising teacher, etc.), parents, and the student.[1] Each of these persons will bring a different, yet important, perspective to the decision-making process. In recent years the role of the parents in the decision-making process has become more and more significant, an important and appropriate trend. Although many parents don't assume it, the major responsibility for making the placement decision is theirs.

The decision to be made is an extremely difficult and complex one. In a responsible role, parents serve in many ways as a combination of a judge and a labor arbitrator A reasonable probability of making a decision that will serve the student well can be achieved by carefully considering the available information. Parents must listen to testimony including technical and professional opinions as well as educated guesses. They must listen and question the testimony in order to distinguish fact from fiction. They must be critically inquisitive without alienating those upon whom their child must depend for a future education, and they must inject common sense into educational jargon and fanciful projections and hopes.

It is easier by far for parents to take an unconcerned and passive role while test scores are conveniently used to make a decision for their child's future. Contrastingly, it is possible for parents to take an overactive, belligerent role in making demands for their child's rights. The best alternative is for parents to take an active, well informed, common-sensical role as their child's advocate; sifting through the evidence and working with professionals to give their child the best possible long-term opportunity. That way everybody wins — especially the child.

If properly utilized by professionals, parents can be a tremendous asset to the child and to the educational system in making decisions and in supporting and participating in educational programs. One of the most challenging questions facing professional educators is how to foster the involvement of parents in this whole process.

---

[1]How extensively the student participates in this process depends largely on his/her age. The remainder of this chapter will be written with 13- to 14-year-old students in mind, i.e., students just beginning their secondary education. In most cases, the older the student, the more she/he should participate. As students become of legal age, they may replace the parent in the entire process.

Gathering a Variety of Data

In addition to multiple perspectives, the assessment process requires a variety of data. Information from the best available standardized achievement and nonverbal IQ tests, academic records, speech and speechreading test results, and audiometric assessments should be carefully considered, keeping the shortcomings and limitations of such testing information in mind. Because such scores come in nice, neat packages with precise-looking numbers, it is easy to put too much confidence in these assessments.

Equally important are observations and opinions of professionals and parents who deal with the student on a daily basis. Inconsistencies between the observations of a classroom teacher and the results of an IQ test regarding a student's aptitude for learning should not always be decided in favor of the standardized test. It may well be that the IQ score in this case is not an accurate measure of aptitude because the student misunderstood the directions of the test. On the other hand, standardized test scores should not be dismissed. As a general rule, when appropriately done, testing is one of the best indicators of skills, achievement, and aptitude. But just as competent people may make errors in judgment, testing information is fallible and has limitations. However, it bears repeating that the key to making good decisions is a well balanced variety of assessment information which can be used as a system of checks and balances to arrive at a proper decision.

Balancing Common Sense and Technical Expertise

It is also important that an appropriate balance between common sense and technical expertise be achieved in the interpretation of the data. Particularly when dealing with a handicapped population such as the hearing impaired, it is critical that people administering and interpreting standardized tests be both competent and experienced in testing hearing-impaired children. The same applies to classroom teachers and consulting specialists. Their technical expertise is invaluable if it is augmented with experience in dealing with hearing-impaired students. Equally important is the common sense to use this expertise and experience appropriately. We all know professionals in many fields so bound up in theory and technology that they are unable to solve practical problems. Again, the key is in achieving a balance.

Collecting Assessment Information

We have discussed the importance of becoming familiar with available program options, of acquiring various perspectives, and of gathering a variety of data. We have presented the underlying principles of collection, interpretation, and decision making which we believe are important in making an assessment to determine educational placement. Now, we will discuss the specifics of assessment data collection by presenting the specific variables which should be considered in each of two major areas referred to earlier—*student variables* and *school variables*. In each of these areas, the importance of various specific pieces of information will be discussed, as well as suggestions and guidelines for collecting such information. These data should be considered in most instances where options such as those presented in Table 6.A are being considered. Depending on the situation, some of these may be excluded and/or others added.

Student Variables

The importance of obtaining an accurate assessment of various student variables should be obvious. As part of Project NEED (Bitter, Johnston, & Sorenson, 1973), questionnaire information was collected from 100 educators of the deaf from programs where students were integrated to some degree. In the questionnaire, respondents were asked to briefly describe the criteria used by their programs to determine who would be integrated. Almost all of the responses cited student variables as the criteria. The most frequently mentioned were overall communications skills (31 percent of the responses), academic skills (23 percent), and social/emotional skills (22 percent). Using a breakdown such as this facilitates the assessing of student variables.

Communication Variables

Many people consider an assessment of the communication variables as the most important information to be considered in making placement decisions (Griffing, 1970; Ross, 1976). Obviously, hearing-impaired students are in a position requiring special educational attention because of a breakdown in the normal process of communication. Thus, the importance attached to these variables by most people is not surprising; but consider the following viewpoints.

Audiological assessment. The hearing loss of a student *is* the first consideration in determining a student's communication status, and the importance of this variable is predominantly emphasized by articles discussing the educational placement of hearing-impaired students (Brill, Merrill, & Frisina, 1973; Griffing, 1970; Hayes & Griffing, 1967; Ross, 1976; Yater, 1977). Ross (1976, p. 104) suggests that "the single best predictor of a hearing-impaired child's (academic) performance is the degree of hearing loss." In support of this statement he cites a number of empirical studies (Luterman, 1974; Quigley & Thomure, 1968; Stark, 1974). However, the position of importance given to this variable must be considered carefully. As Ross (1976) pointed out, most deaf educators "know children with severe or profound hearing losses who are doing beautifully in public schools and others with mild or moderate losses who are doing horribly." In addition, NTID research with postsecondary hearing-impaired students has shown only moderate to weak correlations between average puretone loss in the better ear and various measures of academic success (Welsh & Wilson, 1977; White, 1978a; White, 1978b).

A broader view on the importance of the hearing loss variable was presented by Johnson (1967) in his article, "Let's Look at the Child, Not the Audiogram." Johnson argues that "it is how the hearing-impaired child functions, not the degree of his hearing loss, which should determine the type of educational system to which he is assigned." Since hearing-impaired children are handicapped precisely because of their functional loss, it would be foolish to ignore this variable as one part of the assessment process. On the other hand, it would be equally foolish to establish rigid cut-off points of decibel loss or configuration as the criterion for choice of placement.

It is essential that the analysis be conducted by a certified or licensed audiologist experienced with hearing-impaired clients. The analysis should include such factors as degree and configuration of hearing loss, onset of hearing loss, the amount of residual hearing, and the professional judgment of the audiologist as to how the particular hearing loss would affect the student's ability to function in the proposed setting.

Receptive communication. Factors such as speechreading, use of residual hearing, reading comprehension, and simultaneous communication skills are all potentially important assessment variables depending on the placement options which are being considered. The assessment of these variables interacts significantly with the characteristics of school and support services which will be discussed later. In actual practice, student, school, and support variables must be considered simultaneously rather than in the linear fashion in which this chapter discusses them. For example, a student's skill in manual languages is not important in determining whether or not a student should be placed in a regular classroom unless a manual interpreter is available for use. In which case such skill becomes very important in determining the ability of a student with weak speechreading skills to follow a manual interpreter.

Whatever the educational situation, a large amount of information will be directed at the student. It is important that the student's receptive skills complement the modes of communication which are utilized in the setting being considered. A variety of tests can be useful in measuring these skills. Johnson (1976) describes a set of tests developed at NTID to measure hearing discrimination, speechreading with and without sound, manual reception, and simultaneous reception among postsecondary deaf students. The most important characteristic to look for in tests of receptive skills is that they provide meaningful information about the student's use of receptive communication skills in practical situations. Too frequently we allow ourselves to be lulled into a false sense of security by a barrage of numbers that do not tell us about the student's actual functional abilities.

As always, test scores should be interpreted in the context of opinions from teachers, parents, and specialists who know how the student functions in various situations. In fact, there are many times when the tests described by Johnson (1976), or other similar tests, will not be available or practical for local educators to use. In such situations the judgment of teachers and consultants who have worked with a range of hearing-impaired students is an acceptable substitute for test scores. Work by White (1978a) demonstrates that teachers' ratings of hearing-impaired students' simultaneous reception and speech intelligibility skills correlated .65 and .71 respectively with the actual scores on the more sophisticated tests described by Johnson. The important thing is that decision makers find some way to consider the appropriateness of the students' receptive communication skills for the various placement alternatives.

Expressive communication. Ideally, the process of education involves interaction. To participate fully in any educational setting, the student needs to express ideas, thoughts, and feelings. As was the case with the receptive communication variables, the level of skill required depends to some degree on the characteristics of the settings under consideration. Relevant student variables of expressive communication include speech intelligibility, simultaneous or manual communication, and writing. Johnson (1976) describes tests developed at NTID for measuring speech skills. The scores on such tests should be considered in conjunction with the opinions of past teachers, parents, and specialists to decide whether or not the student's expressive communication skills are adequate for the potential educational setting. Again, in the absence of any such test scores, the professional judgment of experienced people may have to suffice.

Language base. Recently a number of people have been investigating the overall English language base of deaf students. Obviously, it is unimportant how good a student's expressive and/or receptive skills are if there is no language base to support these skills. Quigley and associates (Montanelli & Quigley, 1974; Power, 1971; Quigley, Smith, & Wilbur, 1973; Quigley, Wilbur, & Montanelli, 1974; Wilbur & Quigley, 1972) have developed a Test of Syntactic Ability (TSA) that was designed to measure hearing-impaired individuals' comprehension of specific syntactic structures occurring in English. The test seems to be a fairly good measure of how well a person is able to use and comprehend the standard English language, although there has been little work on how results of the TSA are related to academic success. The test was recently published and is available from DORMAC, Inc., P.O. Box 752, Beaverton, OR 97005. Although untried at this point for aiding in educational placement decisions, such a test represents a potentially valuable tool that could be applied in the future.

Academic Variables

The student's ability to learn. Many labels are used to refer to a student's ability to learn: IQ, aptitude, learning potential, etc. Regardless of what term is used, the student's ability to learn is one of the most important variables in determining where a student should be placed. Unfortunately, it is also one of the most difficult to assess. Psychometricians have debated for years over methods for defining intelligence, and tools for measuring intelligence separate from achievement. Also debated was the possible bias of intelligence tests for or against certain cultural or minority groups (Block & Dworkin, 1976; Mercer, 1972). Most of these issues are still unresolved, but intelligence remains an extremely important variable when gathering information relative to student placement.

The use of individually administered standardized tests of intelligence (or IQ) should be used as one measure of the student's ability to learn. If used cautiously by qualified people, such tests are a good general indicator of a student's ability to profit from instruction. The most valid measure of a deaf student's intelligence will be obtained by using nonverbal performance measures of intelligence (Burchard & Myklebust, 1942; Lane & Schneider, 1941). When used with hearing-impaired individuals, measures of verbal intelligence may lead to misjudgments regarding placement.

Understandably, the scores obtained from verbal intelligence tests are often spuriously low estimates of students' ability due to the confounding of language deficiencies resulting from the hearing loss with intelligence (Brill, 1962; Levine, 1960, pp. 2A–221; Myklebust, 1954, pp. 25, 237). As an example, in their excellent article evaluating the use of psychological tests and testing procedures with deaf populations, Vernon and Brown (1964) cite the case of a deaf girl who was committed to a hospital for the mentally retarded based on her score of 29 on the Stanford Binet verbal IQ test. Five years later, upon reevaluation, a performance test measured her IQ as 113. Subsequently she was dismissed from the hospital and enrolled in a school for the deaf. Although not frequent, such misclassifications of handicapped and disadvantaged individuals do occur.

It should be noted that not all nonverbal measures of ability are appropriate for use with hearing-impaired students because, in many cases, the verbal content of the instructions is still so high as to present a serious obstacle for students with low verbal skills. In administering such tests, the chance for serious errors will be significantly reduced if the examiner is experienced in working with hearing-impaired students. Moreover, since the performance section of most IQ tests is relatively short, it is preferable to use the results from two such tests whenever possible.

There are a number of performance IQ measures which can be used appropriately with deaf populations. Among those recommended are the Wechsler Intelligence Scale for Children (1949), the Wechsler Intelligence Scale for Adults (1955), the Leiter International Performance Scale (1948 revision), and the Raven Progressive Matrices (1948). Each of these scales has been used successfully with hearing-impaired populations in the past. For example, Brill (1962) obtained a correlation of .55 between Wechsler Intelligence IQs and scores on standardized academic achievement tests of 185 graduates of a residential school for the deaf. Birch and Birch (1956) reported correlations of .71 and .86 between Leiter International Performance Scale intelligence scores and supervising teacher ratings of academic achievement and intelligence, respectively. In a further study, years later, these same measures of IQ correlated .63 with Stanford Achievement Test scores (Birch, Stuckless, & Birch, 1963).

The reader should not assume that other measures of IQ are never acceptable. There are probably a number of other equally appropriate measures. Care should be taken, however, to assure that the test has been successful when previously used with hearing-impaired populations. It is also important to make sure that the test selected is appropriate for use with the particular age group being tested.

The student's previous academic achievement. A second important measure of a student's ability to learn should come from a classroom (or consulting) teacher who has worked extensively with the student in the past. This input may be obtained through a formal rating scale or through more informal discussion. This kind of professional judgment is critically important in making the best placement decisions for the greatest number of students and should not be neglected.

As mentioned earlier, properly administered and appropriate IQ tests have, in general, been shown to be fairly good predictors of subsequent academic performance. This means that IQ tests are good predictors for most people; are only moderately good predictors for some; and, for a few, such measures of IQ are not at all related to subsequent achievement. Teachers who have had frequent contact with the individual in a learning situation are in an extremely good position to offer insights about the student's learning potential. Significant discrepancies between the teacher's opinion and the test scores will cast real doubt on the validity of that particular assessment and should be investigated thoroughly.

Because ability is always influenced by such factors as motivation, a student's past academic achievement will give important information about the probability of a future level of achievement. Again, the best beginning point is with one of the commercially available standardized measures of academic achievement. Minimally such a test should include some measure of reading comprehension, vocabulary, and math.

Most of the standardized achievement tests used in school testing programs today are of acceptable quality. Although there are certainly differences among the tests, the pros and cons of the different available tests are overshadowed by the advantage of being able to compare an individual's results on the test with the results of other students in each of the various programs. Consequently, the best test is usually the test which has been administered in each of the other programs being considered. If the student scores significantly below the range of other successful students in a particular program, it would probably not be advisable to place the student in that program unless extraordinary supportive tutoring was planned. The accuracy of this statement, of course, depends on how well the standardized test parallels the curricula.

The student's grades in previous courses provide another source of information about past levels of academic achievement. In order to be considered for a program which will probably be more challenging than previous programs in an academic sense, the student should normally have demonstrated an ability to achieve average or better than average grades in his/her previous setting. In order for this criterion to be meaningful, decision makers must guard against programs which give good grades to or socially promote virtually all students.

As is the case with measures of intelligence, previous teachers and/or consulting specialists are another excellent source of data about past achievement. They will be able to provide information about the credibility and meaning of past grades and whether the student's achievement test scores are consistent with the classroom experience.

Personal/Social Variables

As important as any of the other student variables are the personal/social aspects of the educational setting. Although school is often considered to be primarily an academic pursuit, and hearing impairments require special consideration of the communication variables, some of the most lasting outcomes of the educational experience for hearing-impaired students are neither academic- nor communication-related. Particularly during the secondary and postsecondary years, students formulate and solidify many of the attitudes, behaviors, and personality characteristics which will remain with them for life (Astin, 1977). These years are a time of real growth, change, and maturation, making the personal/social variables extremely important in the process of deciding educational placement.

Student preferences and motivation. The first consideration in this area is the preferences of the student. The old American work ethic, "You can do anything you really want to do," has some validity in predicting the academic success of students. White (1978b) found that faculty ratings of how motivated students were to succeed correlated between .50 and .75 with various measures of academic success among postsecondary deaf students. Intuitively, this is not surprising. There are limits to what certain students are able to accomplish, no matter how hard they are willing to work. Still, student preferences and motivation should be one of the primary considerations in making educational placement decisions at the secondary level.

Behavior problems. Occasionally students are placed in a particular educational setting or discouraged (or even excluded) from another educational setting because of particular behavior problems such as hyperactivity, lack of attendance, disruptive behavior, etc. Except in the most extreme cases, where such behavior has been clinically diagnosed by competent professionals as ongoing emotional or psychological problems requiring specific treatment, such behavior problems should not play a significant role in the placement decision.

Yater (1977) points out that there may be a tendency to keep some students from being mainstreamed because of what are labeled "immature" behaviors. While mature behavior is advantageous in any setting, there is little if any evidence that keeping a child in a self-contained classroom for the deaf will result in more mature behavior.

Many of the so-called behavior problems may result from the student's lack of interest or motivation in the educational process. In such cases, a change of setting might actually help instead of aggravating the problem. Although there should be an awareness of such behavior patterns, with the intent of structuring the environment so improvements can occur, such behavior should not play a significant role in the final decision, except in the most extreme cases.

Personality tests. There are a number of standardized commercially available tests designed to measure various personal/social variables, and their results would seem logically important in making educational placement decisions. Such variables as academic self concept, self esteem, defensiveness, achievement motivation, impulsivity, general maladjustment, etc. are frequently represented in these scales.

Vernon and Brown (1964) recommend against the frequent use of such tests and point out a number of problems that may occur when using these measures with hearing-impaired individuals. Most of these problems stem from the difficulties created by the inadequate language skills possessed by many hearing-impaired students.

Garrison, Tesch, and DeCaro (1978) found that hearing-impaired students at NTID had substantial trouble understanding and appropriately responding to items on the Tennessee Self Concept Scale (TSCS, Fitts, 1965). From a sample of students who had previously completed the TSCS, 30 students were individually interviewed. During the interview each student was presented with a subset of items from the original test. Students were asked to explain in their own words what the item meant and to give examples of the behavior or feelings of people who would answer the item positively and negatively. Students' responses were recorded for each item and subsequently analyzed by three judges as to whether the students had understood the item. The results showed that on the average: (a) on any one item, only half of the students understood its meaning; (b) of all items, any single student understood only about half of them. The resulting message should be clear. It is our recommendation that such invalid personality measures not be used in making assessments relative to educational placement decisions.

Personal/social competencies of greatest concern. As stated in Chapter 1, there seems to be broad agreement among educators of the hearing impaired that their students are deficient in certain important areas of personal/social competency. In a series of workshops held with almost 300 educators of the hearing impaired around the country during 1977, White (1978c), in summarizing the results, reports a great deal of consistency as to what educators were identifying as the areas of personal/social competency most urgently in need of improvement. From a list of 24 major competency areas, these educators consistently emphasized the importance of students improving in their ability to: (1) accept responsibility for their own actions; (2) have an awareness of their own values, strengths, weaknesses, and goals; (3) make sound decisions; (4) have self confidence; and, (5) demonstrate initiative.

As was discussed previously within the area of behavior problems, we do not suggest that students be rated on variables such as these with the intent of estimating their ability to succeed in various educational settings. Certainly not all hearing-impaired students need significant improvement in each of these areas. Yet the consistency with which these areas were identified indicates that these are important areas of consideration for hearing-impaired students in general. This information can be useful in the assessment and decision-making process by alerting decision makers to some key areas of personal/social competency in which many hearing-impaired students need improvement. This helps to delimit an area which most people feel is important but which has remained vague and undefined. These five areas may be used as a starting point (without excluding other areas that may arise). If various decision makers believe an individual student needs improvement in one or more areas, it would be wise to look for program alternatives that are structured in such a way as to foster that improvement.

School Variables

All of the information gathered about the individual student is brought into focus by the various school variables. Without the information about specific program options, the interpretation of the information provided by the student assessment would be extremely difficult and incomplete. For example, how good do the students'

FIGURE 6.1
Illustration depicting the relationship between student and school variables in placement decisions. The weaker the student is in a given category, the stronger the school needs to be in that category.

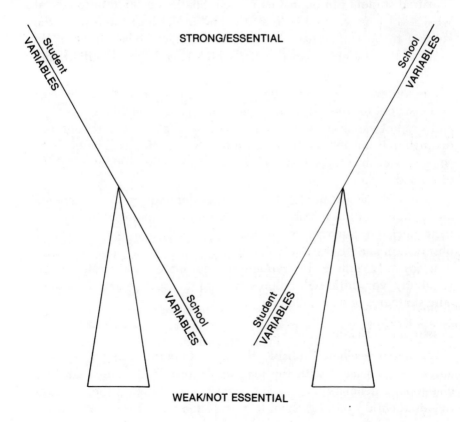

speech skills need to be? That depends on the experience of the classroom teacher, the availability of speech pathologists, the experience of the other students with the hearing impaired, and the demands of the program. The same kind of interaction happens with most, if not all, of the other student variables.

In many ways, the relationship between student variables and school variables is like the teeter-totter pictured in Figure 6.1. The weaker the student is in the various categories which have been outlined, the stronger the school must be in the various classroom and support variables which will be discussed in this section. The reverse is also true; a student with very strong skills can function adequately with very few exceptional classroom or support variables. Theoretically, given the proper classroom and support variables, any hearing-impaired student can be mainstreamed. So, the question becomes: at what level it is reasonable, realistic, and in the best interests of the student to be mainstreamed? This question must be answered in terms of the student characteristics which have been identified, and the resources at the school.

The following section discusses the most important characteristics of the school to consider in making a placement decision. Classroom and support variables will be dealt with separately even though the distinction is not always that clear in reality. An effort will be made to show how each of the school variables relates to the student variables discussed earlier.

Most of the assessment of the variables depends on the judgments and opinions of the members of the team participating in the placement decision. Such an assessment is basically a simple process of observation and discussion which in many cases would only be made unnecessarily complex by trying to make it more sophisticated. Consequently, very little will be presented in this section about the specific strategies of data collection.

Classroom Variables

Classroom teacher. Probably the most important classroom variables are associated with the teacher. Yater (1977) states that "the classroom teacher is the pivotal professional affecting the hearing-impaired child's public school learning situation." Yater continues:

> To the teacher will fall the task of making modifications in his/her classroom teaching methods which will benefit the child with a hearing loss and the entire class. Upon him/her will fall the ultimate responsibility

for creating an atmosphere in which each student will be able to effectively participate in all educational offerings. To the teacher will fall the daily task of making immediate decisions about whether hearing loss or other aspects of the child's functioning are causing difficulties. Upon him/her will primarily depend whether the other children basically view the presence of the child with a hearing loss in their classroom as a positive or negative experience (p. 49).

It is important that the experience, skill, and attitude of the classroom teacher are carefully assessed in making educational placement decisions. The stronger the teacher is in a particular setting, the more likely the student is to be successful. Experience with the hearing impaired is very important; compensations can be made, however, by an inexperienced but skillful teacher who feels good about the challenge and is committed to having a hearing-impaired student in the classroom. The reader interested in a detailed statement of the ideal teacher's competencies is referred to Griffing's chapter in Berg and Fletcher (1970). Such an ideal should be used only as an approximate guideline because, in comparing the teachers in various situations, we run the risk of excluding all potential teachers.

Nature of the curriculum. The second school variable to be considered is the nature of the curriculum in the various settings. The school will need to be flexible enough to incorporate the special curricular needs of the hearing impaired into its existing curricula. Media may need to be used more extensively, existing media may need to be captioned or modified, supplementary texts may be required, etc.

A related issue is the instructional style which dominates the particular setting. If individualization is strongly emphasized, there is a greater probability that the individual learning needs of a hearing-impaired student can be more readily accommodated. Someone should determine how much lecturing, class discussion, reading, computer-assisted instruction, etc. is typically used in the class and how well the student deals with the most commonly used modes.

Finally, the match among the curriculum from which a student is coming, the curriculum in the particular setting, and anticipated future needs should be considered. For example, if the student does not anticipate postsecondary education, will the potential high school situation help him/her to develop the skills and knowledge necessary to enter meaningful employment? If the student is planning to attend college, is there appropriate college preparatory work that can build on the student's present skills in key areas? The answers to many such questions are necessary. The appropriate specific questions will vary from situation to situation and will be best established by the committee of people participating in the placement of a particular student.

Characteristics of other students. Since we are almost always considering a group educational situation, the characteristics of other students play an important role in making a placement decision. We have already discussed the fact that the student being considered for placement should be within the range of academic achievement represented by other students in the class. This should be assessed by an examination of the results of standardized tests, by the curriculum within which the student has been working, and by the opinion of past teachers. When the student is significantly below the academic achievement of all other classmates, the situation will be almost impossible for both the student and the teacher.

The size of the class is another important variable. Students with significant hearing impairments usually require much more time from the teacher than do most normally hearing students. As a result, class sizes need to be correspondingly smaller. In their report recommending organizational policies in the education of the deaf, Brill, Merrill, and Frisina (1973) suggest that secondary classes consisting of all deaf students should not be larger than 10. Although integrated classes do not need to meet this criterion, it is still important that this principle be applied when hearing-impaired students are placed in a class with normally hearing students. Thereafter, depending on the number of hearing-impaired students in the class and on the number of supports being employed, integrated classes should generally be smaller than nonintegrated classes. It is also important that there not be too many severely handicapped children in a single integrated classroom, competing for the teacher's attention and energy.

Support Variables

Regardless of the educational situation in which they are placed, almost all hearing-impaired students will require some additional support. Obviously, the degree of support will vary depending on the needs of the student and the type of program in which he is placed.

Direct support services. In almost all instances some direct support services will need to be provided to the student. The range of potentially required services includes audiology, speech therapy, counseling, tutoring, notetaking, and interpreting. If organized and supervised correctly and staffed by competent people, some of these services can often be provided on a district or regional basis when there are not enough students to justify the expense for a single school. The training and skills of the people providing the services are a key factor. Audiologists and speech pathologists are more likely to provide quality services if they hold the Certificate of Clinical Competence from the American Speech-Language-Hearing Association or the equivalent state licensure. In addition, it is highly desirable that such professionals have experience working with prelingually deaf hearing-impaired persons in an educational setting. Because of the relatively low incidence of severe prelingual hearing loss among the variety of problems with which audiologists and speech pathologists work, it is not unusual for them to have little or no experience with hearing-impaired students in an educational setting. A lack of awareness of this situation could be particularly damaging.

Depending on the student and the setting, it may be necessary to provide interpreting, tutoring, and/or notetaking support. As is discussed in Chapter 9, educational interpreting (oral or manual) is a demanding task requiring thoroughly trained professionals. Ideally, interpreters should possess comprehensive certification from the Registry of Interpreters for the Deaf which will allow them to meet both the expressive and receptive needs of the student.

Experience working with the prelingually hearing impaired is the key to success for the well trained counselor or resource room teacher. For the competent professional who is willing to learn, such experience can be gained "on the job," but it places students at a distinct disadvantage for the first few years. For some students it will be necessary to provide tutoring and notetaking support.

As pointed out by Osguthorpe and Whitehead in Chapter 10 and by the experience at NTID (Osguthorpe, Whitehead, & Bishop, 1978), properly trained and supervised hearing peers can provide most, if not all, of the students' tutoring and notetaking support needs. Whether or not students are trained and used for this purpose, some provision will have to be made to meet these needs.

Administrative support. For hearing-impaired students to be mainstreamed to any degree among their hearing peers, substantial administrative support must exist. Decision makers must attempt to assess the reality of an organization's administrative commitment to the needs of hearing-impaired students. Realistically, a commitment requires purchasing and maintaining communication aids, providing special curriculum/instructor/evaluation schemes, funding and/or training the appropriate support personnel, supporting reduced class sizes, rescheduling of classtimes and classroom, etc. Even though P.L.

94-142 requires that the necessary supports be provided, if the administrative commitment is more in theory than in fact, the support for such provisions is made difficult to enforce and the requirement will soon fade among other administrative priorities—while students' educations suffer.

Ideally, direct support personnel and classroom teachers should have experience working with the hearing impaired. Realistically, at least in the near future, this will not be the case. In those cases where experience is lacking, it is essential that a trained, experienced educator of the hearing impaired be placed in a consulting, supervisory position. Even when classroom and support personnel do have experience, such a person can provide valuable service. Griffing (1970) discusses the importance of such persons, the role they should play, and the characteristics they need.

Family support. Even though it is not really a school variable, the support of the family is discussed here because it is such a crucial factor. Certainly, many hearing-impaired students succeed without the support of their families. Yet, properly encouraged, families can contribute substantially to the probability of the student's success. Parents and siblings can not only provide emotional support and encouragement at home, but also they can participate extensively in the student's educational program by tutoring, providing complementary experiences, acting as a liaison with the school, etc. School personnel need to recognize this and do more to encourage the involvement of parents and family in the educational process. At the same time, family members need to accept the fact that they have a responsibility in the educational success of the student.

Using Assessment Information in Selecting a Program

In the beginning of this chapter we emphasized that assessment is a combination of measurement (the quantification of variables) and evaluation (making judgments of relative worth). We have discussed in some detail a great many variables which should be considered in the assessment process. These variables include objective and subjective information from standardized test scores to personal opinion. The purpose of all of this assessment should be to strengthen the validity of the placement decision. To be worth doing, assessment must lead to a better educational experience for the student.

Conceivably, the number of variables we have discussed can become overwhelming. Because of the broad range of educational set-

TABLE 6.B
Summary of the critical areas which should be considered in making placement decisions.

A. **Academic variables**
  1. Student's ability to learn
  2. Previous academic achievement
     a. Standardized tests
     b. Previous grades
B. **Communication variables**
  1. Audiological assessment
  2. Receptive communication
     a. Residual hearing
     b. Speechreading
     c. Simultaneous communication
     d. Reading comprehension
  3. Expressive communication
     a. Speech intelligibility
     b. Writing
     c. Simultaneous communication
  4. Language usage
C. **Personal/social variables**
  1. Student preferences and motivation
  2. Personal/social competencies
     a. Responsibility for own actions
     b. Awareness of values, goals, strengths, and weaknesses
     c. Decision-making ability
     d. Self confidence
     e. Initiative

D. **Classroom variables**
  1. Classroom teacher
     a. Experience
     b. Skill and training
     c. Attitude and willingness
  2. Nature of curriculum
     a. Instructional style and maturity
     b. Matches student's current level of development and future needs
  3. Characteristics of other students
E. **Support variables**
  1. Direct support needs
     a. Audiologists, speech pathologists, and resource room teachers
     b. Tutors/notetakers
     c. Interpreters
  2. Administrative support
     a. Commitment of upper-level administration
     b. Supervising teachers and specialists
  3. Family support

tings which are potentially available, each of the variables applies to one student or another, even though every variable may not be important for a given individual student. It is important, however, that conscious decisions are made about *which* variables to assess for a given student—by first considering all of the variables. To help the reader organize the assessment information presented in previous sections, Table 6.B summarizes the critical areas which should be considered in making placement decisions.

As pointed out previously, the selection process should involve a group of people. It is not important who is in charge of calling the group together and organizing the meeting, as long as there is significant participation from parents and student, previous classroom teachers, and consulting and/or supervising specialists. These people have the responsibility of deciding what information will be required, of initiating or supervising the data collection, and of carefully weighing the resulting information to reach a placement decision.

It would be wonderful if the determinants of success in each placement option were so well defined and the process of assessment so precise that decision makers could be completely confident that the selected program was the best possible one for that particular student at that particular time. Human behavior is not so predictable, however, and the science of education is not so precise that such a state of affairs is even foreseeable. Every decision will be accompanied by some degree of risk. The better the assessment the less the risk, but risk will never be eliminated. Probably the most powerful factor in making better decisions is experience. As groups of decision makers gain experience in the placement process and couple the wisdom and common sense gained from that experience with the best we know about measurement and assessment, better decisions will result.

It is also important to remember that no placement decision should ever be viewed as final and irrevocable. Sabatino (1972a, p. 344) points out the importance of continually reassessing the educational placement of handicapped children in order to best meet their needs.

> The handicapped child's education is dependent upon a continuously changing instructional pattern, based upon his needs and functions. There is no one diagnostic statement that can cover any more than one educational planning period . . . Educational diagnosis is dynamic, continuous. The one-shot approach to psychoeducational child study sadly lacks the capability to validly sample behaviors leading directly to the instructional management of handicapped children.

This statement applies well to determining the placement of the hearing-impaired child. The group determining the placement must carefully weigh all of the available evidence and make their best decision. When wavering between two options, we recommend that they opt for the alternative which seems to be most challenging for the student. Given the proper support and encouragement, students have a way of rising to meet challenges.

Once a decision is made, the assessment process is not finished. As the student enrolls in whatever option has been chosen, the assessment process begins all over again. If those persons interacting with the student are alert and perceptive, they will be able to gather the most valuable information possible in making the next decision about that student's educational placement. Parents, teachers, and consultants who interact frequently with the student will be able to judge whether the setting is appropriate for that particular student, what variables seem to be leading to success or failure, what the student's strengths and weaknesses are, etc. Not only will the information thus acquired benefit that particular student, but also the experience gained will make those decision makers more confident and competent in the placement of other students.

Dunn (1968) points out an additional advantage of such a diagnostic approach to the instructional setting:

> Different modalities for reaching the child should also be tried. Thus, since the instructional program itself becomes the diagnostic teaching, failures are program and instructor failures, not pupil failures . . . . this diagnostic procedure is viewed as the best available since it enables us to assess continuously the problem points of the instructional program against the assets of the child.

Thus, whatever alternative is chosen, that setting should become the seed bed or the incubator for germinating ideas and perceptions which will lead to making even better future decisions.

Summary

This chapter has discussed the assessment process and how it relates to making educational placement decisions. The student and school variables, which should be simultaneously considered in the placement of hearing-impaired students, have been discussed in some detail including guidelines, recommendations, and cautions which should be considered in each case. We have argued that such placement decisions are never without some risk. The degree of risk, however, can be substantially reduced by structuring the assessment and decision-making process so that a balance is achieved between technical expertise and common sense and by asking people with different backgrounds and different points of view to consider a wide variety of data. The resulting decisions will not be easy. But proper assessment dramatically increases the probability that each hearing-impaired student is being placed in an appropriate educational setting. ☐

CHAPTER VII

Suggestions for the Regular Classroom Teacher

Barry R. Culhane and Lawrence L. Mothersell

This chapter identifies the special needs of hearing-impaired students, emphasizing their need for language development. Factors involved in decision making for development of an individualized education plan are discussed. We present specific suggestions which have been found helpful to regular classroom teachers in establishing a positive physical and emotional climate which will enhance students' communication, personal/social, and academic skills. The practical suggestions put forth in this chapter encourage the use of existing resources in the regular classroom.

Introduction

The preceding chapter was written with concern for those faced with making decisions about the placement of students. This chapter is written with a great deal of concern for you, the classroom teacher, who, regardless of philosophical perspective about mainstreaming, may be challenged with one or more hearing-impaired students in your classroom. We have assumed that most classroom teachers will be confronted with the challenge of teaching hearing-impaired students without the benefit of special training, special resources, or support services which, under ideal conditions, would be available to them. You may come to feel uncertain, angry, fearful, frustrated, challenged, and helpless. But, if you are a capable teacher, you will overcome your anxieties with information and experience. As a compass of encouragement, we offer information gained from our experiences as educators of the hearing impaired.

We empathize because we know that teaching hearing-impaired students can be both very frustrating and very rewarding. Hopefully, many of the suggestions presented will also benefit normally hearing students in your class. We do not consider ourselves as *the* experts in teaching hearing-impaired students. We respect individual teaching styles. Neither do we perceive our suggestions as a cookbook, but rather as potential ways to facilitate learning for hearing-impaired students. One final comment to you, the "regular" classroom teacher, from us, the "irregulars": we enjoy teaching hearing-impaired students and hope you will, too.

Communication Deprivation

Most of us have five functioning senses. Although they are complex biological systems, we take them for granted until something "goes wrong." This is especially true of hearing, until the effect of its loss becomes a traumatic realization. As discussed in the first chapter, deafness separates people from people. In that context, hearing impairments can (with exceptions) severely handicap learning, for hearing is the beginning link in a vital chain. Hearing enables verbal communication which affects one's identity of self (which is basic in relating oneself to one's vast and rich heritage); this, in turn, leads to the ultimate relationship of self and heritage with others.

Indeed, the most limiting aspect of hearing impairment is communication inhibition. Williams and Sussman (1971) indicate that communication impairment affects every aspect of life, and that most other problems exist in relationship to the impairment. The realization that adjustment and achievement are primarily dependent on communications skills leads directly to the importance of the teacher's perspective in meeting the needs of the hearing impaired.

Loss of hearing restricts a ready grasp of heritage, environmental influences, and the present situation. Hearing-impaired students start life at a disadvantage that continues—in fact, the gap between these students and their normally hearing peers has every chance of widening. To minimize communication deprivation, hearing-impaired students need help and understanding from teachers and everyone else in the environment. Empathy is fundamental to teachers' work with these students. As Furth (1973) suggested:

> Acceptance of the thinking and feeling deaf child who is growing into an adult is priority number one for education. These three (four) forms of acceptance of deafness—at home, at school, (at work), and in society—would effectively reverse our perspective on deafness.

Special Needs of Hearing-Impaired Students

"Special" needs of hearing-impaired students must be assessed on an individual basis. Most of their needs are common to all your students but, for a hearing-impaired person, meeting those needs becomes an additional challenge in light of communication problems. Specific needs remain to be identified. But first, one overriding guideline must be realized.

That guideline is the certainty that P.L. 94-142 was never intended to pose new barriers for students. It seems clear that the law was intended for students who would benefit from being placed in the regular classroom. If, after in-depth evaluations, the student clearly *cannot* benefit from such placement, perhaps mainstreaming (beyond that of a special class in a public school setting) is not the best option for that student. If overwhelming deficits manifest themselves throughout the student's spectrum of learning activities, it is beyond the scope of this chapter and this book to address the highly specialized methodology, remedial language, and reading techniques demanded for the severely handicapped.

When all evaluations suggest that possibility, the greatest kindness classroom teachers can show to the severely handicapped, language-deprived student is to make a call for help. On one level, this will mean enlisting the aid of special personnel either on the present school staff or external to it. At the extreme, it will mean initiating discussion that will result in removing the student from the regular classroom into an actually less restrictive environment where learning is possible.

For those situations where the hearing-impaired student can benefit from mainstreaming, school personnel must take the initiative to learn about the characteristics of the hearing-impaired population and meet their special needs. Some of these needs are listed in Table 7.A.

1. Hearing-impaired students need both teachers and resource people who understand the ramifications of hearing losses. A recent hearing test by a certified audiologist will be required, and the diagnosis and prognosis will need to be explained. The correction value of the hearing aid and what can and cannot be expected from an aid should be understood.

2. Because a hearing impairment can so easily produce isolation, hearing-impaired students need many opportunities to communicate with family, peers, teachers, and other significant people in their environment. Students need them to help with schoolwork, to answer questions, and to offer information which the normally hearing student picks up incidentally about current events, personal hygiene, occupations, consumer economics, community resources, government, peer norms, slang, etc.

TABLE 7.A

Specific needs of hearing-impaired students which are important for regular classroom teachers of the hearing impaired to understand.

1. People who understand the meaning of impaired hearing
2. Opportunities to communicate
3. Visual access to information
4. Opportunities for experiential learning
5. Opportunities for incidental learning
6. Opportunities to develop self-esteem
7. Deaf role models
8. Multi-level learning opportunities
9. Successes
10. Opportunities for successful social functioning

3. Hearing-impaired students need visual access to information. Although it is important for them to use whatever residual hearing they may have, it is is also important that they capitalize on an intact visual system.

4. Hearing-impaired students need opportunities for experiential learning. Instead of "talking about it" the class should "do it" whenever possible. For example, a class can learn how a newspaper is printed by visiting a newspaper facility and how government functions by visiting one level of government; then, the activities can be simulated in a classroom exercise. One class actually bought a share of stock and followed the stock market for an entire year, selling the stock at year's end.

5. Hearing-impaired students need to have their natural curiosity fostered. They need time for nonstructured, real-life opportunities for incidental learning (a major way we learn); to observe, to guess, to categorize, to generalize, to tease, and to evaluate. They need to be provided with opportunities that appear to be incidental. They need allowance for trial and error.

6. Hearing-impaired students need to value themselves, their ideas, and their opinions. Too often they view knowledge as emanating from external authorities only. They need to trust their own thoughts and feelings.

7. Hearing-impaired students need role models who are both hear-

ing impaired and normally hearing. They need contact with other hearing-impaired people for companionship and for an opportunity to understand their own deafness.

8. Hearing-impaired students need an opportunity to experience all levels of understanding. They may need to be taught basic life skills, which others learn incidentally, just as they will need to deal with complex theoretical issues at appropriate times in their cognitive development. (Contrary to a popular opinion, hearing-impaired students *can* think in abstract terms.) The point is that they need a variety of levels of instruction.

9. Hearing-impaired students must be placed in programs suitable for their entry-level skills and proceed from there to achieve success. Least of all they do not need devastating feelings of incompetence due to the absence of successful experiences or a series of failures.

10. Hearing-impaired students may need to be reminded, or perhaps even taught, about customs and courtesies established by a predominantly hearing society. They sometimes miss subtle distinctions in manner, which aid in establishing and maintaining positive interpersonal relationships.

11. Above all, hearing-impaired students need your understanding that they are individual human beings who happen to have a hearing handicap.

There are numerous types of functional hearing impairments. In addition to recognizing physical characteristics of the loss, teachers must learn to understand, in each individual case, how the loss has been accepted by the student and what the psychological, social, and educational ramifications may be.

Language Growth for the Hearing-Impaired Student

Easy use of a language by a native user normally involves the processing of an extremely large and complex body of information. A person is expected to learn everything from simple vocabulary, grammar, and syntax all the way to the semantics and style involved in rhetoric. In between is an array of pronoun substitutions, article signals, possessive determiners, regular word-inflective endings, active and passive voices, comparatives, intonations, the difficult English idioms we use daily, and a "feedback" system which provides the dialect of the community.

The English language is especially complex, for in spite of what we learned in school, English is highly irregular. Phonetic play encourages one to spell the word "fish" as follows: "ghoti" (using the "gh" sound in tough, the "o" sound in women, and the "ti" sound in attention). The simplest vocabulary words, if analyzed only minimally, will produce results which make us dizzy. "Sit down" and "sit up" often mean the same thing; "take a bath" and "take a piece of candy" do not. A "player" is one who plays, yet a "cooker" is an appliance. Something that is pretty may be "hot," Florida even in summer may be "cool." This parlor game of inconsistency could continue indefinitely. Yet, the native-speaking, normally hearing student sorts most of this out naturally and *incidentally* because our English language is primarily auditorily based.

In order to understand adequately the nature of your hearing-impaired student's language background, you will want a description of his hearing impairment. Regarding this, you are urged to review the material in Chapter 1 dealing with the two kinds of hearing loss (conductive and sensorineural), degree of loss (amplitude and frequency), and age of onset (prelingual or postlingual). Currently, more hearing-impaired students are prelingually deaf than are postlingually deafened (Schein & Delk, 1974). The prelingually impaired are, in general, the ones with whom you and other specialists need to work especially hard to provide learning experiences to facilitate language development.

Loban, Ryan, and Squire (1961) help us appreciate language-use complexity and the necessity of an individual's experience in language development through the simple diagram shown in Figure 7.1. This model is presented, not because we ascribe to it as the most

FIGURE 7.1

Simplified model showing the complexity and necessity of an individual's experiences and interactions with others in developing language.

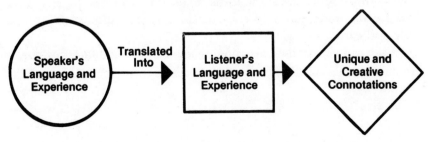

useful model of language development, but rather to demonstrate the essential relationship between language and experience.

Teamwork is essential in building experience and language in the hearing impaired. The successful education of hearing-impaired students in any educational setting—mainstreamed or otherwise—will require an orchestration of resources and a truly interdisciplinary effort of student, family, and professionals. The good news is that most hearing-impaired persons, even those with a profound hearing loss, have some residual hearing. However, they need very special diagnosis and prescription to enhance their listening skills. These are the realms of the educational audiologist and the speech therapist, who will serve as key resources for you and the student. After audiological assessments, the therapist will address the matter of improving the student's speech reception and speech production skills. Reading specialists and other language arts specialists will have various skills to share with you.

Coordination of efforts is important. Developing science vocabulary may be worked on by the science teacher, reading specialist, speech therapist, and family concurrently. Vocabulary classifications lend themselves to topics and experiences that each member can address at the same time. If several teachers are working with the same hearing-impaired student, word lists and significant experiences of the student can be shared and used as a springboard for other learning experiences. The point is, the *coordination* of life experiences and language development, several activities with one focus, is obviously more beneficial than a fragmented approach.

In the words of Moores (1978):

> The greatest problems faced by deaf individuals are related to problems of communication with the dominant society and to the insensitivity of most hearing individuals to the problems of deafness and the resultant lack of empathy for deaf individuals.

In reality, we are not concerned with language development alone but with students' ability to think, to establish values, to analyze and synthesize information, to solve problems, and, ultimately, to live a life and earn a living.

What can you as the classroom teacher do to facilitate this goal?

*　　*　　*

Helpful Hints for the Classroom Teacher

You, the classroom teacher, are the person on the firing line. While educational planning for the hearing-impaired student is a responsibility shared by many professionals and the family, you are the primary person to implement program and evaluate progress. To meet the student's individual needs, you will be called upon to provide major input into the development of an individualized education program (IEP). An IEP must be developed to describe: (a) the student's actual performance in each subject area, (b) specific goals and objectives of the current program, (c) materials and effective teaching strategies to be used, (d) how much contact the student will have with nonhandicapped students in the school, (e) when and how long special education services will be provided, (f) and how your student's progress will be evaluated. One thing a classroom teacher does *not* need is more paperwork. However, the law requires that a program plan be designed; making it explicit will be helpful to those who are instrumental in the orchestration of the plan, now and in the future (Torres, 1977). You should provide a copy of the IEP for the parents, for the student's file, and for all other professional personnel involved in delivering the program to the student.

When setting goals, it is helpful to have a list of curricular areas on hand. When meeting parents, it is essential to communicate in an atmosphere of mutual respect and at a level where there will be a clear understanding of the student's program. The more specific the information is, the more useful the plan will be.

We must emphasize that our discussion is not to provide a recipe for development of an IEP or a solutions approach to teaching hearing-impaired students. Rather, we want to share some practical suggestions for effectively facilitating learning in the classroom. Some will work for you, others may not. Regardless of what we know about teaching hearing-impaired students, we all make mistakes. We inadvertently block visual access to information, forget to control the pace of the classroom, and lose opportunities to motivate our students. "Regular" and "special" classroom teachers share the human characteristic of fallibility. To share our classroom experiences with hearing and hearing-impaired students, we have examined several important aspects of the teaching/learning process and tried to provide useful hints for successful facilitation of learning. The taxonomy we use includes hints regarding physical characteristics of the classroom; communication in the classroom; methods, materials and media; peer interaction; experiential learning and motivation, and the role of the teacher in a variety of situations.

Physical Characteristics of the Classroom

When you have a hearing-impaired student in your class, special consideration must be given to the physical aspects of the classroom. As the classroom teacher, you need to be aware of the effects of seating arrangements, lighting, noise level, and factors related to visual and auditory access to information.

It is important that you give special attention to the physical location of the hearing-impaired students in the classroom. Some special educators advocate preferential seating in the front of the class, but there are many factors to consider. Students may feel more comfortable sitting in the back of a small room with a better view of all classmates and visual access to material presented by the teacher. Although the term "preferential seating" itself implies a priority of rights of exceptional children, this is hardly a healthy situation in a classroom where the hearing-impaired student is likely to draw the attention of classmates. Jealousy may develop if the hearing-impaired students seem to be getting special privileges. A misunderstanding of preferential seating, along with provision of support services, could disrupt your efforts to create a positive sensitivity to and understanding of the nature of deafness; if hearing students perceive hearing-impaired students as receiving special privileges, the socialization process could break down.

For the above reasons, we prefer to use the term "advantageous seating" and recommend that you start your classes by explaining hearing impairments, their implications, and the subsequent special needs of hearing-impaired classmates. This in no way suggests favoritism, and puts an emphasis on maximal positive use of the hearing-impaired student's capabilities. Young adult hearing-impaired students can and should determine their own seating arrangements; however, the teacher can guide students of any age to be considerate and to use common sense. More is said about this in the chapter on interpreting. Several considerations about the physical setting of the classroom are outlined in Table 7.B.

In large group instructional settings, encourage the hearing-impaired student to sit within 15 feet of the instructor to maximize use of residual hearing, speechreading skills, and visual access to instruction. This is particularly helpful in industrial arts, home economics,

TABLE 7.B
A description of physical characteristics of the classroom to be considered for the hearing-impaired student.

1. Place the student with residual hearing near you
2. Be aware of student's "better side"
3. Avoid seating in heavy traffic areas
4. Avoid vibration and lighting difficulties
5. Reduce general noise level
6. Consider the best amplification system for your situation

and science courses where demonstrations and laboratory work occur frequently. In small group instructional settings, seat the hearing-impaired student so that you are on the student's "better side"—the side where the student has the better hearing. For students with severe or profound hearing losses, this is usually the side on which the hearing aid is worn.

Guide the student away from areas of traffic or physical movement: seats near classroom doors, frequently used storage spaces, project areas, drinking fountains, and special activity areas.

Be aware of vibration and use of lighting. Many hearing-impaired students have become accustomed to vibrations or light movement used as methods to attract their attention. Thus, constant changes in vibrations and light (from electric lights and sunlight/shadow variations) can be a real disadvantage to the hearing-impaired learner. Consequently, you will want to guard against seating these students near areas where room lighting is often adjusted or where there is intense sunlight. To help all of your students, eliminate blackboard reflections with a shade or drape. No student, particularly one who must capitalize on visual access to information, should be required to face a light source, a window, or disturbing reflections.

Strive to reduce the noise level of the classroom. Be conscious of adjusting the timing of activities so that periods requiring intense concentration on the part of the hearing-impaired student will not coincide with disturbing audio-visual equipment, loud sounds, or noisy group efforts.

It is important to understand that most hearing aids are not selective in the sounds they amplify. Background noises from heat or cool air registers, doors, desk drawers, background conversations and sneezes, will be amplified as much as your voice will be amplified, causing confusion as the auditory message is transmitted. Use of carpeting and sound-absorbing materials such as draperies and acoustic tiles helps reduce background noise and helps the hearing-impaired student discriminate speech sounds and better understand your message.

Procure the best equipment you can to facilitate oral communication. We do not, of course, intend to advertise specific equipment, but we do urge you to explore various amplification systems with your audiologist and administrator. Some systems, because they are completely wireless and the microphones are close to the talkers' mouths, do not require installation procedures and as such are extremely versatile. They operate on the principle of FM broadcasting and allow the hearing-impaired student to receive the oral/aural message in a variety of settings. Such systems have the capacity to reduce background noise and transmit to the student's hearing aid only the speaker's voice. Many teachers of the hearing impaired, at all levels of instruction, have found such systems helpful.

However, other systems may offer specific advantages for your particular situation. As pointed out by Bishop *et al.* (1972), factors such as comfort to wear, cosmetic effects, and ease of use appear to have a significant influence on teacher and student attitudes, factors which were highly correlated with the amount of time amplification systems were used. Improved systems are continually being developed and tested, so it is important that the decision to use any amplification system be one made with the audiologist's support.

Communication in the Classroom

Many of the above suggestions for facilitating communications relate to physical characteristics of the classroom. During information exchanges there are additional practices that can help. We have divided these hints into two categories: communicating with the hearing impaired in one-to-one situations, and communicating in group settings in the classroom. Your attention to these factors will enhance the effective teaching/learning process, and with the exception of the first suggestion, they will probably be helpful with all of your students. Culhane and Curwin (1978) suggest several ways to facilitate communication with individual students. Their suggestions are listed in Table 7.C.

Becoming knowledgeable about hearing losses and their potential impact and about what specific correction an aid will bring to a specific student is your responsibility in a mainstream situation. Any ef-

TABLE 7.C
*Practical suggestions for communicating with individual
hearing-impaired students in a teaching/learning situation.*

1. Know about hearing losses
2. Use visual cues
3. Speak clearly and normally
4. Avoid standing in front of a window or other light source
5. Face the student when you speak
6. Present one source of visual information at a time
7. Do not block visual access to your mouth
8. Encourage all forms of communication
9. Use movement purposefully
10. Obtain feedback regularly from your student

fects of prior language deprivation will not find immediate compensation through the use of an aid. Inserting a hearing aid into a student's ear will not correct language and experience deficiencies overnight, nor will a hearing aid restore perfect hearing. No one should expect the student to hear perfectly just because he has an aid. You may wish to attract the student's attention by using a visual sign as well as a vocal signal, if necessary. A wave of the hand, a thump on the desk, or a flick of a light switch (in addition to your voice) is helpful in gaining the student's attention.

Speak clearly, at a moderate pace, but without exaggeration or over-enunciation. Too rapid or too slow speech or delivered with exaggerated lip movements can actually hinder the speechreading process. Good speechreaders depend on the quality of the articulation of the speaker and the context of the dialogue; obviously abnormal speech production decreases reception of speech. At best, speech-reading is an approximation since only about 25 percent of speech is clearly visible on the lips.

Do not stand in front of a lamp or window, for standing in front of a light source silhouettes the speaker and makes visual cues impossible.

Look in the direction of the student when you speak. The student depends on direct visual contact with you for assistance in speech-reading and obtaining nonverbal cues.

Try to present only one source of visual information at a time, i.e., do not talk while writing on the blackboard or putting written material up to be read. The student cannot "read" two things at the same time—he must watch your lip movements and also read the material you present in written format.

Hold your hands, papers, pencils, and all other materials away from your mouth. Objects in or in front of your mouth inhibit communication through speechreading and facial cues.

Encourage all forms of communication and use written English as often as possible to communicate directly or to supplement each form of communication. Write key words on the board or an overhead. Repetition and reinforcement of the various modes of communication can lend verification and provide a means to confirm the message.

Use body language, mime, and gesture that is purposeful and enhances instruction. Avoid unnecessary movement such as pacing back and forth, but also avoid standing in one place for a class period; pacing forces the student to keep shifting visual attention, while a stationary figure is boring.

Obtain feedback from your students at every opportunity with every mode of communication. Listening to or seeing the students' modes of expression are indicators of the students' level of understanding. But the best measure is their response to a well planned and timed question which will provide feedback without embarrassing the student.

When you are involved in group discussions, you may find yourself in the position of providing support and being a facilitator of com-

TABLE 7.D
Communication techniques for successful
teaching/learning in a group situation.

1. Identify speaker
2. Point to sources of information
3. Use repetition and rephrasing techniques
4. Use paralanguage
5. Control discussion pace
6. Provide written outlines and written assignments
7. Inform the student of any changes in routine
8. Sensitize others to communication needs
9. Build information about deafness into your curriculum in a positive way
10. Work with support service personnel prior to class
11. Provide guidelines for group activities

munication. Certain practices which will maximize communication of information are described in Table 7.D.

It is important to identify who is speaking to whom. This allows a hearing-impaired student to know who asks questions and who answers them. In addition, encourage dialogue in the classroom so the hearing-impaired student does not feel hopelessly isolated.

When charts, diagrams, overheads, maps, objects, and other forms of visual information are used during instruction, the communicator should point to the source. When pointing, pause long enough for the student to see the specific visual information.

Rephrase and repeat discussion points and questions regularly. Changing words or sentence patterns can often clarify a question or comment. This practice also serves as a teaching tool for expanding vocabulary and knowledge of English idioms. (See details about choice of words and sentence patterns in Chapter 8.)

Remember to use paralanguage, the nonverbal accompaniments or adjuncts in our communication system. Gestures, pantomime, body language, and facial expressions are important factors in communication. Moreover, they add to the fun of teaching and learning.

Control the pace of discussions. In the heat of a good debate, the hearing-impaired student can easily become lost during rapid-fire exchanges of information. Recognize speakers, and should there be an interpreter, allow him to finish interpreting for each speaker.

If possible, provide written outlines of discussion topics, films, lectures, or other materials before the learning experience. Such handouts can provide a context for film sound tracks or discussion plans and keep hearing-impaired students from becoming lost in a presentation. Write assignments for students to take home; give ample time for copying. This practice gives parents, other staff, and students a clear understanding of what you expect them to accomplish.

Repeat messages announced over the public address system. Too often the hearing-impaired student can become frightened or confused when a fire drill or bus change has been announced. He may be the only one in the group who is unprepared for changes in the environment. While the need to inform students of emergency information should be obvious, the hearing-impaired student needs to be informed of any changes in your daily routine.

Sensitize others in the class, including classroom visitors, to the special communication needs of the hearing-impaired student who may ask a question or make a comment out of context. Once your class is sensitized to the potential time delay in communication, an empathy can evolve, with all your students participating. Often, understanding of the special needs of hearing-impaired students can be built into the curriculum. If you are addressing communication as a process, or studying a scientific subject related to perception, you might use the electronic operation of hearing aids as subject matter.

Work with interpreters, notetakers, counselors, and tutors before class. Informed support personnel are better equipped to handle various classroom situations if they have a context for classroom presentations and are aware of your expectations and teaching style.

Discuss group dynamics procedures with all students and staff involved. Group activities can run more smoothly when all participants know and follow certain guidelines. Pettinghill (1977) suggests some basic steps that are necessary to ensure full and equal participation of hearing-impaired people in the group situation. Among them are that hearing-impaired people should be involved in planning meetings to maximize communication. The moderator of a meeting must control the dialogue by recognizing speakers one at a time. Even a very skilled interpreter is usually a sentence or two behind the speaker. Therefore you need to allow time for the hearing-impaired person to receive the whole message and give that person the opportunity to respond. Knowledge of these group dynamics will facilitate communication and prevent embarrassment.

Methods, Materials, and Media

While written words, cartoons, diagrams, and drawings enhance everyone's learning, they are of immeasurable value to the hearing impaired. We encourage you as the classroom teacher to capitalize on hardware and software available to you in every conceivable way. Think in terms of what we call "multiple manipulation"—numerous exposures to new information presented in a variety of formats. Few persons internalize information after one presentation, and this is particularly important to understand when a student does not have full access to information through the auditory channels. Multiple manipulation of instructional materials is a response to the student's request: "Show it to me in a variety of ways, and let me manipulate, handle, and experience it." Some suggestions are provided in Table 7.E. for development and use of materials and media.

Use the blackboard or large sheets of newsprint to outline, itemize, or summarize and synthesize class activities. Various colors of chalk add interest and help to focus attention on specific points of impor-

TABLE 7.E

*A variety of practical suggestions for material and media
development and use.*

1. Use your blackboard and newsprint
2. Write legibly
3. Use handouts
4. Use glossaries
5. Develop coursebooks
6. Maximize use of media
7. Use real-life activities in class
8. Encourage students to share media finds
9. Use your team

tance. Regardless of the media used, write legibly in letters large
enough to be clearly read by all.

Use handouts such as time lines, graphs, charts, and maps. Explain
their purpose *before* submitting them to students. Allow students time
to read a handout or overhead: do not pass materials out and im-
mediately begin talking! Distribute a written outline to reflect your
lesson plan, and leave room on the outline for answers or discussion
points to be written by the learner. Allow the learner to fill in the
"holes" in the notes so that he can be active in the learning process in
terms of the notetaking process. This provides yet one more student
manipulation of the information.

Vocabulary lists can be helpful, and students might develop such a
resource themselves. A glossary serves as a guide to the jargon and
concepts of special subject areas.

Develop a "coursebook"—a skeleton of your curriculum—which
sequentially outlines the material of a specific unit of instruction. The
student may glance at this before class and gain a preview of anticipated topics, vocabulary, and your expectations. The student may
write in it during class, using the blackboard or newsprint summariza-
tions. In addition, there should be space to enter diagrams in the
coursebook. Finally, such a device serves as a tool for review.

Maximize the use of media. If available, use an opaque overhead
projector to display a student's paper, a picture, notes, or other printed
material. Use colored marking pens for transparencies. Do not block
students' views from any visual presentation, and do not speak while
you are writing, even when you are facing the student. Construct

models and bulletin board displays which supplement and concretize units of work. Use filmstrips and films. A summary of the film, issues, and points can be made and given to the students before the class in which the film is shown. In addition, Captioned Films for the Deaf in Washington, D.C. has a comprehensive listing of free instructional films with captioned sound track provided.[1]

Use "real life" activities in class. Collect free or inexpensive materials which may lend authenticity to the classroom objective. Road maps, catalogues, telephone books, and driver-training manuals are helpful, as are directions on how-to-assemble or how-to-do something. Community agencies, often free sources for experiential learning materials, may prove invaluable. Use an instant picture camera to help record in-class and experiential learning activities. In addition to providing a visual record of the event, the pictures may act as a springboard for more writing activities and classroom discussions.

Ask your students to help by bringing pertinent pictures and materials from magazines or travel folders. Your students can be very helpful in identifying useful media, and their selection aids you to informally evaluate their understandings of the concepts.

Use your whole team. Remember that the art teacher and media specialist may add their skills in helping you develop appropriate media. Parents should know of their child's special interests.

Peer Interaction

Positive social behavior is directly related to peer interaction. Gronlund (1955) states that "early in a child's life his peers form an impression of him, and on the basis of such impressions, he is assigned status within a group." One goal of the teacher is to provide for social development of each student.

With the new laws focusing attention on mainstreaming hearing-impaired students into regular classroom settings, the teacher may have some anxiety regarding interpersonal relationships between the hearing-impaired student and his classmates. There is a history of conflict in the literature on this topic. Elser (1959), Force (1956), and Justman and Maskowitz (1957) indicated that hearing-impaired children in regular classrooms are not as socially accepted as their hearing

---

[1]Captioned Films and Telecommunications Branch. Bureau of Education for the Handicapped, U.S. Office of Education, Washington, D.C. 20202.

TABLE 7.F
Practices for maximizing interaction in a group of normally hearing and hearing-impaired students.

1. Serve as a role model
2. Demonstrate sensitivity to handicapping conditions
3. Discuss implications of hearing impairments
4. Alternate group size and makeup
5. Teach rules that are normally implicit
6. Evaluate students on an equal basis

peers. However, Kennedy and Bruininks (1974) found that young hearing-impaired children did gain social acceptance among their peers in regular classrooms:

> The results from the three sociometric scales used revealed there was no significant difference found between the level of peer status for the total hearing handicapped and normally hearing groups, although children with severe to profound losses enjoyed the highest degree of peer status (among hearing students).

In any event, the classroom teacher can do much to foster desirable socialization and peer interaction. Several suggestions as outlined in Table 7.F may serve as examples.

Act as a role model for your students, especially with regard to communications skills. Stressing the worth of each individual in your class can help overcome potentially stigmatizing effects of a communication gap. Students, both hearing and hearing impaired, must take the initiative to establish an effective communication system with each other, and you can help by modeling those behaviors.

To demonstrate your sensitivity to and acceptance of people with handicapping conditions, incorporate such persons performing normal tasks into your plans for media development. Guidelines for representing them in educational material can be obtained from the Council for Exceptional Children, Reston, Virginia 22090.

As mentioned earlier, your awareness of the implications of hearing impairments can set the stage for peer empathy and acceptance. By incorporating information about hearing into the content areas of your curriculum, a cognitive understanding can evolve. Teach a unit on fingerspelling and signing (the manual alphabet can be learned in about half an hour). Invite an interpreter for the deaf to demonstrate and teach both manual interpreting and oral interpreting techniques.

If you have difficulty finding a resource, refer to the local chapter of the Registry of Interpreters for the Deaf (RID) and to Appendix B at the end of this book. To convey concepts and help peers experience some of the implications of hearing impairments you can use drama, mime, and role playing. Try having periods of silence in the classroom where writing is the only acceptable form of communication other than gestures or mouthing words. Provide an opportunity for hearing students to experience what it is like to be hearing impaired. For example, you show a movie without the sound. Perhaps your class could try communicating without voice for a period of time. Obviously, you do not want to endanger any student's hearing by placing an object in his ear, so you will want to consult your audiologist or the local speech and hearing clinic for a safe means to achieve the simulation by "plugging" ears and masking out sound.

Have children work in various sized groups, depending on the task. Rather than allowing rigid peer patterns to be established for an entire school year, provide opportunities for adaptability and multiple interactions. One of your more difficult tasks will be to prevent close friendships from becoming dependency relationships. Varying class group size can help prevent this, as well as providing hearing-impaired students with opportunities to define their roles in small and large groups.

Many of the rules we learn are perceived through incidental verbal learning. You can help by teaching social conventions, expectations, manners, and even why people have a set of manners. You may find it necessary to teach rules for games and extracurricular activities so that the hearing-impaired student is not left out.

Problems which may result from a hearing impairment are not always visible. How you deal with your hearing-impaired students can affect their peer relationships. Overprotection may cause jealousy or resentment on the part of their hearing peers. At the same time, students should be evaluated by equal measures of achievement and be given an equal opportunity to share class responsibilities.

Experiential Learning and Motivation

Earlier in this chapter we noted that, whenever possible, the class should *do* an activity rather than simply talk about it. In our previous context, the emphasis was on language development through experiential learning. We suggested that real-life learning experiences motivate students to learn specific information. Here are several suggestions we would like to share: (a) employ hands-on materials; (b) use containers to study volume; (c) actually measure or weigh objects; (d) demonstrate the effects of certain chemicals or ingredients in classes such as chemistry laboratory or home economics; (e) provide opportunities for students to experience the sequence of step-by-step activities in the process.

Invite guest lecturers to demonstrate some task or share an experience. Ask both normally hearing and hearing-impaired students to make presentations periodically. Ask representatives of schools, community clubs, and organizations to explain their purposes to your class. Plan units to include field trips such as exploring land features around your school for geology and visiting a museum or historical point of interest in your community. Have two teams of students go to a grocery store to buy food and learn about consumerism. If budgets are restrictive, simulate activities.

In addition to providing "real life" experiences, you will need to use representations of actual places and times to simulate activities. Make maps to be followed and reward students for successful navigation of a route. Teach students to use a compass.

You will need to help students develop a sense of the past, present, and future. Discuss a current event, historical event, or literary work and ask, "What do you think happened then?" Write the beginning of an example from any literary genre and ask students to finish it. Ask students to simulate historical events in a dramatic presentation.

The Role of the Teacher

In sharing helpful hints in this chapter, we have focused on the teacher who is faced, without preparation, with teaching a hearing-impaired student. However, we believe that sound principles of teaching apply for all students, regardless of their hearing status. Our position has been that the "good" teacher of the hearing impaired in the mainstreamed classroom is also the good teacher in the regular classroom. And the converse may be true. Teachers have multiple responsibilities and are required to play a variety of roles.

The effective teacher is:
1. a planner who involves the student, the parents, and all other school personnel and community people who are able to contribute toward the child's education.
2. an implementer who utilizes a variety of methods, materials, and media in the utilization of a teaching plan.

3. a trusted transmitter of information.
4. a trusted receiver of information.
5. a conscientious and continuous evaluator.
6. a facilitator for learning who provides access to information for the student and supports other teachers and specialists in their respective roles.
7. a moderator and leader of group discussion.
8. a role model.
9. a manager of people.
10. a very busy person.

Using the Resources Available to You

Because of the multiplicity of roles and responsibilities which you shoulder, it is imperative that you make maximal use of the resources available to you. With the wide variety of services and resources available, we cannot prescribe specific solutions for teaching individual hearing-impaired students in individual schools. We respect individual teaching styles and acknowledge your responsibility to other students in your classroom. Regardless of your specific situation, you need to use all the help available to you, the classroom teacher. A successful program for hearing-impaired students demands an interdependent and interdisciplinary approach of administrators, other classroom teachers, school psychologists, interpreters, counselors, tutors, notetakers, audiologists, social workers, reading teachers, itinerant teachers, physicians and nurses, teacher aides, classmates, and the student's family. Northcott (1973) provides a description of how to use the resources available to you at various educational levels.

Bitter (1976) emphasizes the need to involve parents in communication development and educational planning as part of the interdisciplinary approach to educating hearing-impaired students. Spradley and Spradley (1978) point out that parents need help accepting and understanding their children's hearing losses. Communication with parents must be straightforward, with minimal use of educational jargon, and must reflect an empathy toward the special burdens placed on parents. Healy (1976) enumerates many factors to be considered in a successfully integrated educational setting, including the need for parent instruction and participation in programs. Clearly, the classroom teacher is confronted with a challenge in teaching the hearing impaired . But you are not alone in your encounter with the hearing-impaired student: the challenge is shared by everyone involved.

Summary

We are hopeful this chapter has helped you understand the special needs of hearing-impaired students, especially in terms of language development. While the task of teaching a hearing-impaired student in the regular classroom can be an awesome challenge, it can be met through a concerted effort by an interdisciplinary team. Specific suggestions based on our experiences and related to physical setting, communication, methods, materials, media, peer interaction, and an experiential learning situation have been shared with you. We are confident that you, the regular classroom teacher, will be a primary force in helping hearing-impaired students acquire educations that will enable them to join the mainstream of our society as adults. □

CHAPTER VIII

Suggestions for Assessing Reading Levels and for Preparing Written Materials

Loy E. Golladay

Hearing impairment from birth or early age, with its lack of verbal input, typically leads to severe linguistic and communication disadvantages for the secondary and postsecondary student. Development of vocabulary, idiomatic and grammatical English, sophisticated sentence patterns, and understanding of abstract concepts in the "tapestry" of linguistic competence may be severely retarded. This chapter assesses briefly some of these special problems. It presents in outline form approximately 20 principles, based on practical experience, for preparing written lessons and other materials to meet the special needs of language-handicapped hearing-impaired students.

Introduction

Historically, many hearing-impaired students with only mild to moderate hearing losses have attended public schools. They may have had the advantage of front-row seating and properly fitted hearing aids, along with some support service such as resource room aid, speechreading training, speech therapy, auditory training, and tutorial assistance. Students with greater hearing loss have generally attended self-contained day or residential schools, with small classes and highly organized programs to meet their needs.

Now, under Public Law 94-142, the public school teacher may be faced with students with various degrees of hearing loss, and unless she is receptive to the challenge, some of these students could "sit out" their school years with minimal learning and inadequate preparation for intellectual fulfillment or economic independence.

Although the inexperienced teacher will realize that deaf students cannot absorb knowledge by listening as normally hearing students

120

do, she may not realize that hearing aids are generally of limited benefit to most students with a severe or profound hearing loss.

The Impact of Prelingual Hearing Impairment

Except for persons who are both deaf and blind, prelingually hearing-impaired students are considered to have the greatest educational disadvantage (Boatner, 1947). Other types of handicapped students—the blind, the wheelchair-bound, the spastic, or whatever—can be expected to start school with a vocabulary and command of standard American English that is near, if not fully equal to, that of students without a handicapping condition.

As described in Chapter 1, this is obviously not true of the severely or profoundly hearing-impaired student. Prelingual loss of hearing from birth, or from before language has been acquired, typically leads to severe linguistic, communication, and academic disadvantages by the time the student reaches adolescence. The development of vocabulary, idiomatic and grammatical English, and sophisticated sentence patterns, and the understanding of abstract concepts are severely retarded. And so is reading.

One might assume that a person who cannot hear would find enjoyment in reading and satisfaction in writing. For persons deafened after establishment of language and basic reading and writing skills, this is generally true; but this is not generally true of persons who are prelingually deaf. Nevertheless, experience has shown that even prelingually deaf individuals, with only marginal reading skills, can derive great benefit from written communication when they have a teacher who applies ingenuity in preparing written materials which compensate for their reading deficiencies.

Deafness and Reading—an Educational Challenge

It is axiomatic that one learns to read by reading; language, however, is a prerequisite to the process. Reading is not simply looking at familiar words in a book; it involves associating sequencing of the words or symbols with one's experience. For example, someone has an experience to relate and expresses it by writing words describing the experience. Someone else reads the words and, drawing on a personal concept of English syntax combined with personal knowledge and experience, mentally reconstructs the writer's experience. As such, reading comprehension requires not only facility with language, but also a reclaimable base of knowledge and experience. Typically, prelingually deaf readers lag behind less handicapped peers in all three areas.

Vocabulary and related concepts, idiomatic and colloquial expressions, ways of saying things which are part of the culture but not strictly structured—all contribute to a sophistication which is common to those who hear normally and comprehend sound without special effort. Unlike normally hearing children, prelingually hearing-impaired children cannot receive the sound of words and match a naturally acquired vocabulary. Frequently they are not even aware of current idiomatic and colloquial expressions.

Normally hearing children glean information and experience from radio and television, in a store, riding in a car, even from incidental conversation around the dinner table and during inadvertent eavesdropping which occurs in the daily environment. Much of our environmental information escapes the severely hearing impaired. While the hearing-impaired person attends the same place and shares the same surface experience as the normally hearing person, the concept of the experience may not be related in the same way to a meaningful verbal symbolization.

When a teacher considers this combined linguistic, factual, and experiential background deficiency—which is not shared by other types of handicapped students who may be mainstreamed—it should be evident that hearing-impaired students present a unique educational challenge. This is emphasized by the fact that so much of the educational process depends upon reading and listening. In meeting this challenge it is important that the teacher be able to evaluate adequately each student's reading ability in relation to texts and be prepared to devise supplementary learning aids and written materials. The teacher must devise ways to assist the student in bridging the experience and information gap.

In searching for such bridges it is important to understand that frequently, by the time hearing-impaired students reach high school, a sense of inadequacy in vocabulary, sentence structure, and general linguistic sophistication may have "turned them off" to reading as a recreational activity. Reading skills seem to level off, or "plateau," at adolescence, yet my many years of classroom experience have shown that the plateau can be raised if students will acquire the habit of reading large quantities of interesting materials. There seems to be no argument concerning the effectiveness of meaningful reading in the education of the hearing impaired.

Startling improvements following the acquisition of good reading habits have been too numerous for coincidence. Experienced teachers as well as educated hearing-impaired persons will attest to this fact.

In the 1940s there was a tendency to provide high-interest, low-difficulty recreational reading for elementary and secondary students with serious reading problems. These were in a sense antedated by books especially written for deaf students (Jenkins, 1888; Crane, 1890, 1916; among others).

I recall many hearing-impaired high school students "cutting their teeth" on a dozen or more adapted classics, with some going on to read with relish such formidable challenges as *Gone With the Wind*. Anken and Holmes (1977) found especially adapted classics brought respectable gains in word meaning and paragraph meaning compared to other reading programs using basal reader systems.

As in all learning, a student's special interest in subject matter can produce great differences. I have known students to develop such a consuming interest in some special subject that they would somehow successfully muddle through difficult printed material that, from all practical considerations, should have produced complete frustration.

It is sometimes said that children teach themselves to read if supplied with materials at a level which they can enjoy and to which they can relate. Not all deaf children will do this, but those who acquire a love of reading through appropriate materials and the encouragement of some tactful, knowledgeable, and enthusiastic parent or teacher may be on their way to solving their educational and linguistic problems, if not to breaking the "sound" barrier.

Assessing Reading Performance

Standardized Tests

While standardized tests have been and will continue to be used with deaf students, assessing the reading level of prelingually, profoundly hearing-impaired students presents significant problems. As pointed out in Chapter 6, when tests standardized on a hearing population are administered to hearing-impaired students, the results in terms of grade or age levels should be used with considerable caution. This is especially true with standardized reading tests. Administering alternative and equivalent forms of a reading test will often show substantial variations in such a student's results. In general, only the most able upper-grade readers will achieve test results which may be considered valid measures of their reading ability in the factors which the test measures, and these students may not rank with their hearing peers. In the mainstreamed situation, this discrepancy in apparent achievement may be a traumatic experience for the deaf student, if not also for the teacher. The situation might be considered worse, since Moores (1970) showed that some standard tests of reading ability give spuriously high estimates of the reading ability of deaf students. In all fairness it should be noted that reading authorities have recognized such tests also usually give normally hearing students at least one grade higher level than their functional reading.

In considering assessment, it is helpful to know that the most commonly used standardized test for measuring the reading ability of hearing-impaired students is the Stanford Achievement Test (SAT).[1] A new special edition of the SAT has just been nationally standardized on hearing-impaired students ages 8 through 20 (Office of Demographic Studies, Gallaudet College).[2] Other frequently used standardized tests include the Metropolitan Achievement Test, which has norms for both deaf and hearing populations (Moores, 1970; Wrightstone, Aranow, & Moskowitz, 1963), and the American School Achievement Series, which puts more stress on reading for understanding than on multiple choice opportunities for guesswork (Lane, 1976). The California Achievement Test, Jr. High School Level, Forms X, 4, 2 (1957) Reading and Language subtests have been used with freshman students at NTID.

When standardized tests are used with hearing-impaired students, regardless of the test, the administrator of the test needs to be certain that students understand what they are to do before taking each subtest. The directions may not be clearly understood, so a demonstration of correct procedures for each change of subtest directions is suggested, perhaps on an overhead projector or a blackboard.

In this connection, Moores (1978) implies that survey results may be adversely affected by the examiner's inability to communicate with the students being tested. Nevertheless, the magnitude of the challenge is reflected in a report by the Office of Demographic Studies[3] that the average 16-year-old hearing-impaired person had attained the reading skills of the average fourth grader. According to Wrightstone, Aranow, and Moskowitz (1963), who used the elementary-level bat-

---

[1]Office of Demographic Studies, Monograph 1972b, Gallaudet College, Washington, D.C., 20002.

[2]For information contact Arthur Schildroth, Achievement Testing Services, Office of Demographic Studies, Gallaudet College, 7th and Florida Avenue, N.E., Washington, D.C. 20002.

[3]Office of Demographic Studies, Stanford Achievement Test (SAT), Gallaudet College, Washington, D.C. 20002.

tery subtest of the Metropolitan Achievement Test, fewer than 10 percent of the deaf population tested were said to read at or beyond a seventh-grade level.

Reading Ability and Cognitive Ability

Before discussing other procedures for assessing reading ability, it is important to caution against generalizing low reading performance to broader cognitive ability.

Results of numerous studies that explored the issue of language and thought clearly demonstrate that it is the faculty to read the English language which is limited, not the ability to think (Blank & Bridger, 1966; Furth, 1966, 1970, 1973; Furth & Youniss, 1965, 1969, 1975; Pufall & Furth, 1966; Ross, 1966; Weigl & Metze, 1968; Youniss, 1964; Youniss, Feil, & Furth, 1965). Absence of language skills does not necessarily lower a hearing-impaired student's cognitive skills (Furth, 1961; Rosenstein, 1960; Oléron, 1957).

Hearing children from a cognitively impoverished environment, such as rural Appalachia (Furth, 1973), have cognitive performance levels similar to those of the hearing impaired. Schlesinger and Meadow (1972) saw similarities between hearing-impaired children and children who were victims of discrimination because of race or social class. Furth linked implications of his study to a hypothesis that a slightly retarded nonverbal performance of hearing-impaired children comes from the traditional stress on language and reading in the elementary school, where their psychological need for intellectually challenging activities may be neglected.

It must be noted, however, that more formal thinking may focus on concepts that can only be articulated in a linguistic medium (Furth & Youniss, 1975). Abstract concepts in general have long been recognized as difficult for hearing-impaired students when presented in verbal form.

Non-Standardized Procedures

Traditionally, in education, hierarchies of reading difficulty have included four basic levels. An early definer of these levels was Betts (1950, 1957).

The independent or basal level. Materials are so easy that there is at least 90 percent reading comprehension and freedom from tension in the reading situation.

The instructional level. Material is challenging but not too difficult to understand (at least 75 percent comprehension). Some teacher assistance may be needed in clarifying concepts and vocabulary.

The frustration level. The lowest level of readability, at which the student's comprehension is under 50 percent and he is frustrated and dislikes the reading material.

The potential or capacity level. The highest level of readability of material which the hearing student can understand when the material is read to him. For hearing-impaired students, an estimate of this might be derived by looking at what the student can understand through non-reading means: material presented in picture or pantomime, films, cartoons, or in manual language with which he may be familiar. However it is done, I feel that performance by a student over larger quantities of reading materials is generally more valid than any brief informal inventory or standardized test for determining his level. Once the student's reading level has been established, the next step is to select reading material suited to that level. To do so one needs to determine the "readability level" of written materials.

Problems of Textbook Readability

Depending on the authority, we are told that secondary and postsecondary textbooks are becoming easier—or more difficult—to read.

Technical and scientific fields inevitably and continually increase their vocabularies and conceptual loads in texts. Santa and Burstyn (1977) analyzed 1953, 1962, and 1975 editions of a best-selling college text, *Introduction to Psychology*, by Hilgyard, Atkinson, and Atkinson. In the latest edition—compared to the 1953 edition—they discovered 56 percent more terms and 37 percent more major theoretical viewpoints or concepts. These investigators commented, "Professors should choose books that present new material in simple form. Only when technical vocabulary becomes familiar and its meaning understood can students absorb a greater density of information or a greater complexity of sentence structure."

It is doubtful whether any single textbook can be completely suitable for every student in a typical public or high school class. Considerations of readability for hearing-impaired students (Golladay, 1951) include such things as:

1. Vocabulary load, usually expressed in terms of vocabulary diversity or rarity according to lists of words selected as to frequency of use. In general this has been the most significant single element for determining readability, according to research with hearing children.

2. Sentence structure, usually measured in terms of sentence

length; complexity and rhetorical inversions count against the deaf child even more than the normally hearing student.

3. Idea density, appraised in different ways: number of nouns or verbs; concrete and abstract words; simple and obscure words; prepositional phrases.

4. Human interest, usually evaluated in terms of directness of approach. Among measures used are: number of personal pronouns; words of human interest; words associated with early learning or homely experiences. Other things being equal, the more human interest, the less difficulty to the reader.

5. Conceptual difficulty. The ideas in a passage may be written in simple English, yet still be too abstruse because they are remote from the experience of the reader. Many history and science texts and books dealing with remote periods of time, such as the Middle Ages, have this drawback.

6. Organization of the text. This may present difficulties to the reader when, for example, a writer starts a story at some exciting point, then flashes back to the beginning and fills in the missing parts of the plot.

7. Miscellaneous difficulties, some peculiar to the deaf. Included are: figures of speech; colloquial or idiomatic language; excessive dialogue which carries the plot along; plots which hinge on a single key sentence or two which may not be detected or understood by the reader; excessive use of substitute words in place of the name of some character, or too many characters to remember. Some older books do not begin to be interesting for a chapter or two and thereby discourage the reader at the start. Some deaf children also seem to have shorter-than-average attention spans which handicap them when they are reading long selections.

Most of the problems relate to literary study as well as to textbook readability.

The Informal Reading Inventory

The basal readers used in most elementary schools are written to conform with rather strict readability formulas. Each publishing company appears to have its own system for producing reading texts of graduated difficulty, from preprimer through at least eighth grade. Vocabulary, syllable count per sentence, concepts, level of interest, sentence patterns and lengths are among the considerations used to determine a selection's grade level.

As described by Betts (1950, 1957) and others, the Informal Reading Inventory is used by many public elementary schools to determine the suitability of one of several basal readers in a single series put out by one publisher. Starting with a reader estimated to be well below the student's reading ability, the student reads and answers questions about short selections in succeeding books which become progressively more difficult until he is obviously on his frustration level in that series.

Selections should permit questions based on fact, inference, and vocabulary. Samplings from vocabulary lists on each level may be used as screening devices before the reading. The student is motivated to read each selection by informal discussion and clarification of the background without the answers to the questions being "given away."

Evidences of frustration in the hearing student (who is required to do the reading orally) include hesitations, mispronunciations, word substitutions, fidgeting and finger pointing, retrogressions, as well as failure to answer questions.

The frustration level would be at a point where, besides the above-mentioned symptoms, the student would show less than 50 percent comprehension. The instructional level would be 75 percent or better comprehension with minor help from the instructor.

Obviously, the hearing-impaired student should read silently and the examiner should watch closely for visible evidences of frustration. Reading orally would be more of a mechanical test of speech than a test of reading for meaning, and it would defeat the purpose of the procedure for all but, possibly, the very slightly hearing impaired. Follow-up questions should be worded as simply and briefly as possible and preferably presented in written or typed form to prevent misunderstanding.

This author has used the Informal Reading Inventory to evaluate the suitability of reading materials for hearing-impaired high school students, generally with helpful results when combined with other observations. As teachers gain skill and confidence in using the inventory procedure, they will make better judgments as to whether material is suitable for the student in question. A number of teacher preparation texts, such as those by Betts (1950, 1957), give full details of the IRI procedure.

Spache (1962) has published similar graded paragraphs, with follow-up questions, which can be used as a variation of the IRI procedure.

Other Evaluation Methods

Some attention has been given to developing newer methods to evaluate the reading abilities of deaf students. Besides Moores and Quigley (1967), Kazmierski (1973) has experimented with the "cloze" technique. Cloze involves omitting words from material which becomes progressively more difficult (as in selections from basal readers in the Informal Reading Inventory). Words are omitted in a regular pattern, usually every fifth or seventh word. The student reads this and fills in the blanks with words according to his concept of the intended meaning, and the percentage of acceptable words determines his probable reading level.

However, in any evaluation using graded materials or materials to be evaluated for other purposes, there is some danger that individual selections used for testing may contain stylistic or conceptual problems which make them unsuitable and misleading as test materials, or which in effect upset the order of difficulty of graded materials. For example, a seventh-grade selection may actually be more difficult than an eighth-grade selection if the content is too remote from the experience of the student (therefore, too abstract), if the language itself is too difficult, or if there are complications such as a play on words, underlying humor that is not detected, colloquialisms, or unfamiliar idiomatic usages.

Readability testing formulas, for the reasons just cited, should be used with care when intended to evaluate materials for hearing-impaired students. They are at best a rough screening device for comparing reading materials. I am personally wary of depending on formulas unless other factors are taken into consideration.

Use of Supplementary Materials

Handouts and Other Materials

A most useful, although generally impractical, project for teachers knowledgeable in pedagogy would be to write textbooks for hearing-impaired students. Texts paralleling the regular class texts, using only the essential technical terms in an otherwise simple style, are a possibility, as suggested by Santa and Burstyn (1977).

A more practical option is for teachers to write study guides or syllabi to accompany a regular textbook. *Cliff's Notes* on certain literary classics is a current example of study guides popularly used by high school and postsecondary students, with or without their instructor's approval. The technique could be adapted to content-area texts.

Other special helps on a day-to-day basis can include shorter types of study guides, objective or lesson sheets, outlines, guiding questions, and the like. I have used such handouts as aids to understanding quite difficult materials with satisfactory results in terms of interest, learning, and attitude. In fact, designing and using supplementary materials and procedures to facilitate student understanding can make even relatively difficult textbooks into effective sources of learning.

Some Principles for Preparing Written Materials

The following is not an outline for teaching reading skills, nor do I advocate simplifying all instructional reading materials to the lowest common denominator of reading difficulty. Rather, the items are intended as suggestions for techniques in developing supplemental materials and tests with which to "bridge the gap" between reading materials and the cognitive ability of hearing-impaired students:

1. Break up too-long sentences.
    a. Rewrite as two or more shorter ones.
    b. Use a simple conjunction in a compound sentence.
    c. Less skilled readers tend to be "word readers" or "surface readers." Longer sentences provide more opportunity for misuse and misinterpretation of the wording and difficulty in internalizing the total meaning. This lack of linguistic sophistication is sometimes blamed on a short memory span.
2. Reduce difficult vocabulary load as much as possible.
    a. Retain only essential technical vocabulary.
    b. For the rest of the context, use simpler words.
    c. With training, students may be enabled to unlock the meaning of an unfamiliar word through context clues. But if two or more unfamiliar words appear close together, unlocking meaning from context clues becomes extremely difficult.
3. Reduce concept density.
    a. Too many unfamiliar concepts in a single new lesson are difficult to master.
    b. This may mean breaking down the lesson into two or more steps, with one new concept at a time.
    c. Where practical, use illustrative material (pictures, sketches, graphs, media) as a supplement.
4. Endeavor to enlist the student's background of experience and knowledge. Verbally related experience is especially helpful.

a. Bring the student's experience into the process of understanding a new concept.

b. Communicate with the student (expressively and receptively) to explore and relate new facts to the student's background.

c. Use movies or television to relate to a new concept. Media may be useful for this.

5. If you use a pronoun or other word that refers to a word previously used, be sure that the antecedent or referent is very clear.

a. If in doubt, repeat the referent word.

b. In trying to avoid repetitions, don't confuse the student by using too many synonyms for the same word.

c. The use of a pronoun (such as *this*) to refer to a complex proceeding, general situation, or series of events can be confusing. Such usage may be a difficult order of linguistic sophistication for many deaf students.

6. Don't omit words such as *that*, where they will clarify a sentence connection.

a. While colloquial usage sanctions this omission, deaf students may not be able to mentally supply the missing word.

b. Example: "We make sure *that* all material is ready before we start our project."

7. Stay with simple coordinating conjunctions (*but, so, for, and*) and try to avoid less common transitional words (*however, as a consequence, nevertheless, although*). *Since,* having more than one common meaning, should be avoided as a synonym for *because.* Be alert for similar misleading usages.

8. Keep cause-and-result expressions very simple in form.

a. Deaf students have seldom mastered the more sophisticated of these forms.

b. Experience seems to show that there is a general weakness in understanding of cause-result, reason-result constructions. This is part of the hearing-impaired person's language problem.

9. Conditional expressions which influence the meaning of a statement (such as *if, when, assuming that, suppose, provided that,* etc.) should be used carefully.

a. Use in sentences which are as brief and clear as possible.

b. It is generally preferable to place the conditional expression before, rather than after, the main statement which it modifies.

10. In choosing a synonym to replace a difficult word, word-frequency lists may be helpful, but:

a. If the same concept has a manual sign and corresponding

word known to the student, you're safer to choose the sign-related word.

b. This is another way of enlisting the student's symbol-related experience.

11. If there is no other way to avoid using a difficult word, why not put a brief explanation beside it in parentheses, preferably a simple, familiar synonym or synonyms? However, don't pepper your lesson with too many parenthetical explanations! Footnotes or marginal explanations might be used in formally prepared materials.

12. Certain language forms are generally to be avoided.

a. Passive voice verbs. Some students have forgotten this usage through disuse.

b. Negative forms of verbs and other expressions of negation where a plain statement of positive fact would suffice. One should avoid shifting back and forth between positive and negative forms.

c. Too many modifying forms, such as prepositional phrases, relative clauses, etc., inserted in a sentence. (Shorter sentences will help you to avoid this.)

d. If a relative clause must be used, the relative pronoun (*who, which, that, where*, etc.) should as a general rule be next to the word to which it refers.

e. Stylistic embellishments, such as rhetorical inversions and plays on words, can be confusing.

f. Colloquial and idiomatic expressions which have become embedded in the English language, but which do not lend themselves to structural regularity, are a special problem for the student who has never heard them (Boatner & Gates, 1966, 1975).

13. The English language is full of redundancies and wordiness. Try to cut wordiness to the bone while retaining simple English.

a. However, this does not mean that adding words where necessary for clarity is taboo.

b. Remember to "say what you mean, mean what you say."

14. If an important basic or technical word is to be taught:

a. Make sure its meaning and application are understood from the beginning.

b. Vividness and clarity of presentation in a typical context are a memory aid.

c. If it can be analyzed by meaningful word parts—prefix or known root-word—so much the better.

d. Once well mastered for a primary meaning, spaced repetition of the word in a variety of contexts is helpful.

e. While hearing students are said to require from 30 to 60 encounters with a new word to make it their own, the deaf student may require several times as many encounters.

f. The use of word flashcards is one good way for a student to memorize a new word economically. Meaning enrichment in varied context should follow, because such students tend to accept only the first meaning they have learned. They need to become aware of the influence of context in changing the meaning of a new word.

15. A handout list of guiding questions may be used to help in studying new text materials. Some basic questions could involve:

a. Important facts

b. Inferences which require thought, judgment, application of prior experience

c. Vocabulary that is important, including some that can be understood from context clues

d. Main-idea, theme, or summarizing question (very difficult for many deaf students)

e. Sequence questions which can sometimes involve cause-effect relationships.

f. In literary study, a class may be stopped at some point and asked to speculate on the outcome. In an open-plot story, a new ending can be written.

16. Long, involved questions almost invariably cause confusion because a student may not be able to separate the question from the background material (See 1c). This is analogous to using too-long sentences.

a. Break it up by presenting a hypothetical situation; then

b. Ask a simple question about it.

17. In introducing a new and strange process or technical operation, don't depend on verbal directions alone.

a. Demonstrate, step by step.

b. Let the student get hands-on experience.

c. This may provide some flow-back of experience to the student when he re-reads the text material or directions.

18. Place illustrative sketches, graphs, etc., as near as possible to the text matter which they explain. Keep them simple. Don't worry about being artistic if they are clear.

19. Remember the D.I.G. concept.

a. *Direct* information first;

b. *Indirect* and trivial information next, if needed;

c. *General* information last.

d. This may have to be disregarded where complex new concepts require added background material.

20. Mnemonics may sometimes be helpful.

a. They are essentially a crutch, to be discarded.

b. Most effective for short-term learning.

c. The most efficient "mnemonic" is probably *vividness* in lesson presentation and relating concepts to a student's own experience background.

21. Familiarity with standard cognition principles will help the teacher in preparing meaningful materials.

a. A student with language handicaps obviously will have trouble mastering more abstract concepts. A single word, such as "commercialize" or "feudalism," brings in a whole complex of ideas and experience. Audiovisual materials can be of great value in helping to clarify concepts.

Conclusion

There can be little question regarding the importance of matching students' ability to read and the level of the reading materials if learning is to occur. The importance is just as great in our efforts to assess what it is that students have learned. It is not uncommon to find test questions in a content area such as history or science are more a test of the student's reading ability than a test which assesses the student's knowledge of the subject content. Similarly, an essay question may turn out to be more of a test of writing than of knowledge. While the magnitude of the challenge facing a regular classroom teacher of a hearing-impaired student is great, the prognosis need not be bleak. It is important to point out that there are literally thousands of deaf adults with varying degrees of English and reading deficiencies functioning at a high level of citizenship, social and occupational success. There are thousands of prelingually deaf persons in America with practically flawless English, many with advanced professional degrees. The challenge is not beyond the reach of the talented, dedicated teacher.

There is always danger in stereotyping members of any subgroup such as the hearing impaired, because individuals may vary widely. As teachers, we should prefer to evaluate and capitalize on student strengths and not dwell on their weaknesses. We must take students where they are and have faith that their potential can be developed. If we do not have this faith in and dedication for a student, then we have no business undertaking that student's education. □

CHAPTER IX

Principles of Interpreting in an Educational Environment

T. Alan Hurwitz and Anna B. Witter

This chapter discusses the position of an educational interpreter in a mainstreamed setting. Basic principles are suggested for effective utilization of the educational interpreter by students and teachers. Special interpreting situations (e.g., oral interpreting, reverse interpreting) are explained. A model interpreter is briefly described, and a list of institutions offering interpreter training programs is provided in Appendix C (pages 193-197).

Introduction

In 1968, with the advent of NTID and other federally funded postsecondary programs for the deaf, a new concept in education—the educational interpreter—began being recognized across the country. The implementation of P.L. 94-142 and Section 504 of the Vocational Rehabilitation Act of 1973 has called to the attention of school authorities the fact that the hearing-impaired student must not be denied the use of auxiliary aids (e.g., interpreters) if such support is needed in the regular classroom.

The role of the educational interpreter is to facilitate communication for hearing-impaired students. Interpreters serve as a link between deaf individuals and their hearing counterparts in many different respects: it may be an educational link between a deaf student and a learning process, or it may be a communication link between a deaf person and a hearing person. Either way, interpreters serve to provide a "bridge" for communication between both parties. It is reasonable to expect that many regular classroom teachers may be uncertain about how this is done, what the specific role of the interpreter is, and how to best use interpreting services.

This chapter will address several major topics related to the interpreting process: limitations of interpreting, terminology of interpreting, the interpreter's role, the role of the classroom teacher, the student's role, and interpreter preparation.

Limitations of Interpreting

At NTID approximately 25 percent of the deaf students are fully mainstreamed into the baccalaureate programs of Rochester Institute of Technology (RIT), the host institution for NTID. About half of the remaining students take five or more courses in the regular classrooms. Although most of these students receive interpreting services, many of them still encounter considerable difficulty keeping pace with their normally hearing peers. Contributing to this difficulty is the tendency of teachers to move around, speak too rapidly, use terminology with too much abstraction, and neglect to use appropriate visual aids in their lectures. It is also difficult for many of the deaf students to conceptualize the meaning of particular spoken content in a lecture or discussion even though it is interpreted.

Interpreting may be one medium of support service that will help improve the educational process, but it can not solve all problems. It only reduces the impact of the handicap.

Interpreter Terminology

A review of the interpreting communication process will clarify the role of the interpreter and introduce some helpful guidelines which have been developed through experience at NTID and RIT. There are various methods an educational interpreter may use:

1. *Translate.* Present a spoken, or a combination of spoken and signed/fingerspelled, word-for-word representation of a speaker's actual message. The exact wording may be changed so that it can be conceptually understood by the student. For example, if a speaker said, "I am running this meeting and I want you to run to the café and buy me a cup of coffee," a translation might be, "I am controlling this meeting and I want you to go quickly to the café and buy me a cup of coffee."

2. *Interpret.* Present the spoken word in the communication mode used by the individual hearing-impaired student, which may include American Sign Language (ASL) or other sign language systems. This requires both a familiarity with the content material and a diversity of language skills, as well as a knowledge of the attributes of mouthing

words—as can be used in oral or combined interpreting—which may enhance lipreading.

3. *Reverse interpret.* To repeat in spoken English, the signed and/or spoken message of a hearing-impaired student. This is done when normally hearing people cannot understand the signs or the speech of a hearing-impaired person. Traditionally, this is the most difficult skill for an interpreter to develop.

Role of the Interpreter

Generally, in a classroom an interpreter sits on a chair a few feet from the teacher in front of the class and not away from the blackboard or the screen for overhead projection. A deaf student sits where he has access to the line of view of the teacher, the interpreter, and the blackboard/screen. Some deaf students prefer to sit in the second or third row, at one side of the room, so that they can have access to a broader view of the classroom activities and are able to see which student is talking. In practice, the interpreter interprets ("translate or interpret") everything the teacher says as well as questions/answers or discussions made by other students. Normally, this is done using a combination of sign language, fingerspelling, clear mouth movement (without voice), good facial/eye expressions and expressive body language. In situations where the deaf student wants to participate in the classroom discussion, the interpreter reverse interprets the student's signed or spoken words into understandable speech.

At the postsecondary level, some interpreters are able to "interpret" the speaker's message, but most will have to "translate" since they do not have sufficient skill with both the subject matter and with sign language. However, more interpreters will develop that skill as they are assigned to classes in which they have some knowledge of the content and as their opportunities for advanced interpreting training are increased. Few interpreters have advanced reverse interpreting skills due to the difficulty in mastering this skill. This is evidenced by records of the Registry of Interpreters for the Deaf (1978), which state that out of a membership of almost 4,000 individuals, only 586 have certification measuring reverse skills at 70 percent accuracy. More training opportunities should provide regular classrooms with more interpreters with reverse skills.

Regardless of the method that the interpreter uses—translating, interpreting, or reversing—the role of the interpreter is not to teach or assume responsibility for the hearing-impaired students. The teacher has this responsibility at all times. It is helpful for teachers to think of the interpreter as a support for their communication, rather than as a substitute for it.

> The interpreter is a facilitator of communication between two or more individuals using different languages or communication modes. It is imperative that this communication be unhampered by the presence of the third party, i.e. the interpreter. He/she must be able at all times to function in an objective and impartial way. The interpreter must be able to faithfully transmit the ideas presented without minimizing, exaggerating, deleting or in any way distorting the original message. (Rudser, Witter, & Gillies, 1978)

If interpreters are to effectively serve in a support capacity for teachers, they must work with the teacher and student to answer some basic questions:

1. How can the hearing-impaired student's full participation be assured?

2. What are the hearing-impaired student's specific communication needs?

3. Do others involved in the communication process, such as the teacher and students (both hearing and hearing-impaired), fully understand the role and responsibility of the interpreter?

The answers to these questions provide the interpreter with a needed awareness of the students and the classroom situation.

The Role of the Classroom Teacher

Classroom teachers can help the interpreter find answers to these questions, provide time for the interpreter to assess the student's communication needs, or just be aware that these concerns are important for successful classroom communication. Teachers can increase both their own effectiveness in teaching hearing-impaired students and the effectiveness of the interpreter by:

1. *Taking time at the onset of the class to discuss with the interpreter and students the interpreter's role in the classroom setting.* This will help alleviate one of the biggest problems an interpreter faces— being asked to assume a role that he is not qualified for and/or ethically can not assume (such as providing information to the teacher without the student's knowledge; or advising the student or acting as the student's defender, protector, or informer). It is the interpreter's role to facilitate, not replace, communication between the hearing and hearing-impaired in the classroom.

2. *Informing the interpreter of the class format.* Will it be a discussion or a lecture? Will there be films or media employed? Knowing the answers to these questions in advance will allow the interpreter to prepare appropriately.

3. *Minimizing movement whenever possible.* This will allow the student to have a full view of the teacher, interpreter, and blackboard concurrently. A hearing student receives oral messages and at the same time receives visual ones from the facial expressions and body language of the teacher. Often the subtle nonverbal cues have as much, if not more, impact on how the message is received than the spoken word. If the teacher moves away from the interpreter, or stands in such a way that the hearing-impaired student cannot watch both the interpreter and the teacher's visual cues, then much of the important part of the message may be missed. Also, a student may rely on speechreading for understanding the teacher. Occasionally such a student may miss a word or two and watch the interpreter to catch the missing word. Since the interpreter is lagging three to eight words behind, it is difficult for the student to speechread if the teacher is not close by.

4. *Being sensitive to the "lag time" that occurs.* The interpreter needs time to identify who is speaking, especially in discussion groups. When questions are being asked, it is important to remember that there is a lag between what is being spoken and what is being interpreted. Make sure that the deaf student has time to respond. Also, when using media, a deaf student needs time to receive the message from the interpreter and then look at the overhead, slide, or blackboard information since he cannot receive both forms of visual information concurrently.

5. *Providing periodic checks to make sure the student understood the information.* A teacher might assume that a student is comprehending all information, regardless of the interpreter, because he appears responsive. In many instances a student may nod his head rather than ask for clarification in order to avoid appearing foolish or being misunderstood. Teachers are encouraged to seek out reinforcement of a student's comprehension by asking the student to repeat information or encouraging more active classroom participation.

If you are not certain after initiating these suggestions, then it may be a good idea for you to talk with the student and find out exactly how he feels about his role in the classroom. He may want to discuss his problems with you, or he may prefer to talk it over with his counselor or someone from the resource room, if one is available in your school.

He may be reluctant to admit that he has difficulty understanding the classroom activities. In fact, he may even have difficulty accepting the fact that he has a hearing problem. If this is the case, further discussion with his counselor and his parents should be initiated to help the student (and possibly help the parents) to realize the benefits of special assistance through interpreters.

Communication is often difficult. Understandably, it becomes more complex with the introduction of the third dimension of an interpreter. Remember, it is important to the teacher that an accurate message be sent and that the message be received by the student. It is critically important for the teacher to understand how the interpreting process works and to cooperate with the interpreter in making sure that hearing-impaired students receive and understand the essence of all classroom communication. We have found that the following simple guidelines can make the difference between understanding or not.

1. *Speaking too rapidly.* It is not necessary to speak at an unnatural, exaggeratedly slow pace, but it is important to speak slowly enough for the students to read the interpreter. Often the student may have more trouble than the interpreter with a rapid pace.

2. *Using a lot of idioms or too much abstraction.* Some hearing-impaired students are not familiar with English idioms, which makes it difficult for them to conceptualize through an interpreter.

3. *Using technical terminology which may be unfamiliar to the interpreter or student.* In both of the above points, it is very helpful for the interpreter and the students to be given any concepts or technical vocabulary well in advance of the class so that they can prepare to use the most effective means of communication.

In order to make the interpreted situation a successful one, it is important to perceive the process as a teacher/interpreter/student team effort. To help you review these points, they have been summarized in Table 9.A.

There are some concerns about how an interpreter may be utilized in the mainstreaming situation. An extreme example of how an interpreter may be used in a school was the case of a hearing-impaired student who was taken out of a residential school for the deaf and placed in a regular school at the wish of his parents. This took place in a very small town, so qualified interpreters were not available. The parents knew an elderly lady who was a daughter of deaf parents and used signs fluently. She was hired by the school to perform as the student's interpreter on a full-time basis. She interpreted in every class where the student was enrolled, including physical education

TABLE 9.A
Summary of hints for teachers and problems which may hinder the interpreting process.

Hints for Teachers
1. Taking time at the onset of the class to discuss with the interpreter and students the interpreter's role in the classrooms
2. Informing the interpreter of the class format
3. Being sensitive to the "lag time" that occurs

Problems that may hinder interpreting process
1. Speaking too rapidly
2. Using a lot of idiomatic terminology or too much abstraction
3. Using technical terminology which may be unfamiliar to the interpreter or student

and other enrichment sessions (e.g., art). In addition, the interpreter followed the student everywhere he went—his locker, dining room, study hall, book store, etc. In the dining room the interpreter made sure that the deaf student was involved in every communication activity with his hearing peers.

In this situation the interpreter had become a full-time chaperone or "mother" figure. There can be serious consequences with regard to a student's social development with his peers if an interpreter assumes, by request or arbitrarily, full responsibility for a deaf student's involvement in the communication process.

Students need to develop skills which will enable them to grow into independent and responsible citizens when they leave the school environment.

Role of the Student

The responsibility for optimizing the chances that an interpreted classroom presentation is understood rests not only with the teacher and the interpreter but also with the student.

It is essential that the deaf student be well prepared for each class. This means reading the textbook in advance, doing homework on time, and listing relevant questions to be asked during class. In addition, the student must be knowledgeable about the role of the interpreter and various principles to ensure appropriate utilization of an interpreter.

When NTID searched for methods to motivate students to effectively use the interpreting staff, it became increasingly important for students to internalize the role of an interpreter and to realize their own responsibilities in the interpreted process.

One method found to be helpful in informing students of their role is the use of visual reinforcement of established principles through a comic book format. The comic book serves to stimulate the student's imagination and to motivate learning with regard to the utilization of an interpreter and other support services at NTID. The material is presented in logical steps, and the deaf student has frequent opportunities to respond to the meaning of printed words. As Stark (1974) has pointed out, a student gets immediate feedback to an interpretation of printed words, because a picture either does or does not confirm an interpretation. Many well-educated deaf individuals have remarked that comic books have significantly contributed to their language development (Bowe, 1974).

The comic book was designed by a deaf student in the Art program at NTID and contains principles NTID has identified for effective utilization of an interpreter and explanations of the roles of all communicators—the student, the teacher, and the interpreter—in an educational setting. These principles and explanations are the culmination of efforts begun in 1971 by interpreters, faculty, and deaf students. The purposes of the comic book are:

1. To explain to the student his own responsibilities, as well as the teacher's and the interpreter's, relative to classroom preparation.

2. To describe techniques which will facilitate optimal classroom activity and lighting.

3. To show the students how they may go about getting volunteer notetakers.

4. To show the student how to listen in class, and to show the interpreter and the teacher how to make it easier for the student to listen to them.

5. To familiarize students, interpreters, and teachers with factors related to reverse interpreting in the classroom.

6. To help students' understanding in special interpreting situations, i.e., TV lectures, labs, group discussions.

7. To show students potential problems that may arise with interpreters and how to solve them.

8. To show students and interpreters their respective responsibilities in interpreting telephone calls.

While the comic book looks very promising and has been received

FIGURE 9.1

Illustration from NTID comic book (1978) showing students the problems that may arise with an interpreter and what the students' responsibilities are.

RESPONSIBILITIES OF THE STUDENT:

1 IF YOU HAVE TROUBLE UNDERSTANDING THE INTERPRETER TRY TO FIND OUT WHAT THE PROBLEM IS:

ⓐ UNCLEAR FINGERSPELLING.

ⓑ LACK OF MOUTH MOVEMENT.

ⓒ NO FACIAL EXPRESSION, OR TOO MUCH FACIAL EXPRESSION.

ⓓ LANGUAGE IS TOO HARD TO UNDERSTAND.

ⓔ TECHNICAL SIGNS ARE NOT USED.

ⓕ DIFFERENT TECH SIGNS USED.

I THINK SHE'S DEAD!!

2 THINGAMAJIG?

SHOW THE INTERPRETER ANY TECHNICAL SIGNS SHE MAY NOT KNOW.

3 NEW CLEAR FISHING?

NUCLEAR FISSION

KNOW THAT OFTEN INTERPRETERS DO NOT HAVE THE BACKGROUND IN THE AREAS THEY INTERPRET.

4 DO YOU UNDERSTAND?

MASK

Z

LACK OF ATTENTION WILL MAKE IT HARD FOR THE INTERPRETER TO INTERPRET.

5 GRAH! THIS IS THA LAST TIME I'LL COME TO A NIGHT CLASS DURING A FULL MOON!

REMEMBER THAT THE INTERPRETER IS HUMAN AND HAS GOOD AND BAD DAYS JUST LIKE YOU.

with enthusiasm by students, there is a need to more formally evaluate this approach and to determine ways to improve its effectiveness for deaf students and faculty. Based on the information currently available, it is expected that the comic book medium will serve as an exciting tool to help students become more sensitive and aware of their responsibilities. Hopefully, this will lead to more open discussion among students, teachers, advisers, and interpreters about effective implementation of support services. Samples from the comic book are shown in Figures 9.1 and 9.2.

Knowledge of these principles will assist in minimizing the problems that arise during an interpreted process. It is also imperative that a teacher and a student work together to determine a student's communicative style and mode so that the most appropriate interpreter can be selected to meet the communication needs of a student.

Various Interpreting Methods

It often has been assumed that interpreting means sign language or that a deaf student must learn sign language to use an interpreter. This was true for many years until 1964, when a group of oral deaf adults formed the Oral Deaf Adults Section (ODAS) of the Alexander Graham Bell Association for the Deaf. These individuals organized to provide their support to the association's philosophy that the use of speech, speechreading, and residual hearing be promoted for those hearing-impaired children who have the potential for oral/aural development. They have expressed a need for a qualified oral interpreter in large assembly meetings where it is difficult to read the lips of the speaker at the podium. In recent AGBAD meetings, two interpreters—one who uses a combination of mouthing and signing and the other who uses mouthing exclusively—have been provided so that deaf people in the audience could have the choice of using either or both of the interpreters. Training for oral interpreters has increased over the past 10 years. Northcott (1977) stated that individuals who might request an oral interpreter fall into two subclassifications, auditory/oral and visual/oral:

Auditory/oral: Any individual who receives his linguistic information primarily through the auditory channel, with or without amplification. This type of person will generally settle back, turn his or her hearing aid (if worn) to the desired volume, and listen to the speaker, while occasionally glancing at the oral interpreter. If the speaker turns away from the audience or someone asks a question out of hearing

FIGURE 9.2

Illustration from NTID comic book (1978) showing problems that may arise with an interpreter and what the students', interpreters', and teachers' responsibilities are.

range, the interpreter is useful temporarily. Here, the specialist's role is one of watchful waiting to supply cues when necessary (e.g., "A woman in the back of the room asked if the same play would be given again tomorrow") in a checks-and-balance kind of supportive role.

Visual/oral: The person who relies on speechreading plus amplified hearing, or speechreading alone, is apt to turn off his or her hearing aid to circumvent the problem of a dual or garbled message (due to delayed feedback if the hearing aid is turned on). Such a person needs the oral interpreter for group discussion situations and for audience situations where he is too far from the speaker to speechread easily.

It has also been realized in the last few years that there are other forms of interpreting, depending on the individual needs of deaf people. For instance, one may wonder how interpreting can be provided to a deaf-blind person. This is accomplished through the tactile process when the interpreter fingerspells in the deaf-blind person's hands. In many cases a deaf-blind person can "read lips" by pressing a thumb on the lips of a speaker while feeling the voice vibrations on the speaker's neck with the rest of the hand. Some deaf-blind persons can comprehend sign language by placing their hands on the back of the hands of the interpreter.

Some deaf people who do not understand signs/fingerspelling and are unable to read lips, much less use their residual hearing, may benefit from a printed form of interpreting. The interpreter may use a pad and pencil to convey messages to the deaf person. A blackboard may be used as a medium in this process. A deaf person who has limited language skills may benefit from a graphic display or a pantomime in the interpreting process. The student and teacher must work together to determine the interpreter who will best meet the needs of the individual student.

The Model Interpreter

The model interpreter of today must be versatile, knowledgeable, and extremely competent to meet the ever-growing challenge of the profession. The population he serves demonstrates a variety of communication needs, and the skills required to meet these needs can no longer be acquired by "chance." The professional, model interpreter is prepared to meet the communication needs of all deaf persons, regardless of their communication mode, and is able to assess any interpreting situation and adapt accordingly.

An interpreter functioning in the academic environment must possess a variety of competencies to meet the needs of a diverse population. An overview of these skills is as follows:

1. A good command of the English language
2. Excellent memory retention skills
3. Above-average hand/mind coordination
4. An in-depth understanding of the population being served (e.g., etiologies of deafness, audiology, psychosocial aspects of deafness)
5. Content knowledge of the subject matter being taught
6. Fluency in the language used by deaf people
7. Ability to interpret/translate at 140/200 words per minute
8. Ability to reverse interpret from signed English to verbal English, ASL to verbal English, combine ASL and signed English to verbal English, and spoken words of a deaf person into more understandable speech
9. Comprehensive understanding of the role of an interpreter and the ability to communicate this role to students, staff, and faculty
10. Ability to orally interpret/translate the spoken words of a speaker
11. Ability to use mime, pantomime, gesturing, and written communication appropriate to the setting.

This overview is not ranked in order of importance and is not all-inclusive. It serves as a general overview of the type of skills an educational interpreter should possess in order to fully perform his tasks. Acquisition of these skills requires a combination of ongoing training, practicum, on-the-job experience, and evaluation. Experience at NTID has demonstrated the need for ongoing training and application in a well supervised environment for at least two or three years.

Interpreter Preparation

For the past 11 years NTID has sponsored an intensive interpreter training program which focuses primarily on preparing interpreters for an academic/educational setting. This program is 10 weeks in length and serves as the introduction to the interpreting profession. Most graduates require one to three years of additional training/ practicum before becoming proficient interpreters. The curriculum is designed to prepare the interpreter to meet the communication needs of all deaf persons, regardless of their communication mode.

It is also NTID's intent that the training efforts be supportive of the existing certification of interpreters sponsored by the National Registry of Interpreters for the Deaf and degree programs established in

interpreting. Ways this can occur are to:
1. Provide opportunities for specialization in educational interpreting and oral interpreting
2. Provide internship/practicum opportunities for interpreters in training
3. Adapt curriculum expectations to the certification requirements of the National Registry of Interpreters for the Deaf.

There are a number of short-term training programs, as well as A.A.S. and B.S. degree programs offered throughout the United States. To aid in recruiting qualified interpreters, a listing of these programs is provided in Appendix C. Experience demonstrates the need for formal training and supervision of those individuals functioning as interpreters in an educational setting. To offer less to a deaf person, child or adult, is prohibiting their right to equal educational opportunities.

Certification of Interpreters

Any academic program using educational interpreters should make every effort to recruit competent, certified interpreters. The Registry of Interpreters for the Deaf (RID) National Certification Board has established the following levels of competency:

(ETC) *Expressive Translating:* Ability to simultaneously translate from spoken to manual English (verbatim).

(EIC) *Expressive Interpreting:* Ability to use sign language with hearing-impaired persons who possess various levels of language competence.

(RSC) *Reverse Skills:* Ability to render (manually, orally, or written) a hearing-impaired person's message.

(CSC) *Comprehensive Skills:* Includes expressive translating, expressive interpreting, and reverse skills.

(MCSC) *Master Comprehensive Skills Certificate:* Includes all skills measured for a CSC but requires a higher degree of competency.

Ex(LSC) *Legal Specialist Certificate:* Includes CSC skills plus specialized evaluation to qualify for interpreting in a variety of legal settings.

(PP) *Provisional Permit:* Knowledge of sign language and beginning interpreting skills, apprenticeship (one year or less) prior to applying for certification by the National RID, Inc.

Note: It is possible for an individual to receive a combination of the first three certificates.

To employ interpreters who do not possess any of these *levels* of competency jeopardizes the deaf student's opportunity and right to an equal educational opportunity. It is vital—imperative—that the interpreters utilized in the educational setting possess a high degree of competency and professionalism, and this is of even greater importance in a nonsupervised setting. Often a lack of understanding by the student can result directly from the inferior skills of the interpreter.

Summary

This chapter has introduced some basic principles relevant to the use of interpreters in the educational environment. The roles and responsibilities of the interpreter, student, and teacher were elaborated on as well as the competencies interpreters must master through interpreter preparation programs.

The use of an interpreter is one means of support service to a hearing-impaired student in a mainstreamed environment. It is important that the interpreter possesses the degree of competency necessary to encourage confidence—in the teacher, in the hearing-impaired student, and in peer students—that the job will be done well.

For many people, the incorporation of the interpreting dimension is a new and somewhat awesome experience. Appropriate selection of an interpreter, and a close working relationship among all individuals involved in the interpreted process, will ensure the smooth, productive, and effective implementation of this support service. ☐

CHAPTER X

Principles of Tutoring and Notetaking

Russell T. Osguthorpe and Beth Duffin Whitehead

For those interested in establishing a tutoring and/or notetaking support service for hearing-impaired students, this chapter may serve as a brief handbook. We summarize the research and evaluation data, and discuss several methods of providing proper training and evaluating and improving any tutor/notetaker support system. More extensive guides to quality training programs are referenced.

Introduction

School districts have two basic options in providing tutoring and notetaking support services. The first is to augment the professional staff by hiring additional special education teachers as tutors and notetakers. Although cost should not be a factor, it is understood that most school systems would not be able to hire enough professionals to provide adequate services. The second option is to train an existing staff member to assume the role of "support manager." As a manager of tutoring and notetaking services, this person trains and supervises a corps of paraprofessionals who provide individualized tutoring and notetaking support for each mainstreamed deaf student. The use of paraprofessionals as tutors and notetakers is not new to education. But their use with physically disabled students (deaf, blind, orthopedically handicapped) *is* relatively new and much less carefully researched. This should not discourage school districts from exploring the feasibility of using paraprofessionals with deaf students. On the contrary, there is every indication, from research with other populations, that paraprofessionals should be capable of improving a deaf person's chances of success in a mainstreamed situation (Devin-Sheehan, Feldman, & Allen, 1976).

150

In this chapter we will describe effective processes to be considered as school districts and educators of deaf people begin to implement paraprofessional support systems for mainstreamed deaf students. The processes are drawn from empirical studies conducted with deaf people (Osguthorpe, 1976) and other populations (Melaragno, 1976). From this research it appears that one of the most important ingredients in any paraprofessional support system is the development of a quality training program.

Evidence, as well as logic, suggests that paraprofessionals must be properly trained to be effective providers of educational support (Harrison & Cohen, 1969). Common mistakes otherwise occur when untrained or improperly trained paraprofessional tutors are placed with low-achieving learners. Among the problem areas are:

1. "Overprompting"
   a. Giving too many hints
   b. Never requiring the student to work alone
   c. Telling rather than explaining
2. Lack of patience
   a. Expecting the student to succeed on the first try
   b. Looking disappointed
   c. Punishing incorrect responses
3. Lack of record keeping
   a. Neither planning nor evaluating tutoring sessions
   b. Not keeping a record of student progress

Another problem area for those working with deaf students is the whole area of communications skills.

At first glance it may appear that the problems of involving paraprofessionals in a supportive role are not worth the effort that must be devoted to the design and implementation of a quality training program. But experience has suggested otherwise. Parents have been successfully trained to use structured materials to help their young children acquire beginning reading skills (Osguthorpe & Harrison, 1976). Retarded adolescents have been trained to tutor younger retarded children in basic life skills (Wagner, 1973).

NTID's Tutor/Notetaker Training Program

At NTID, an ongoing program focuses on training normally hearing college students as tutors and notetakers for their mainstreamed deaf classmates (Osguthorpe, 1975). The four-day training program emphasizes the tailoring of notes and tutoring techniques to specific learning characteristics and communications skills of individual deaf students. Tutor/notetakers become familiar with the unique personal and educational effects of deafness on students they support.

By the close of our training period tutor/notetakers have:

1. established a working relationship with their support manager
2. practiced tutoring and taking notes
3. had follow-up diagnostic evaluations
4. an understanding of the individual students they will be supporting
5. learned which classes they will cover
6. set up regular meetings with their manager for purposes of skill development and program monitoring.

As the use of paraprofessionals for mainstreamed deaf students increases, a variety of training programs will undoubtedly emerge. The specifics of these training program needs will vary, depending upon several factors:

1. the particular needs of the deaf students receiving support
2. the age and experience of prospective tutors/notetakers
3. the availability of appropriate materials (or resources for the development of materials)
4. the skills and experience of those conducting the training program and those who will subsequently manage the total support system.

For example, at NTID the paraprofessionals must be prepared to deal with a variety of content areas, for they may be assigned to a different course each quarter. Efforts are made to place tutor/notetakers in courses they have already taken or to place them in courses closely related to their area of expertise. Because college courses include a broad range of content areas and the skill level of the paraprofessional is relatively high, structured teaching materials for each course are not provided for tutor/notetakers to use when working with deaf students. Emphasis is placed on training tutors to encourage and facilitate students' self-learning efforts, rather than going through a fixed series of lessons with the student.

If we look at what is required for training sixth graders to tutor second graders, we see something quite different from the NTID (college) situation. In this case notetaking may not be needed and tutoring must be more structured. A sixth-grade student will probably not be expected to be effective as a tutor of both reading and math. A separate tutoring corps for each content area will be preferable. A significant amount of the training will likely be devoted to familiarizing tutors with the math or reading materials to be used and the teaching strategies attached to each learning activity. Without carefully planned and sequenced learning activities, young cross-age tutors normally do not effect much learning in students they support.

Training Tutors and Notetakers

Tutoring Skills

When designing a program to train paraprofessionals as tutors for mainstreamed deaf students, consider developing a section of the training program around each of the following content areas:

1. Establishing rapport
2. Communications skills
3. Diagnosing, teaching, assessing
4. Providing feedback
5. Specific content skills

Establishing rapport. An important skill for any tutor, whatever the age, is the ability to be both a friend and a teacher to the student. Paraprofessionals who tutor deaf students need to become aware of deafness as a handicap and be trained in the role they will play with both professionals and students. As a part of this training, the support service manager and deaf students, by role playing, can emphasize the importance of establishing rapport. Once the manager has demonstrated the proper techniques of establishing rapport and has emphasized the importance of sincerity, trainees should have an opportunity to role-play meeting a deaf student for the first time.

Communications skills. Obviously, an effective tutor is one who has learned to communicate well with students. While this does not necessarily mean a skill in manual communication, it does mean an awareness of the communication difficulties of deaf people and a willingness to augment one's communications skills in order that learning will occur. If a majority of students requiring tutoring rely on sign language, then basic skill in manual communication should be acquired as a prerequisite for entering the training program.

Diagnosing, teaching, assessing. If the tutor trainees are secondary or postsecondary students, and if they will be working within a variety of content areas, it is important that a segment of the training program focus on improving skills in diagnosing, teaching, and assessing. At the close of the training program, trainees should have a clear understanding that most tutoring sessions will require the diagnose-teach-assess cycle. They should receive ample practice in working with students during the training program, either in a role play session or in an actual tutoring session in order that their skills in this area will improve.

In the case of younger cross-aged tutors, it is recommended that most of the diagnosing and assessing be handled by a professional manager. This means that the majority of the training program for young tutors should focus on specific teaching techniques for specific content areas (such as math or reading).

Providing feedback. One of the most critical skills for any teacher or tutor is that of providing appropriate feedback to students. This means providing positive feedback when students do well and answer correctly, but not providing discouraging feedback when students do not do well. For example, it is not unusual for most of us to become impatient or upset when the student seems not to be grasping what we are trying to teach. This type of behavior on the part of the tutor inhibits the student and may prevent any meaningful future contacts between the tutor and the student. When students give incorrect responses or continually fail to grasp a particular concept, tutors should lead the student to correct answers and thereby avoid frustration. Skilled tutors are sensitized to the problem of dependency as it relates to the handicap of deafness and to the types of tutoring behavior that will increase independence on the part of the student.

Specific content skills. When tutoring programs are established in the lower grades, it is usually best to focus on specific content areas, for each content area has instructional techniques that are specific to that area. In math, for example, the tutor should be trained in the specific techniques for helping students through different types of math problems. The techniques for helping a student through a long-division problem may be slightly different from the techniques for helping a student through a simple subtraction problem. There might also be drills and exercises specific to the math area. In the case of elementary reading instruction, training might include specific techniques for teaching sight words or for teaching comprehension skills.

Table 10.A illustrates a sample tutoring skills check list designed for use by older peer tutors. It can be used as both an evaluation tool and as a base for developing an appropriate set of training objectives.

Notetaking Skills

When designing a training program for paraprofessional notetakers,

TABLE 10.A
A tutoring check list designed for use by older students.

Tutor _____ Student _____

Course _____ Date _____

1. How effective is the rapport
   you have developed with your
   student(s)? If you tutor more   1 2 3 4 5
   than one student, respond sep-   negative   positive
   arately for each.

2. Is the student becoming more
   independent or less independent   1 2 3 4 5
   of you and your services?   more   less

3. How effective are your communication skills?

                                            1 2 3 4 5
   Expressive   poor   excellent
                                            1 2 3 4 5
   Receptive   poor   excellent

4. How effective are you at using
   visual aids (books, diagrams,   1 2 3 4 5
   pictures)?   poor   excellent

5. How often do you use praise and
   encouragement when the student   1 2 3 4 5
   performs well?   never   very often

6. How often do you punish incorrect
   answers (verbally or by a dis-   1 2 3 4 5
   appointed facial expression)?   very often   never

7. How competent do you feel at
   handling incorrect responses or   1 2 3 4 5
   poor performance?   incompetent   competent

8. After each tutoring session, how   1 2 3 4 5
   often do you fill out a Tutor Log? never   always

9. How confident do you feel in
   your ability to determine the   1 2 3 4 5
   student(s)' instructional needs? unconfident   confident

it is advisable to focus on three basic areas: 1) Functions, 2) Mechanics, 3) Instructional helps.

Functions include such things as being on time to class and leaving personal bias out of the notes. In this segment of the training program, it is important to help notetakers understand what their specific roles and responsibilities will be in relationship to both professionals (faculty) and students. Notetaking mechanics include such things as writing legibly, using dark ink so that notes can be mechanically copied, and spelling accurately. Although the mechanics seem fairly straightforward and are very important to deaf students, they are often overlooked.

The most comprehensive part of notetaking training centers around some· broader techniques and instructional helps. These techniques include defining difficult vocabulary, using complete sentences, and emphasizing important points. Because these are the techniques most seldom used by notetakers when they are taking notes for themselves, they deserve special attention in any training program. Table 10.B is a notetaking check list with a more complete listing of each of the specific skills within each of the three areas just discussed.

How Paraprofessionals Can Best Gain the Skills

Several different methods for training paraprofessionals as tutors and notetakers are discussed in the following section, which describes the advantages and disadvantages of each major type of program.

Intensive training. One of the most common ways of imparting tutoring and notetaking skills to paraprofessionals is through an intensive training program. Such a program has several advantages:

1. A support system can be quickly established.

2. Notetakers and their managers have an opportunity to develop close working relationships.

3. Tutors/notetakers gain basic skills and understandings which enable them to benefit more from experience following the program.

4. Tutors/notetakers have sufficient exposure to the requirements of their new roles that they are able to provide quality services early in their tutoring/notetaking careers.

One of the difficulties with such a program is that tutors are often not able to practice their new skills with deaf students in an actual classroom setting. In an intensive program it is usually necessary to rely on simulated practice sessions such as role playing for tutoring, and audiotapes of lectures for notetaking practice.

TABLE 10.B
A notetaking check list designed for use by older students.

Tutor/Notetaker _____ Students _____

Course _____ Date _____

	YES	NO
FUNCTIONS		
1. I am on time to class.	____	____
2. I ask for feedback on the quality of notes from:		
students	____	____
teacher	____	____
3. I have discussed my role as a T/N with the teacher.	____	____
4. I support student rules concerning attendance and notes distribution.	____	____
5. I try to leave my own biases out of the notes.	____	____
MECHANICS		
1. Each page has a number, title, and date.	____	____
2. The paper is 8½ × 11 written on one side only.	____	____
3. I use dark ink.	____	____
4. My writing is legible.	____	____
5. When I am unsure of a word or an idea, I leave it blank and then fill it in later.	____	____
6. My spelling is accurate.	____	____

	YES	NO
INSTRUCTIONAL HELPS		
1. I use white space effectively.	____	____
2. I have the ability to listen and store while I write.	____	____
3. I make maximum use of the cues given by the teacher.	____	____
4. I mark points of emphasis so that they are more noticeable.	____	____
5. I define difficult vocabulary.	____	____
6. I use complete sentences.	____	____
7. I use meaningful examples.	____	____
8. I use diagrams and illustrations effectively.	____	____
9. I try to organize the information in the most understandable way.		
10. My notes are complete.	____	____
11. In a discussion, I indicate who is speaking.	____	____
12. I use only abbreviations that students understand.	____	____
13. I have tried reworking the notes after class.	____	____

The length of the intensive training program depends upon several factors: (a) the level of skill the paraprofessional possesses, (b) the breadth of training objectives (tutoring, notetaking, or both), (c) the complexities of the population being served, (d) the level of structure provided in tutorial learning aids or the number of content areas covered in the case of notetaking, and (e) the degree of and kinds of supervision provided following the training.

Let us examine several examples of intensive training programs for tutors and notetakers. At NTID tutors and notetakers are trained in a 30-hour, four-day intensive program, grouped according to broad content areas. A professional manager is assigned to each of the content areas and participates in the training program as a trainer/monitor. Within each of the broad content areas, tutor/notetakers must have the ability to cover several different courses. Because of this broad content coverage, the possibility of providing structured tutorial learning aids for each content area becomes impractical. Learning aids designed to train deaf students in study skills are provided, however. Following the training program, managers assume a close relationship with tutor/notetakers and continue to help these paraprofessionals improve their skills.

Let us now examine a program quite different from the NTID situation. At the Texas School for the Deaf in Austin, Texas, eighth-grade deaf students are trained to tutor other middle school students in math skills. Because the tutors bring with them the prerequisite skills of communications and a knowledge of deafness, the training consists of general techniques of tutoring and specific techniques for tutoring in math. For example, some tutors are trained to tutor other students in their memorization of math facts. This training includes a two-hour practice and demonstration session on flash card techniques used in memorizing math facts. Due to the content area being limited, the training objectives are narrow, close supervision is provided following the training, and the middle school students can be trained as tutors in a relatively short period of time (four to six hours).

Apprenticeship training. Another effective way to train paraprofessionals is to do it while they work. When this mode of training is used, it is assumed that the paraprofessionals bring with them the important prerequisites of communication skills and content expertise. In other words, an untrained tutor would not be paired with a manual deaf student if the tutor did not already have manual communications skills. An untrained notetaker would not be placed in a course in which the notetaker did not have content expertise. When the paraprofessional brings these critical tutoring prerequisites into the position, the manager can provide ongoing training throughout the first year of the paraprofessional's work.

Apprenticeship training can take several forms. San Diego Mesa College offers a course on tutoring skills for credit and prepares a paraprofessional to be a tutor of deaf or learning disabled students. At NTID courses are offered for tutors and notetakers in communications skills during their entire tenure as tutor/notetakers. It is expected that communications skills will improve (if they are not already possessed) by each paraprofessional each academic quarter.

Self-training. A third option for paraprofessionals wishing to gain tutoring and notetaking skills is through self-training. At Brigham Young University, Provo, Utah, paraprofessionals may register for a home study course in tutoring skills in reading or math. These courses prepare students to act as paraprofessional tutors to learning disabled students in the younger grades. NTID has published a training manual for college-age tutors and notetakers wishing to give support to mainstreamed deaf college students. While this manual was not designed to be used in isolation, it may be of use to those working with deaf college students where organized support systems are not available. For example, if one or two deaf students are enrolled in a junior high school, high school or university setting, and organized support services do not exist, the notetaker or tutor can benefit from the study of the NTID tutoring and notetaking manuals.[1]

In the case of self-training it is emphasized that paraprofessionals should make every effort to have contact with a professional. This contact should occur both during and following the training.

Evaluating Tutoring and Notetaking Support Systems

Educational evaluation will probably never live up to the promises its proponents have made during the past decade. There are two basic reasons for this. First, evaluation has been oversold and, hence, improperly defined. Second, most evaluation has been conducted by those who know little about research or evaluation methodology. Because of these two factors, educational administrators have either been disappointed or misled by many of the evaluation studies conducted in their school systems.

---

[1]The NTID Tutor/Notetaker Manual can be obtained by writing the Office of Educational Extension, NTID, One Lomb Memorial Drive, Rochester, New York 14623.

Few evaluation studies conducted in the area of tutoring or notetaking have yielded definitive results. In a recent review of the literature on tutoring, the authors have concluded that few, if any, of the existing research studies in the area of tutoring have been carefully enough conducted to warrant any broad conclusions (Devin-Sheehan, Feldman, & Allen, 1976). Perhaps because tutoring and notetaking are individualized forms of support service, many people erroneously feel that the effects of the programs will be easy to evaluate. Before discussing some of the ways to successfully evaluate tutoring and notetaking support systems, it may be of value to review some of the difficulties that may be encountered as you attempt to evaluate such a system.

First, there is the problem of appropriate comparison groups. Obviously, the most important outcome of any support system is the system's effects on student learning. With that in mind, it is natural for most evaluators to proceed by selecting an experimental (supported) group and comparing that with a group who receives no support services. Anyone who has evaluated a support system knows well the problems of finding an appropriate control or comparison group. If such a group can be identified, one wonders if the more appropriate comparison is not with those who receive no support at all, but with those who receive some other kind of support or personal study time.

A second difficulty in evaluating any support system is in the appropriate selection and administration of tests. There may be uncertainty as to whether or not the test is measuring what it proposed to measure. This does not mean that tests developed by evaluators themselves should not be used, for this is often the best and possibly only alternative. It does mean that (1) we should be aware of any tests that might be appropriate in our evaluation design, and that (2) when we choose to develop our own instruments, we should be certain that those skilled in the area of test development assist us in that effort.

If we intend to measure the worth of a support service through learning outcomes, a third and very important consideration is the content that the students are intended to learn. In an elementary or secondary school setting, this content might be fixed. In other words, we might be attempting to measure the effects of a tutoring system or a notetaking system in one content area, such as reading. We might compare the reading growth of students who receive tutoring and notetaking in their reading course with students who do not receive those services. This might be a logical first step in an evaluation of a fixed content support system. The problem becomes more difficult, however, when multiple content areas are included in the support system. If we look, for example, at a tutoring and notetaking support system in a postsecondary setting, we find that a variety of content is being supported in many different courses. If one or two handicapped students are being given tutoring and notetaking services in each one of 50 different courses, and each of those courses differs in content, it is difficult to compare learning outcomes with students in 50 other courses with different content who are not receiving the services. For these reasons, using learning outcomes as the final evaluative measure is not appropriate in most postsecondary settings.

The fourth concern in evaluating support systems is with ethics. In order to identify an appropriate comparison group, it is often necessary to withhold a support service from a certain number of students. Ethically, we must carefully think through the advisability of withholding service. We seldom consider it appropriate, for example, to withhold interpreting services from students in order to evaluate their effectiveness. The dilemma can be compared in some ways to the challenge faced by health officials who are unsure of the spread of a flu germ and not completely positive about the effectiveness of their vaccine. But these health officials seldom consider it appropriate to randomly withhold the vaccine and then tabulate the number of deaths in order to evaluate the effectiveness of their treatment.

After reading through all of these difficulties, you may feel that it is impossible to evaluate tutoring and notetaking support systems. That is not the intent of defining the difficulties; rather, our intent is to make evaluators aware of the problems associated with this type of study. It is also hoped that the discussion of these problems might encourage evaluators of support systems to think more carefully about the reasons for which they are conducting their evaluations. There should be two basic reasons for gathering such data. First, to answer the question, "How can we make this program better?" Second, "Is the program doing what we want it to do?" The first type of data, commonly called formative data, is important to collect early in the program's development. It is usually gathered in order to make program revisions. The second question describes what is often called summative data. Such data are normally gathered so that program developers, teachers, and administrators can make decisions that affect the future of the program. A third kind of data that is important to the ongoing success of any program is system monitoring data, the continual data collection that should exist following the formal implementation of a new educational support system. This type of data should be relatively painless to collect, frequent, and not disruptive to program goals. It should be continually collected in order that teachers, administrators, and program supervisors might have the information they need in order to improve, or perhaps replace, the program.

Let us now look at some of the methods you may want to use in order to gather formative and summative data on a tutoring or notetaking program. These methods include: (1) multiple rating schemes, (2) simulated sessions, (3) observation techniques.

Multiple Rating Schemes

One way to measure the effectiveness of any program is to ask the people closest to it to give their opinion. In the case of tutoring and notetaking support systems, those people would include deaf students, tutors/notetakers, and faculty. Collecting data from these three groups can be highly beneficial for several reasons. First, it allows the program developer to gain insights that will otherwise be difficult to obtain. Second, it allows participants the feeling that their input into the program is valued, and that they have the ultimate power to effect change in the new program. Third, if the data are properly collected, none of the groups will feel that they are being "evaluated" and therefore will be more willing to participate in the program in the future.

When you set out to gather data from students, tutors/notetakers, and faculty, you have two primary choices. You might choose to develop and distribute a questionnaire, or you might choose to personally interview each person in each of the three groups. The data you collect will probably be more useful if you emphasize interviews rather than questionnaires. While questionnaires are not inherently inferior, the human contact that is associated with the interview method will aid program developers in gaining the confidence of program users, especially when a program is young. You might choose to use a combination of questionnaires and interviews. In this case, you may want to select at random a small number of people from each of the three groups in order to conduct your interviews.

When conducting interviews or developing questionnaires, you should keep in mind that at the close of the evaluation effort you will need to summarize your data. In order to effectively summarize data, you need to pay special attention to the questions you ask in an interview or the items you include on a questionnaire. When preparing a questionnaire, make certain that the questions you ask do not in any way bias the person responding. When conducting interviews, be sure that you ask the same questions in the same ways to each of the people you interview, and that their responses are carefully recorded in an unbiased manner.

Simulated Sessions

One of the most effective ways to measure the effects of a support system is through the use of simulated sessions. The use of simulated sessions extends your ability to apply experimental controls and, at the same time, reduces markedly the treatment time that you are measuring. In one respect, therefore, your data are "cleaner" but your ability to generalize to the total program can be reduced. Let's look at some examples of the use of simulated sessions in evaluating tutoring and notetaking support systems.

Suppose that you have developed a tutoring program to support deaf college students who are enrolled in classes that were planned primarily for hearing students. You have identified tutors, both deaf students and hearing students, who are capable in a number of content areas, and you have trained these tutors to assist deaf students in their classes. You want to know if the training that you provide these peers is helpful and if the tutoring that they provide is of benefit to deaf students. You know that it would be difficult to measure learning outcomes across the many different content areas that your program is designed to support, and because of this, you decide to use a simulated tutoring session. You select a content area that is fairly neutral, such as an introductory general education course, and you videotape a lecture or prepare a lecture yourself and put it on videotape. You then decide to use an evaluation design with three different tutoring treatments. The first group of students will receive tutoring by the tutors you have trained. The second group of students will receive tutoring by a group of untrained student tutors. The third group of students will receive no tutoring.

During the first simulated session, students will view the videotape. During the second session, a random selection of one-third of the students would receive "trained" tutoring, a second random third would receive "untrained" tutoring, and the final random third of the students would receive some irrelevant activity. Following the tutoring, each group of students would take the same test designed to measure the content delivered in the videotaped lecture. One way in which this design could be improved would be to extend the number of lectures to three or four, and have tutoring sessions following each of those lectures. In this way the treatment time would be extended and the data would be more generalizable to the total support system.

The same type of evaluation design used in a simulated session for tutoring could also be employed to evaluate the notetaking support service. Let's suppose again that you have designed a program to support deaf students enrolled in a secondary or a postsecondary setting. You might decide to again select a neutral type content area and videotape a live lecture from an existing course. Following the lecture you collect the notes taken by hearing students that they would normally take for themselves. You then take the videotape and, in a second session, show it to untrained hearing notetakers. In this session you ask these untrained hearing students to take notes as if they had volunteered to support a deaf student in this class. In a third session you show the videotape to the trained notetakers and ask them to also take the type of notes that they would normally take for their deaf peers. Following the third session, you have collected three different groups of notes. At that point, you randomly pair a set of "trained" notes with a set of "untrained" notes or a set of "self" notes. After you have paired the notes with each other, you give several sets to deaf students or to faculty or both, and have these people rate the notes and tell you which set (the trained or the untrained or the self) is better. It is wise to have more than one student or faculty rating on each pair of notes. You can then summarize the data by looking at the amount of agreement among raters on the same set of notes and also at the relative comparison between trained, untrained, and self notes.

Observation Techniques

Observation techniques can be useful for evaluating the effectiveness of both tutoring and notetaking services. In the case of notetaking, the observation consists of simply looking at notes after they have been taken. In the case of tutoring, observation requires the observer to actually be present while the tutoring is occurring, or that a tutoring session be videotaped and the observer watch the videotape at some later point. Whichever method is used and whichever service is being evaluated, observation can be an extremely useful technique to evaluate and improve support systems.

Let's suppose that a manager has 10 eighth-grade deaf students who have been trained as peer tutors for deaf students who are failing in math. Because the tutoring sessions always occur in the same room, the manager is able to observe each tutor each day. Through this ongoing observation of tutoring sessions, the manager is able to re-mediate any deficiencies in the tutors and continually improve the quality of the service being offered. Now, suppose that a manager is responsible for notetaking services being offered to deaf students in a postsecondary situation. Each week the manager receives copies of the notes that are taken by the trained notetakers. The manager reviews each set of notes periodically to ensure that quality notes are being provided to deaf students. This does not require the presence of the manager. It is a fairly simple but effective way to help notetakers improve the quality of their notes and ensure the delivery of quality notes to deaf students.

Let's imagine that this same manager in the postsecondary setting desires to evaluate the tutoring service being offered. The manager is responsible for 12 tutors, each of whom is covering different courses. Because the tutoring sessions occur in different places at different times each day, it is difficult for the manager to personally observe the sessions. Thus the manager asks the tutors to periodically videotape one of their tutoring sessions. The manager views the videotape with the tutor, and together they suggest areas for improvement. While at first glance, this method may seem threatening, it has been our experience that peer tutors and notetakers are eager to know how they can improve. Since they are not professionals (and do not view themselves as professionals), they need and welcome the guidance that professionals can provide them.

College-age tutors and notetakers are often aware themselves of the areas in which they need to improve. For this reason, it is often wise to ask them to periodically evaluate themselves, using some rating scale. These self-evaluations can then be discussed with the manager, and goals can be set for tutors and notetakers to improve their skills.

Following a training session of tutors or notetakers, it is often wise to take them through a simulated evaluation session so that they can become aware of the criteria for quality notes or quality tutoring. In the case of tutoring, let's imagine an elementary school setting. The manager has 20 sixth-grade students tutoring 20 second-grade students in reading. The manager has provided the tutors with four two-hour training sessions, each a week apart. Following the training, the manager develops a structured role play in order to see if each of them has mastered the techniques covered in the training. This structured role play consists of the manager playing the role of the student and the cross-aged tutor playing the role of the tutor. The manager would use the same role play with each tutor and the same check list to measure tutors' mastery techniques. Following each role play session, the manager individually remediates each tutor's deficiencies and helps the tutor to set goals for improvement.

Summary

In this chapter we have talked about the training and evaluation of tutoring and notetaking support systems. We have emphasized the importance of imparting generalizable skills to those paraprofessionals who aid us in assisting deaf students when they are mainstreamed. Several fairly specific training suggestions have been put forth. It is hoped that these suggestions will expand rather than limit the possibilities that you consider as you develop your own training program for tutoring and notetaking services. Once you have developed a training program appropriate for the specific needs of the deaf students you are supporting, it is hoped that you will give some careful thought to the planning and conducting of an effective evaluation of your program. Again, it is hoped that the specific examples of studies that have been employed previously to evaluate tutoring and notetaking support systems will be of use to you as you design your own evaluation. The important thing is to design an evaluation scheme that will help you to continually improve the quality of the support service that you are offering to mainstreamed deaf students. □

CHAPTER XI

Organizing Support Services

Russell T. Osguthorpe and T. Alan Hurwitz

In this chapter we discuss the principles of organizing a support system for mainstreamed deaf students. The principles include three decision areas:

1. Determining how much and what kinds of support services are needed

2. Selecting appropriate personnel to deliver the supports

3. Managing the total support system.

Guidelines for managing professional interpreters are described, as well as principles for managing paraprofessionals as tutors and notetakers. Finally, schemes for implementing these support systems will be illustrated.

Introduction

In the two previous chapters we discussed the principles involved in selecting and training support service personnel. In this chapter we focus on the organization and management of a support system once you have selected and trained your personnel.

Three primary decisions must be made when establishing a support system for mainstreamed hearing-impaired students. First, you must determine the mix of services you will provide. In this chapter we will focus exclusively on the interpreting, tutoring, and notetaking supports. Second, it is necessary to determine *who* will provide each support service. Will some services be provided by certified professionals and others by paraprofessionals or volunteers? Third, once you have selected and trained your personnel you will need to establish an effective management system.

Determining Services

In Chapter 9, Principles of Interpreting, some guidelines are given for determining when to assign an interpreter to a hearing-impaired student. It is also emphasized that the type of interpreter (ASL, signed English, oral) should be carefully matched to the student's communication preference. Determining whether or not to provide tutoring and notetaking services is an equally important mainstreaming decision. The following is a list of questions you might pose concerning the advisability of providing a tutor to a mainstreamed deaf student:

1. How large is the educational gap between deaf students' performance and that of their hearing peers? (see Chapter 6 on assessment).

2. Has tutoring been helpful in the past?

3. Is the teacher capable of providing the service without assistance from tutoring?

4. Have students with similar skills required tutoring in this course in the past?

The results of different responses to each question are quite obvious. For example, the larger the educational gap between deaf and hearing students, the *greater* the need for tutoring. The more capable the classroom teacher is at communicating with deaf students, the less outside tutoring will be required. It should be noted, however, that questions regarding the availability of tutors, the willingness of teachers to allow outside tutoring, or the potential jealousy of non-handicapped students toward those who receive special services were intentionally omitted. The basic decision of whether or not to provide tutoring services should rest upon *student need* and not on external forces. Some students will be functioning much like their hearing peers and will not need tutoring. Their communications handicap has apparently not created an educational handicap for them. These students should be allowed to pursue learning independent of a tutor.

Most deaf students will need tutoring. In earlier grades this tutoring may focus exclusively on language, reading, and math. As the student matures and course content broadens, different tutoring requirements will arise. Continued attention should be given to each student's needs relative to a particular course or subject matter area.

Careful attention should be paid to student progress so that tutoring services are tailored to the *present* needs of each student. The obvious advantage of tutoring (over large group instruction) is its flexibility among students. Each student should be focusing on the most needed topic or skill and moving at his own pace. If a tutoring program does not achieve these goals, it will not be successful.

Determining the need for notetaking services is equally important. It has been found that hearing-impaired college students often do not need all three services (interpreting, tutoring, notetaking) because one service compensates for one or both of the others. For example, some students prefer a notetaker to an interpreter. They feel that if they don't have to concern themselves about recording the information, they can process the class through speechreading and use of residual hearing. It may also happen that the student has good study skills and can benefit from the notes to the point that tutoring is unnecessary. Another student may need tutoring from a parent or outside teacher's aide. Class notes would then be valuable as a study tool for both tutor and student. Still another student may feel that the text is readable and that notes are not necessary if an interpreter is present. As you approach the decision concerning notetaking services, the following questions may be useful:

1. How important are notes to success in the course?

2. What are the student's notetaking skills?

3. How do the student's reading skills impact on using the text or notes as study aids?

4. Is there evidence that the student has benefited from notetaking services in other courses?

Again, the focus is on student learning style and the ability of the student to benefit from the service. However, there is a critical factor which goes beyond student need in both the tutoring and notetaking services. *This factor is the teacher.* In the case of tutoring, the teacher may be able and willing to himself provide the tutoring service. If this is the case, it would be unwise to automatically remove that responsibility from the teacher simply because a tutor is available. Likewise, it may be unnecessary to provide a notetaker. If the teacher lectures straight from the book or emphasizes experiential learning, notes may be of little worth to any student.

Selecting Appropriate Personnel

Once you have determined the mix of support services you will provide, you should consider the question of *who* will interpret, tutor, and notetake. There are basically three options available: you may choose professionals, paraprofessionals, or volunteers. Each group offers unique advantages for each support service offered.

Let's look first at the notetaking service. At NTID each option has been used. Some notetakers are professional educational specialists, some are volunteer students, and others are paid paraprofessional students (see Chapter 10 on tutoring and notetaking).

During the early years of NTID, a volunteer system was used for notetaking services. A special notetaking book with chemical copying papers was developed for use by volunteer notetakers. Two volunteer notetakers were engaged for each class where a deaf student was enrolled. Deaf students would receive copies of both sets of notes from the two volunteer notetakers so that they could review the notes and develop their own notes based on the information acquired through the class interpreter and from the sets of notes. This option had several advantages. It encouraged contact between deaf and hearing students, it required little supervison, and it was inexpensive. Later, however, it became increasingly difficult to find volunteer notetakers for many classes. And some volunteers were not able to take adequate notes for many deaf students. These conditions gave rise to the use of paid, trained students as notetakers. This option was obviously more expensive than using volunteers, but still much less expensive than assigning full-time professionals as notetakers. The quality of notes was increased at a reasonable cost.

If we now look at interpreting in the same way, we begin to see a more complex picture than that of notetaking. Volunteers have not been found to be a viable alternative. Paraprofessionals should be carefully placed in auxiliary interpreting situations (telephone interpreting, informal group meetings, etc.). Professional interpreters, on the other hand, should make up the bulk of educational interpreters. While notetaking skills can be acquired fairly quickly, a qualified interpreter requires extensive experience and training.

Selecting appropriate personnel for tutoring services requires consideration of the prerequisites for both notetaking and interpreting. If there is a large variance of skill levels among students being served, it is important to develop a broad tutoring support system. For example, some students may be able to succeed with home-based tutoring from a parent or sibling in the home. Others may need frequent contact with a trained peer tutor (who might be one of those more capable hearing-impaired students mentioned earlier). Still others may require intensive tutoring from a professional whose content expertise and/or communications skills are stronger than the paraprofessionals.

Managing the Total Support System

After deciding who should fill each supportive role, you should determine the management scheme. If your hearing-impaired student enrollment is small, the management system will be relatively simple. For larger programs, the system should be more carefully designed, especially when paraprofessionals or volunteers are involved. Since interpreting usually involves a majority of professionals and few peer students, we will discuss the management considerations for interpreting first. Following this discussion, we will describe the principles for managing paraprofessionals as tutors and notetakers; finally, we will provide some illustrations of sample support systems involving these paraprofessionals.

Interpreting Services

The primary barriers to effective management of interpreting services are associated with the following factors: (a) user's (student's and/or hearing teacher's) knowledge and ability to use the interpreter effectively; (b) scheduling interpreting services; (c) skills of interpreters on the staff. (For a discussion of effective utilization of interpreters by students and teachers, see Chapter 9.)

To ease the scheduling difficulties associated with providing interpreting services, you may find the form illustrated in Table 11.A to be helpful. The form is broken down into a listing of context variables and student/teacher (or any speaker) variables. It is necessary to know the type of course being covered and the content discussed at a specific time so that an appropriate interpreter with relevant subject background may be assigned. It is important to know how long the assignment will take so that more than one interpreter may be assigned, if necessary. The form also allows feedback from the requestor and the interpreter after the assignment is completed so that outstanding performance may be recognized or problems can be noted.

When managing interpreters, keep the following guidelines in mind, in addition to scheduling:

1. Ideally, interpreters should not be expected to interpret more than five hours a day and should not be asked to exceed 50 minutes of straight interpreting.

2. Most interpreters need at least an hour's break between blocks of approximately two hours of interpreting.

3. The pay scale for interpreters should be commensurate with the

suggested fees of the Registry of Interpreters for the Deaf and be consistent with the overall faculty/staff salaries in the school.

4. In-service training should be provided as an ongoing program for interpreters in the school or in the community.

5. Interpreters should be assigned according to how well their communications skills match those of the student.

6. Interpreters should possess content expertise in areas in which they are assigned to interpret.

7. Managers of interpreting services should be experienced, competent interpreters, able to evaluate the skills of other professional interpreters.

Managing Paraprofessionals

While similarities exist between the management of paraprofessional tutor/notetakers and the management of interpreters, special considerations should be given to the supervision of these support aides. They should be assigned to a support manager whose role in the total support system is two-fold. Primarily, the manager is concerned with student progress. Managers need to establish a feedback system from teachers and tutors/notetakers concerning the level of performance of each student being supported. Secondly, the manager should concentrate on improving the quality of the tutoring and notetaking supports being offered. In order to accomplish this, managers should regularly evaluate each paraprofessional and provide needed training and/or experiences which will result in improved tutoring and notetaking services. The manager can also work with students receiving support to ensure that they use the services to maximum benefit. Depending upon the size of the program, the trainer and manager could be the same individual.

NTID's Management System

In the NTID tutor/notetaker program for mainstreamed hearing-impaired college students, each major area of study has a different support manager. This person, in each case, is a full-time professional with other responsibilities, including teaching. During the 30-hour training program described earlier, managers become closely acquainted with the tutor/notetakers who will be serving under their direction. Managers participate in the training program as trainers, tailoring some sessions to the unique needs of students in their area.

TABLE 11.A
Interpreting Request Form

INTERPRETING REQUEST FORM

- Fill out all necessary information
- Use pencil or ball point pen, press hard

- Make corrections on all 3 sheets
- Be sure to include code number

Requester _____   Assignment Date _____

Date of Request _____   Day _____

Phone # _____ Office # _____   Time _____ to _____

Dept./Organization_____   Place _____

No. of Interpreters Needed _____   Communication ☐ oral   Light Needed

Total Anticipated Attendance _____   ☐ manual   ☐ yes

Anticipated No. of Deaf Persons_____   ☐ voicing needed   ☐ no

DESCRIPTION OF SETTING (check all appropriate boxes)

☐ lab   ☐ film   ☐ social

☐ final exam   ☐ panel   ☐ student meeting

☐ lecture   ☐ workshop   ☐ faculty/staff meeting

☐ formal course   ☐ seminar/conference   ☐ other (please specify below)

Course or Code #_____   _____

Specify Subject or Topic of Discussion _____

Additional information_____

_____

SCHEDULER fill out and assign

_____ has been scheduled to interpret for the above activity

INTERPRETER fill out and return to **Scheduler**

Total time interpreted_____   Number of deaf persons present _____

Comments _____

Signature _____

REQUESTER fill out and return to Scheduler

Comments _____

Signature _____

WHITE COPY–Interpreter   YELLOW COPY– Scheduler   PINK COPY–Requester

For example, since different content areas pose different notetaking problems, each manager exposes tutor/notetakers during the training program to the types of classes in which they will serve.

Following the training program, managers meet regularly with each of their tutor/notetakers. During these meetings, managers discuss the quality of notes being taken and suggest improvements. The manager also discusses the tutoring contacts the tutor/notetaker has had, and the progress each student is making in the course. These student contacts should be reported to the manager on Tutor Logs filled out by the tutor/notetaker following each tutoring session. As the manager gains confidence that the tutor/notetaker's skills are well developed, meetings are initiated less frequently. Managers are encouraged, however, to observe tutoring sessions and to continually monitor the quality of notes being provided to students. Record keeping is built into the support system to allow managers to keep track of each tutor/notetaker and all of the students receiving service.

Paraprofessional support systems for younger hearing-impaired students in the secondary and elementary grades will differ somewhat from the NTID design. For example, a support manager for cross-age tutoring in an elementary school will likely arrange the program so that all tutoring is scheduled in the same room. This will allow the manager to consistently observe tutoring, conduct mastery checks of learner performance, and provide assistance to tutors and students when problems arise.

Whether the support system is designed for young students or college students, certain management principles should be included.

The manager should:
1. participate as one of the trainers in the training program for tutors/notetakers
2. have experience as a tutor and notetaker
3. periodically evaluate tutor/notetaker performance
4. provide training for skill development based on the performance evaluation
5. get feedback from students, teachers, and tutors/notetakers concerning the program and make revisions in the program based on this feedback
6. monitor student progress and take steps to help ensure student success.

Implementation Schemes

Various implementation schemes may be used for establishing a paraprofessional support system for deaf students. Keeping in mind that most of the systems have been used in actual school settings, it should be understood that many of the schemes have been employed with learner populations other than deaf students. Data remain to be gathered with mainstreamed hearing-impaired students, using some of the following configurations. The schemes are presented simply as types of systems which have proven effective with other special learner groups.

Figure 11.1 describes the NTID tutor/notetaker support system. Tutor/notetakers may be assigned to one, two, or three college classes depending upon the number of students in each class and the tutor/notetaker's schedule. They are paid for taking notes and tutoring, but they are not paid for taking notes in a course taken for credit.

FIGURE 11.1

Illustration of NTID tutor/notetaker (T/N) support system in which T/Ns may be assigned to cover a different number of classes.

POSTSECONDARY: PEER TUTOR/NOTETAKERS

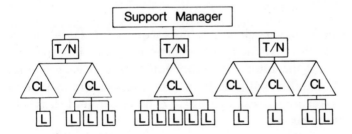

Support Manager-Professional

T/N-Hearing Peer

Learner (L)-Post-Secondary deaf students

CL - class

Figure 11.2 presents a situation where the same person does *not* provide notes and tutoring. In each of these cases, trained notetakers should be assigned to courses being covered by an interpreter/tutor, an adult (community) tutor, or a deaf tutor. Tutoring content would be determined by the specific course being covered.

FIGURE 11.2

Illustration of situation where same person does not provide notes and tutoring.

POSTSECONDARY: VARIATIONS

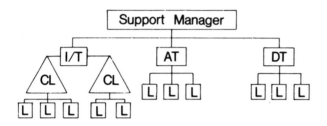

Support Manager - Professional

I/T-Interpreter/Tutor

AT-Adult Tutor- paid aide, volunteer ⟩ trained, paid notetakers

DT - deaf peer tutor

L- Learner

CL-class

Figure 11.3 describes a scheme using several adult (aide) tutors, each with several learners. The number of learners could be expanded to as many as 10 if the tutor is working full time and each learner spends about 30 minutes with the tutor. Tutoring content may be in basic skill areas (reading, math, writing) or centered around class subjects the student is taking.

Figure 11.4 describes peer tutoring/notetaking in the secondary school. As illustrated, tutor/notetakers could be assigned to cover two courses which they are taking for credit and which contain hearing-impaired students, or they may cover only one class. If a study-hall hour exists in the schedule, peers could, perhaps, work with deaf classmates on problem areas during that time periodically throughout the semester.

Figure 11.5 suggests that high school students (perhaps on a work-study program for social work or a special education degree) be assigned as tutor/notetakers for junior high school-aged hearing-impaired students.

FIGURE 11.3

Illustration of scheme using several adult (aide) tutors, each with several learners.

SECONDARY: ADULT TUTORING

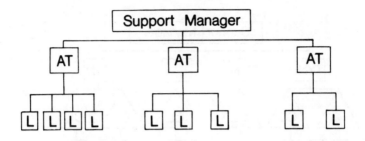

Support Manager-Professional

Adult Tutor (AT)- paid aides, volunteers, interpreter/tutor

Learner (L)-7th- 12th graders

FIGURE 11.4

Illustration of peer tutor/notetakers assigned to one or more classes having one or more learners.

SECONDARY: CROSS-AGE

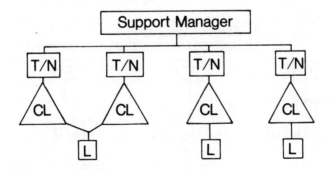

Support Manager-Professional

T/N-Hearing 11th, 12th graders (work-study program)

Learner-7th, 8th, 9th graders

CL-class

FIGURE 11.5
Illustration of high school students being assigned as tutor/notetakers for junior-high-school-age hearing-impaired students.

SECONDARY: PEER TUTOR/NOTETAKERS

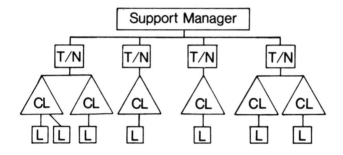

Support Manager-Professional
T/N-Hearing peer (fellow classmate)
Learner (L)-Secondary-age student
CL-class

FIGURE 11.6
Illustration of a support manager with several adult tutors.

ELEMENTARY: ADULT TUTORING

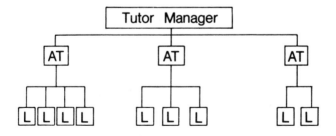

Tutor Manager-Resource Teacher, L.D. Specialist
Adult Tutor (AT)-paid aides, student teacher, Interpreter/Tutor
Learner (L)-K-6 graders

Figure 11.6 depicts a support manager with several adult tutors. These tutors would probably be working with hearing-impaired students on basic skill areas such as reading, math, and writing. The tutors may be student teachers fulfilling their degree program requirements, teacher aides, or interpreter tutors.

Figure 11.7 illustrates a cross-age tutorial system. As in Figure 11.6, notetaking is not required and tutoring content would likely focus on the basic skill development of students. Each student tutor would probably work with only one learner for 20 minutes each day.

FIGURE 11.7
Illustration of a cross-age tutorial system.

ELEMENTARY: CROSS-AGE

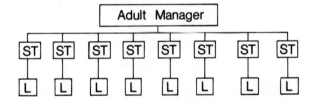

Adult Manager-paid aide, volunteer, professional
Student Tutor(ST)-5th or 6th graders, secondary age students
Learner- 1st, 2nd, 3rd graders

Summary

In this chapter we have discussed some techniques for organizing support services to mainstreamed deaf students that have proven effective. We have emphasized the importance of selecting the appropriate services, identifying qualified people to deliver those services, and managing a program once it has been implemented. A variety of methods for organizing support systems have been discussed. Many of these systems have involved paraprofessionals, but as we consider the benefits of such programs, we should remember that these peer support systems are not meant to replace skilled professionals, but to augment the ability of professionals to provide quality individualized services to hearing-impaired students. As we learn about the most effective ways of training and organizing these supportive programs, we will also learn about the process of helping mainstreamed students develop a feeling of independence and confidence in their own ability to succeed in our society.   □

Figures 11.1 through 11.7 reprinted, with permission, from the article "Training and Managing Paraprofessionals as Tutors and Notetakers for Mainstreamed Deaf Students," by Russell T. Osguthorpe, Beth D. Whitehead, and Milo E. Bishop; the *American Annals of the Deaf*, Vol. 123, No. 5, pp. 567-570, ISSN 0002-726X.

Summary and Conclusions

I n this book we have shared practical ideas on how to implement mainstreaming of hearing-impaired students at secondary and post-secondary levels. Additionally, we have provided information about hearing impairments, the various laws pertaining to mainstreaming, and the goals of education for hearing-impaired students. The ideas and information provided should have an impact upon the complete educational program from planning goals to assessing results.

In the first section, we provided an overview of mainstreaming. Chapter 1 included information on the hearing process, hearing impairment, and on their educational implications. Chapter 2 provided information concerning the various laws which have mandated educational change, and insights into the reasons behind such laws. Chapter 3 presented critical issues related to ensuring that the focus of mainstreaming remains on the student as opposed to on the processes.

It was asserted that our goals must always be specified in terms of the educational attainments of the students and never in terms of the means by which such attainments are achieved. Factors important in the placement of students were discussed. Of significance was the importance of considering the nature and the extent of the gap between the students' abilities and the expectations of the alternative programs. Chapter 5 described common models of educational mainstreaming and reviewed the various processes those models describe. A framework was provided for considering the match or mismatch between the students' needs and the processes provided.

Chapters 6 through 8 focused on specific suggestions designed to help teachers and administrators implement mainstreaming effectively. Important considerations involved in selecting an appropriate placement for hearing-impaired students were discussed. Mechanisms for assessing school variables as well as the more common student variables were provided. The importance of common sense and professional judgment in interpreting data and making decisions was

stressed. Specific hints were given to teachers for enhancing the classroom climate, students' communication, personal/social, and academic
skills. Valuable information on the reading-language problems of secondary and postsecondary profoundly hearing-impaired students was
provided. In addition, approximately twenty principles for preparing
written materials for use with language-handicapped students were
presented.

Chapters 9 through 11 covered various educational support services
frequently needed by hearing-impaired students when placed in a
regular class setting. The various types of interpreting, how to provide
quality interpreting services, and how to select and prepare qualified
interpreters were described. Basic information was provided on the
use and training of notetakers/tutors. Principles of effective tutoring
were described. Specific recommendations were made and alternative plans described for organizing and managing such support services in your program.

As you consider how to apply the information, suggestions, and
guidelines provided in this book, it is important to keep in mind that
they will need to be adapted to your specific situation. Each district,
school, and classroom is unique and presents its own set of dynamics.
It is also important to understand that there are areas important to
mainstreaming which have not been discussed in this book. Some of
the important areas needing more discussion are: (a) the personal/
social aspects of mainstreaming, (b) counseling as a support service,
(c) communication development in the mainstreamed environment,
(d) the use of public relations techniques to facilitate acceptance of
hearing-impaired students to a new educational community, and (e)
teacher preparation. To address some of these important areas, a second volume is being prepared for publication in 1980. In the mean-
time, it is hoped that this book will be of assistance to you as you strive
to mainstream hearing-impaired students.

In the conclusion of Chapter 5 the question was asked, "Will educational integration be successful?" In answering that question, it was
stated:

> The answer is yes, for some students. Can educational integration be
> successful for most students? That depends on several factors. One of
> the most important is whether or not it is viewed by educators and those
> controlling the purse strings as a goal or as one alternative educational
> process. Another factor in its success will be whether or not public
> school systems think of it as a more economical means of educating
> handicapped children. To take such a position is to ignore reality.
> Teachers will have to be prepared. They will need to be supervised.

Adequate support services will need to be provided and supervised. To place a hearing-impaired child in a classroom without properly preparing the teacher and without providing *needed* support services is . . . tantamount to child abuse.

To this could be added: to a large degree, success will be dictated by the attitudes of teachers, administrators, students, parents, school board members, bus drivers, custodians, and secretaries. And, for the most part, the attitudes of such people will be shaped by what is done or not done in setting the stage for effective mainstreaming.

When appropriate preparations are made, being involved in the education of hearing-impaired students is an exciting and meaningfully productive endeavor. When such preparations are not made, it is frustrating and many times nonproductive.

The reality of this statement is reflected in excerpts from a poem by Sergius Kostum, a student at NTID, entitled "My Deafness."

The road through life has been rough
and sometimes downright stormy
With friends I found much happiness
But many days were lonely.

My nursery school teacher was a peach—
She treated me like all the rest.
In Kindergarten I learned they would not teach
A deaf boy in their little nest.

Mrs. King, God bless her soul,
Had room for me in her fold.
Her room was a very happy "hole."
This story I've already told.

A special class for the hearing impaired
Was my room for much too long.
No contact with the rest. I despaired!
To the human race we didn't seem to belong.

Parents listened and parents agreed
This special class was not meant for me.
To the challenge of junior high I was freed
Ah! This challenge was no cup of tea.

There were teachers who were willing and able.
They were tops in everyone's book.
There were others who couldn't forget the label
They could only give me dirty looks. . . .

Blessings always filter through life's darkest moments
With a sister, a father, and a mother who understood and cared.
Love and understanding helped me to fight life's torments
No help in their power was ever limited or spared.

I pray to God that I may be
The best *in everything I do;*
So that others may also see
The value of my life anew.

We trust that your experience will be productive for the students and gratifying for yourselves. □

COMMUNICATIONS RESOURCES FOR THE TEACHER

N. Phillip Weinbach and Linda Bardenstein

Print Materials/Publications

An Annotated Bibliography on Mainstreaming (Volume 1) and *Bibliography on Mainstreaming* (Volume 2). A two-volume literature search by Ronald D. Hein and Milo E. Bishop of the National Technical Institute for the Deaf. Volume 1 includes an annotated author listing for quick identification of the content of each article in the bibliography. Volume 2 includes a cross-referenced cluster of the 15 topics identified and annotated in Volume 1. Specially designed for teachers, administrators, and others involved in implementing programs influenced by Public Law 94-142. Source: National Technical Information Service, U.S. Dept. of Commerce, 5285 Port Royal Road, Springfield, Virginia 22161.

"Career Development of the Deaf Student and Worker," *NTID InfoSeries 1,* edited by David W. Lacey, April 1973. A 50-page compendium of papers presented at a one-week Institute on Career Development for Deaf Students at the National Technical Institute for the Deaf. Serves as a collection of readings on the preparation and establishment of deaf people in careers. Source: Office of Educational Extension, National Technical Institute for the Deaf, Rochester Institute of Technology, One Lomb Memorial Drive, Rochester, New York 14623.

A Parent's Guide to the Individualized Education Program. This publication is a self-instructional package designed to give the handicapped child's parents information about P.L. 94-142. The rights of handicapped children and their parents under this law are carefully explained. The guide is written so that information is presented step by step. Each section is followed by a short self-quiz. The guide also includes lists of references, resource agencies, and organizations that may be of assistance to parents. Source: Alumni/Public Relations Office, Gallaudet College, Washington, D.C. 20002.

Parent's Information Kit. This kit was developed to provide parents with a variety of information about P.L. 94-142 and related topics. It includes articles about mainstreaming deaf children, Section 504 of the Rehabilitation Act of 1973, booklists, lists of resource agencies and organizations, and check lists for evaluating educational programs. The kit helps to expand the information parents can obtain from the *Parent's Guide to the IEP* and *P.L. 94-142 and Deaf Children.* Source:

Alumni/Public Relations Office, Gallaudet College, Washington, D.C. 20002.

P.L. 94-142 Resource Manual. The Resource Manual was originally developed to provide workshop participants with the technical information they needed to understand and interpret the requirements of P.L. 94-142. The manual is a product of the Gallaudet P.L. 94-142 Task Force and is used to assist in the planning of local in-service training activities. The materials may be selected for reprinting and distribution, or can be used as masters from which transparencies can be made. Source: Alumni/Public Relations Office, Gallaudet College, Washington, D.C. 20002.

P.L. 94-142 and Deaf Children. This publication is a special issue of the Gallaudet College Alumni Newsletter devoted to P.L. 94-142 and its implications for deaf children. Topics addressed in the publication include an analysis of the law itself, issues in the assessment of hearing-impaired children, IEP purposes, contents, participants and processes, implications of deafness for mainstreaming, and the least restrictive environment as it relates to deafness. Source: Alumni/Public Relations Office, Gallaudet College, Washington, D.C. 20002.

Communication: What's It All About? Information module prepared by the NTID Public Information Office which provides helpful hints and tips to hearing people on how to communicate with deaf people in both one-to-one and group situations. Also discusses programs for communications skill development programs for deaf people at the National Technical Institute for the Deaf. Source: Public Information Office, National Technical Institute for the Deaf, Rochester Institute of Technology, One Lomb Memorial Drive, Rochester, New York 14623.

"The Deaf in America: Two Hundred Years of Progress," article by Robert F. Panara in *NTID Focus*, Nov./Dec. 1976. Reviews 200 years of deaf people's advancement, highlighting people and milestones in education, literature and journalism, architecture and engineering, business and industry, and modern technology. Source: Public Information Office, National Technical Institute for the Deaf, Rochester Institute of Technology, One Lomb Memorial Drive, Rochester, New York 14623.

The Deaf Population of the United States, by Jerome D. Schein and Marcus T. Delk, Jr., 1974, the National Association of the Deaf. A national study of the numbers and characteristics of deaf people in the United States. Includes information about the deaf person's household, kinds of dwelling units, size and composition of his family, family members' hearing ability, education, occupation, income, communication, health, insurance problems and experiences with vocational rehabilitation. Source: National Association of the Deaf, 814 Thayer Avenue, Silver Spring, Maryland 20910.

"Equipment Designed To Improve the Communication Skills of the Deaf," *NTID InfoSeries 2*, co-edited by Donald D. Johnson and William E. Castle, May 1976. A 76-page monograph concerning the development of special equipment and facilities to help deaf people upgrade their communication skills. Source: Office of Educational Extension, National Technical Institute for the Deaf, Rochester Institute of Technology, One Lomb Memorial Drive, Rochester, New York 14623.

"The Invisible Handicap," article by Bobbi Linkemer in *St. Louis Commerce* magazine. Focuses on the occupational experiences of National Technical Institute for the Deaf graduates at work in organizations in St. Louis, Mo. Also comments on NTID programs to prepare students for the world of work. Source: Reprints are available from the Public Information Office, National Technical Institute for the Deaf, Rochester Institute of Technology, One Lomb Memorial Drive, Rochester, New York 14623.

The Meaning of Deafness, information module prepared by the Public Information Office, NTID. Defines deafness, related terms and jargon. Points out the people-oriented, personal dimensions of deafness and implications of the handicap. Source: Public Information Office, National Technical Institute for the Deaf, Rochester Institute of Technology, One Lomb Memorial Drive, Rochester, New York 14623.

Misconceptions About Deaf People, information module prepared by the NTID Public Information Office. Sets the record straight on commonly held misconceptions and stereotypes concerning deaf people. Focuses on deaf people's intelligence potential, speech capabilities, hearing capabilities, speechreading capabilities, language capabilities, and work performance. Source: Public Information Office, National Technical Institute for the Deaf, Rochester Institute of Technology, One Lomb Memorial Drive, Rochester, New York 14623.

Principles Basic to the Establishment and Operation of Postsecondary Education for Deaf Students, edited by E. Ross Stuckless and published in June 1973 by the Conference of Executives of American Schools for the Deaf. Reviews historical developments in postsecondary education of deaf people and discusses principles warranting consideration by educators in planning and operating a program for deaf students at the postsecondary level. Also useful to elementary and secondary educators involved in preparing their deaf students for successful postsecondary education. Sources: Conference of Executives of American Schools for the Deaf, 5034 Wisconsin Avenue, N.W., Washington, D.C. 20016, and Office of Educational Extension, National Technical Institute for the Deaf, Rochester Institute of Technology, One Lomb Memorial Drive, Rochester, New York 14623.

"A Place and Time of Opportunity," article by Robert Frisina in *NTID Focus*, Nov./Dec. 1976. Reviews advances in technology and education in relationship to new opportunities for deaf people. Source: Public Information Office, National Technical Institute for the Deaf, Rochester Institute of Technology, One Lomb Memorial Drive, Rochester, New York 14623.

Telephone Equipment for the Deaf, information module prepared by the NTID Public Information Office. Although the telephone has been perceived as an obstacle to deaf people, this publication points out that deaf people can use the telephone and telephone-coupled communications equipment. Identifies and describes specific devices, how they function, and sources for the products. Source: Public Information Office, National Technical Institute for the Deaf, Rochester Institute of Technology, One Lomb Memorial Drive, Rochester, New York 14623.

"The Times, They Are a-Changin' . . .," article by Loy E. Golladay in *NTID Focus*, Nov./Dec. 1976. First-person reflections on the "deaf experience" of the author. Offers insight into the experiences and interactions of a deaf person. Told with a sense of humor. Source: Public Information Office, National Technical Institute for the Deaf, Rochester Institute of Technology, One Lomb Memorial Drive, Rochester, New York 14623.

Audio-Visual Materials

Across the Silence Barrier, 57-minute, color, sound, 16mm. film produced by WGBH Television, Boston. Part of the NOVA television series, it explores the many dimensions of the world of deaf people. Covers communications problems, educational and social challenges; reviews various approaches to communications and communications skills development of deaf people; and examines employment and educational opportunities. Includes segments on Gallaudet College, National Technical Institute for the Deaf, and National Theatre of the Deaf. Available with partial captioning and also available in video format. Source: WGBH, 125 Western Avenue, Boston, Mass. 02134.

The Auditorially-Handicapped Child, The Deaf, 29-minute, black-and-white, sound, 16mm. film reviews special problems confronting the deaf child and shows many of the techniques used in teaching deaf people. Uses film sequences to point out characteristics of the deaf child and how his capabilities are strengthened; stresses the importance of meeting the needs of the deaf child. Features Dr. Louis M. DiCarlo of Syracuse University. Source: Indiana University, Audio-Visual Center, Bloomington, Indiana 47407.

Can You Hear Me?, 26-minute, color, sound, 16mm. film narrated by Ingrid Bergman and produced and written for ABC-TV by Lester Cooper. Filmed at the John Tracy Clinic in Los Angeles, this film demonstrates steps in teaching a young deaf child to communicate and shows the many problems of educating and training a child born deaf. This case study can serve to motivate parents and teachers of deaf people; suggested audiences are parent groups, special education classes, nurse and lay training groups, and community groups interested in organizing or participating in clinics for the deaf or perceptually handicapped. Source: International Film Bureau, Inc., 332 South Michigan Avenue (C1), Chicago, Illinois 60604.

Deaf in a Hearing World, black-and-white, sound, 16mm. film. A group of profoundly deaf people and one hard-of-hearing person present problems they meet in trying to establish relationships with the hearing world and discuss (with the aid of an interpreter) how they think their situation might be improved. Source: Media Guild, 7838 San Fernando Road, Sun Valley, California 91352.

Deafness and Communications, 11-minute, color, sound, 16mm. film produced by the National Technical Institute for the Deaf. An aid in informing people who have little knowledge of deafness and who have a high likelihood of associating with deaf people. Deals with the nature and severity of hearing loss and the channels of communications with the deaf. Available non-captioned. Source: Media Services, National Technical Institute for the Deaf, Rochester Institute of Technology, One Lomb Memorial Drive, Rochester, New York 14623.

Deafness in Children, 30-minute, audiotape cassette (1⅞" per second). Deals with the problems of the family and the deaf person within the family. Reveals that people often think a child is retarded when he is really deaf, and shows that with help and understanding the child can lead a relatively normal life. Source: CBC Learning Systems, Box 500, Station A, Toronto, Ontario, Canada M5W1E6.

An Evening on Deafness, 3-hour program, contains 5 16mm. films. "The Silent Majority" explains the general nature of deafness and hearing loss, and the behavioral implications that surround it. The second film focuses on the psychological effects deafness has on children and their parents. "Bridge Over Troubled Waters" deals with teaching very young children to think in terms of verbal communication and sign language. The fourth film deals in more depth with the idea of total communication. "Conversations with Deaf Teenagers" speaks to counselors and future teachers of deaf young people. Source: Maryland Center for Public Broadcasting, Owings Mills, Maryland 21117.

It's Okay To Be Deaf, Denise, 28-minute, color, sound, 16mm. film produced by the David T. Siegel Institute for Communicative Disorders of Michael Reese Medical Center and the Ear Research Institute, Los Angeles. Reviews the first six years of the life of Denise, a bright, attractive child who was born deaf. The film presents a moving and inspiring portrait of a child and her family working to overcome a disability. Available with or without captioning. Source: Viewfinders, Inc., P.O. Box 1665, Evanston, Illinois 60204.

More Than One Way: Chris, 19-minute, color, 16mm. film that shows Chris, a seventh grader with a slight hearing loss in both ears, and his participation in Ontario's special education system for part of each school day. Emphasizes techniques used to help Chris, and shows him progressing as a confident and useful person in society. A special education team works cooperatively with Chris and his teachers, rather than segregating him in a separate school. Source: Wallace Memorial Library, Rochester Institute of Technology, One Lomb Memorial Drive, Rochester, New York 14623.

No Whistles, No Bells, No Bedlam, 20-minute, color, sound, 16mm. film produced by the National Technical Institute for the Deaf. Provides information about capabilities of deaf people for many kinds of employment. Designed to increase potential employers' receptivity to hiring deaf people. Useful to counselors and others in job placement and employer contact. Available both with and without captioning. Source: Media Services, National Technical Institute for the Deaf, Rochester Institute of Technology, One Lomb Memorial Drive, Rochester, New York 14623.

A Quiet Time, color, sound, 16mm. film produced by Nancy Margulies and David Howard for the St. Louis Registry of Interpreters of the Deaf. Designed to bring the worlds of hearing and deaf people closer together, it conveys its message through two deaf St. Louisans in their 70's. Audience focuses on difficulties deaf people encounter during their life, how they communicate, and their feelings in various experiences. Source: Nancy Margulies, 7121 Pershing Avenue, University City, Missouri 63130.

The Silent Drum, 22-minute, color, sound, 16mm. film produced by the National Technical Institute for the Deaf. Introduces the hearing viewer to some basic concepts about deafness. Points out the communications problems and related personal, social and educational challenges that deaf people face. Introduces NTID; explains origins and milestones in NTID's development, and reviews NTID's aims and responsibilities. Available both with and without captioning. Source: Media Services, National Technical Institute for the Deaf, Rochester Institute of Technology, One Lomb Memorial Drive, Rochester, New York 14623.

Understanding the Deaf, 21-minute, color, sound, 16mm. film produced by Portafilms. Can assist teachers and students in regular public schools to understand and communicate with deaf and hard-of-hearing children who enter the regular classroom after having been taught to communicate in a special school or a special class. Shows how hearing people can overcome feelings of uneasiness when interacting with deaf children with special problems. Demonstrates how deaf children are taught to speak, use sign language, and lipread. Available noncaptioned. Also available in Super 8mm. videocassettes. Source: Perennial Education, Inc., 1825 Willow Road, P.O. Box 236, Northfield, Illinois 60093.

APPENDIX B

MEDIA FOR USE IN SIGN LANGUAGE INSTRUCTION

ABC. 20 videotapes accompanying ABC book. NTID Sign Language Department, One Lomb Memorial Drive, Rochester, New York 14623.

Basic I, II, III. 6 videotapes. Teaches sign language. NTID Sign Language Department, One Lomb Memorial Drive, Rochester, New York 14623.

Fingerspelling. 30 film loops, 4 minutes each, teach fingerspelling and drill. Graphic Films Corp., 3341 Cahuenga Blvd. W., Los Angeles, California 90028.

Fingerspelling Is Easy. 9-minute, 16mm. film teaches fingerspelling. Deaf Missions, R.R. 2, Council Bluffs, Iowa 51501.

Manual Alphabet Poster. Fingerspelling. Gallaudet College Press, Gallaudet College Library, Kendall Green, Washington, D.C. 20002.

Manual English Vocabulary List. 120-minute videotape teaches 512 signed English vocabulary words. Gallaudet College Library, Kendall Green, Washington, D.C. 20002.

Pancom Program. Level I: 11 film loops. Level II: 10 film loops. Teaches beginning sign language. Joyce Media, 8613 Yolanda, P.O. Box 458, Northridge, California 91324.

Say It With Hands. 26 films, 30 minutes each, accompany book by Louie Fant. Teaches beginning sign language. Captioned Films for the Deaf, 5034 Wisconsin Avenue, N.W., Washington, D.C. 20016.

Sign Language Flashcards. 500 cards teach basic vocabulary. Alexander Graham Bell Association for the Deaf, 3417 Volta Place, N.W., Washington, D.C. 20007.

Speaking With Your Hands. Ten 30-minute videotapes teach beginning sign language. New York University Deafness Research and Training Center, 80 Washington Square East, New York, N.Y. 10003.

APPENDIX C
INTERPRETER TRAINING PROGRAMS

The following institutions offer a B.A. degree in interpreting:

Madonna College
Interpreter Training Program
Ken Rust, Director
36600 Schoolcraft Road
Livonia, Michigan 48150

Maryville College
Interpreter Training Program
Mrs. Irma Young, Instructor/Coordinator
Maryville, Tennessee 37801

The following institutions offer an A.A. degree in interpreting:

Delgado Junior College
Interpreter Training Program
Ann Guidry, Coordinator
615 City Park Ave.
New Orleans, Louisiana 70119

Madonna College
Interpreter Training Program
Ken Rust, Director
36600 Schoolcraft Road
Livonia, Michigan 48150

North Central Technical Institute
Interpreter Training Program
Miss Margaret James, Coordinator
1000 Schofield Ave.
Wausaw, Wisconsin 54401

Seattle Community College
Interpreter Training Program
Ms. Tereasa B. Smith, Coordinator
1801 Broadway
Seattle, Washington 98122

Golden West College
Interpreter Training Program
Paul Culton, Coordinator
15744 Golden West Street
Huntington Beach, California 92647

Metro Technical Community College
Southwest Campus
Interpreter Training Program
Ed. Franklyn, Coordinator
Omaha, Nebraska 68134

Waubonsee Community College
Interpreter Training Program
Mrs. Chris Alvarez, Coordinator
P.O. Box 508
Sugar Grove, Illinois 60554

DeKalb Community College
Interpreter Training Program
Richard Dirst, Superintendent
Atlanta Area School for the Deaf
850 N. Indian Creek
Clarkston, Georgia 30021

Charles Stewart Mott Community College
Interpreter Training Program
1401 Court St.
Flint, Michigan 48503

Ohlone Community College
Interpreter Training Program
43600 Mission Blvd.
P.O. Box 909
Fremont, California 94638

Central State University
Interpreter Training Program
Ada, Oklahoma 74820

Spartanburg Methodist College
Interpreter Training Program
Barbara S. Garrison, Coordinator
Spartanburg, South Carolina 29301

College of Southern Idaho
Interpreter Training Program
P.O. Box 1238
Twin Falls, Idaho 83301

Gallaudet College
Interpreter Training Programs
John Reinman, Coordinator
7th and Florida Ave. N.E.
Washington, D.C. 20002

The following institutions offer interpreter training programs that are non-degree but train large numbers of interpreters:

NYU/NITC
Janet Avacedo, Coordinator
Deafness & Research Center
80 Washington Square E.
New York, New York 10003

CSUN/NITC
Mel Carter, Coordinator
Special Education Programs
18111 Nordhoff St., Building S
Northridge, Calif. 91324

University of Tennessee
Nancy Kramer, Coordinator
Dept. of Special Education
Knoxville, Tennessee 37916

Gallaudet College
John Reinman, Coordinator
S.L. Programs
7th and Florida Ave., N.E.
Washington, D.C. 20002

University of Arizona
Annette Long, Coordinator
Dept. of Special Education
Tucson, Arizona 85721

National Technical Institute for the Deaf
Interpreter Training Program
Ms. Anna Braddock Witter, Coordinator
One Lomb Memorial Drive
Rochester, New York 14623

R.V.I./NITC
Robert Lauritsen, Coordinator
Interpreter Training Program
235 Marshall Avenue
St. Paul, Minnesota 55102

Columbus Technical School
Interpreter Training Program
Janet Dobecki, Coordinator
550 E. Spring, Box 1609
Columbus, Ohio 43216

Claremont Community College
Interpreter Training Program
Claremont, New Hampshire 07343

Central Piedmont Community College
Interpreter Training Program
Eddie Hodges, Coordinator
P.O. Box 4009
Charlotte, North Carolina 28204

Community College of Philadelphia
Eve West, Coordinator
Interpreter Training Program
34 South 11th Street
Philadelphia, Pennsylvania 19107

University of Wisconsin
Dept. of Exceptional Educational Programs
Dr. Leo Dicker, Coordinator
2400 E. Hartford Avenue
Milwaukee, Wisconsin 53201

Eastfield College
Elizabeth Fetter, Coordinator
Interpreter Training Program
3737 Motley Drive
Mesquite, Texas 75149

Oregon College of Education
Shirley Shisler
Interpreter Training Program
Monmouth, Oregon 97361

References

Abeson, A., Bolick, N., & Hass, J. *A Primer on Due Process: Educational Decisions for Handicapped Children.* Reston, Va.: Council for Exceptional Children, 1975.

Adamson, G. Fail-save continuum model. In K.E. Berry, Ed., *Models for Mainstreaming.* Sioux Falls, South Dakota: Adapt Press, 1972.

Adamson, G., & Van Etten, G. Zero reject model revisited: A workable alternative. *Exceptional Children, 38*(9), 735–738, 1972.

Advisory Council for the Deaf. *A Comprehensive Plan for the Education of Hearing Impaired Children and Youth in Massachusetts.* Boston, Massachusetts: Massachusetts Department of Education, Division of Special Education, 1975.

Anderson, B. R. Mainstreaming is the name for a new idea: Getting the problem child back into a regular class. *School Management, 17*(7), 28–30, 52, 1973.

Anken, J., & Holmes, D. Use of adapted "classics" in a reading program for deaf students. *American Annals of the Deaf, 122,* 8–14, 1977.

Bender, R. *The Conquest of Deafness* (rev. ed.). Cleveland, Ohio: Case Western Reserve University, 1971.

Berg, F. S., & Fletcher, S. G., Eds. *The Hard of Hearing Child: Clinical and Educational Management.* New York: Grune & Stratton, 1970.

Berry, K. E. *Models for Mainstreaming.* Sioux Falls, South Dakota: Adapt Press, 1972.

Berry, S. R. *Legal Considerations in the Education of the Handicapped: An Annotated Bibliography for School Administrators.* Washington, D.C.: National Association of State Directors of Special Education, 1978.

Betts, E. *Foundations of Reading Instruction.* New York: American Book Company, 1950.

Betts, E. *Foundations of Reading Instruction* (rev. ed.). New York: American Book Company, 1957.

Birch, J. R., & Birch, J. W. Predicting school achievement in young deaf children. *American Annals of the Deaf, 101,* 348–352, 1956.

Birch, J. R., Stuckless, E. R., & Birch, J. W. An eleven-year study of predicting school achievement in young deaf children. *American Annals of the Deaf, 108,* 236–240, 1963.

Bishop, M. E., Christopolus, T., & Nielson, M. A. A study of amplification systems used in schools for the deaf. *The Volta Review, 74,* 111–121, 1972.

Bishop, M. E., & Clarcq, J. *Planning and the Career Development Model.* Unpublished manuscript, 1977. (Available from M. E. Bishop, Division of Career Development Programs, National Technical Institute for the Deaf, Rochester, New York 14623).

Bishop, M. E., White, K. R., & Emerton, G. E. *Socialization: Approaches for Doing Something About It* (paper series No. 12). Rochester, New York: National Technical Institute for the Deaf, Department of Research and Development, 1977.

Bitter, G. B. Whose schools: Educational expediency/educational integrity? In Nix, G. W., Ed., *Mainstream Education for Hearing Impaired Children and Youth.* New York: Grune & Stratton, 1976.

Bitter, G. B., & Johnston, K. A. *Review of the Literature: Integration of Exceptional Children Into Regular Classes* (technical report). Salt Lake City, Utah: University of Utah, Department of Special Education, 1973.

Bitter, G. B., Johnston, K. A., & Sorenson, R. G. *Project Need: Facilitating the Integration of Hearing Impaired Children Into Regular Public School Classes* (technical report). Salt Lake City, Utah: University of Utah, Department of Special Education, January 1973.

Blank, M., & Bridger, W. Conceptual cross-model transfer in deaf and hearing children. *Child Development, 37,* 29–38, 1966.

Block, N. J., & Dworkin, G., Eds. *The IQ Controversy: Critical Readings.* New York: Random House, 1976.

Boatner, E. B. Address to parents, teachers, and counselors, the American School for the Deaf, 1947.

Boatner, M., & Gates, J. *Dictonary of Idioms for the Deaf.* Silver Spring, Maryland: National Association for the Deaf, 1966, 1975.

Bowe, F. The DA interview: *Deaf American.* 27(1), 9–10, 1974.

Breunig, H. L., & Nix, G. W. Historical and educational perspectives. *The Volta Review, 79*(5), 263–269, 1977.

Brill, R. G. The relation of Wechsler IQs to academic achievement among deaf students. *Exceptional Children, 28,* 315, 1962.

Brill, R. G. *Administrative and Professional Developments in the Education of the Deaf.* Washington, D.C.: Gallaudet College Press, 1971.

Brill, R. G., Merrill, E., Jr., & Frisina, D. R. *Recommended Organizational Policies in the Education of the Deaf.* Washington, D.C.: Conference of Executives of American Schools for the Deaf, 1973.

Burchard, E. M., & Myklebust, H. R. A comparison of congenital and adventitious deafness with respect to its effects on intelligence, personality and social maturity. *American Annals of the Deaf, 87,* 241–250, 1942.

California Achievement Test. Monterey, California: California Test Bureau/McGraw Hill, 1957–1970.

Crane, J. E. *Bits of History.* W. Hartford, Connecticut: American School for the Deaf Press, 1890, 1916.

Cruickshank, W. M. The development of education for exceptional children. In W. M. Cruickshank & G. O. Johnson, Eds., *Education of Exceptional Children and Youth* (3rd ed.). Englewood Cliffs, New Jersey: Prentice-Hall, 1975.

Cruickshank, W. M., & DeYoung, H. C. Educational practices with exceptional children. In W. M. Cruickshank & G. O. Johnson, Eds., *Education of Exceptional Children and Youth* (3rd ed.). Englewood Cliffs, New Jersey: Prentice-Hall, 1975.

Cruickshank, W. M., & Johnson, G. O., Eds. *Education of Exceptional Children and Youth* (3rd ed.). Englewood Cliffs, New Jersey: Prentice-Hall, 1975.

Culhane, B. R., & Curwin, R. There's a deaf child in my class. *Learning Magazine,* 111–112, 117, October 1978.

DeFrancesca, S. *Academic Achievement Test Results of a National Testing Program for Hearing Impaired Students* (Report No. D-9). Washington, D.C.: Gallaudet College, Office of Demographic Studies, 1972.

Deno, E. Special education as developmental capital. *Exceptional Children, 37*(3), 229–237, 1970.

Devin-Sheehan, L., Feldman, R. S., & Allen, V. L. Research on children tutoring children: A critical review. *Review of Educational Research, 46,* 355–385, 1976.

DuBow, S. Public Law 94–142. *American Annals of the Deaf, 122*(5), 468–469, 1977.

Dunn, L. M.   Special education for the mildly retarded—is much of it justifiable? *Exceptional Children, 35*(1), 5–22, 1968.

Dunn, L. M., Ed.   *Exceptional Children in the Public Schools: Special Education in Transition* (2nd ed.). New York: Holt, Rinehart & Winston, 1973a.

Dunn, L. M.   *The Normalization of Special Education.* Inaugural lecture, Laycock Memorial Lectureship, Saskatoon, Saskatchewan, Canada: University of Saskatchewan, 1973b.

DuPont Company.   Myths about hiring the physically handicapped, reprinted from *Job Safety and Health, 2*(2), September 1974, distributed by the President's Committee on Employment of the Handicapped, Washington, D.C. 20210.

Elser, R.   The social position of hearing handicapped children in the regular grades. *Exceptional Children, 25,* 305–309, 1959.

Emerton, G. E., & Bishop, M. E.   *A Conceptual Framework for Personal and Social Development* (paper series No. 10). Rochester, New York: National Technical Institute for the Deaf, Department of Research and Development, 1977.

Emerton, R. G., Hurwitz, T. A., & Bishop, M. E.   Development of social maturity in deaf adolescents and adults. In L. J. Bradford & W. G. Hardy, Eds., *Hearing and Hearing Impairment.* New York: Grune & Stratton, 1979.

Fitts, W. H.   *Tennessee Self Concept Scale: Manual.* Nashville, Tennessee: Counselor Recordings and Tests, Department of Mental Health, 1965.

Force, D.   Social status of physically handicapped children. *Exceptional Children, 23,* 104–107, 132–134, 1956.

Frisina, R. F., Ed.   *A Bicentennial Monograph on Hearing Impairment.* Washington, D.C.: The A.G. Bell Association for the Deaf, 1976.

Furth, H. G.   The influence of language on the development of concept formation in deaf children. *Journal of Abnormal Social Psychology, 63,* 386–389, 1961.

Furth, H. G.   *Thinking Without Language: Psychological Implications of Deafness.* New York: Free Press, 1966.

Furth, H. G.   *Piaget for Teachers.* Englewood Cliffs, N.J.: Prentice-Hall, 1970.

Furth, H. G.   *Deafness and Learning: A Psychosocial Approach.* Belmont, California: Wadsworth Publishing, 1973.

Furth, H. G., & Youniss, J.   The influence of language and experience on discovery and use of logical symbols. *British Journal of Psychology, 56,* 381–390, 1965.

Furth, H. G., & Youniss, J.   Thinking in deaf adolescents: language and formal operations. *Journal of Communication Disorders, 2,* 105–202, 1969.

Furth, H. G., & Youniss, J.   Congenital deafness and the development of thinking. In E. H. Lenneberg & E. Lenneberg, Eds., *Foundations of Language Development* (vol. 2). New York: Academic Press, 1975.

Garrison, W. M., Tesch, S., & DeCaro, P.   An assessment of self-concept levels among postsecondary deaf adolescents. *American Annals of the Deaf,* 1978.

Golladay, L. E.   Effective reading by deaf children must be meaningful. *American Era, 1,* 1–4, 1951.

Good, C. V., Ed.   *Dictionary of Education* (3rd ed.). New York: McGraw-Hill, 1973.

Gordon, E. W.   Significant trends in the education of the disadvantaged. Clearinghouse on the Urban Disadvantaged, ERIC, New York, 1970.

Griffing, B. L.   Planning educational programs and services for hard of hearing children. In F. S. Berg and S. G. Fletcher, Eds., *The Hard of Hearing Child: Clinical and Educational Management*. New York: Grune & Stratton, 1970.

Griffing, B. L.   Reshaping the role of the state school for the deaf in public education. *The Changing Role of School Programs for Deaf Children: Selected Papers*. Washington, D.C.: Conference of Executives of American Schools for the Deaf, 1977.

Harrison, G. V., & Cohen, A.   *Empirical Validation of Tutor-training Procedures*. Unpublished manuscript, Brigham Young University, September 1969. (Available from G. V. Harrison, Department of Instructional Science, University of Utah, Provo, Utah 84602).

Hayes, G. M., & Griffing, B. L.   *A Guide to the Education of the Deaf in the Public Schools of California*. Sacramento: California State Department of Education, 1967. (ERIC Document Reproduction Service No. ED 022 292)

Healy, W. C.   Integrated education. In R. F. Frisina, Ed., *A Bicentennial Monograph on Hearing Impairment*. Washington, D.C.: The A.G. Bell Association for the Deaf, 1976.

Hein, R. D., & Bishop, M. E.   *An Annotated Bibliography on Mainstreaming* (2 vols.). Rochester, New York: NTID, 1978 (NTIS No. PB280000).

Hoeltke, G.   *Effects of Special Class Placement for Educable Mentally Retarded Children* (Unpublished doctoral dissertation, University of Nebraska Teachers' College, Lincoln, Nebraska, 1969).

Jacobs, L. M.   *A Deaf Adult Speaks Out*. Washington, D.C.: Gallaudet Press, 1974.

Jenkins, W. G.   *Talks and Stories*. Hartford, Connecticut: American School for the Deaf Press, 1888.

Johnson, E. W.   Let's look at the child, not the audiogram. *The Volta Review, 69*, 306–310, 1967.

Johnson, D. D.   Communication characteristics of a young deaf adult population: Techniques for evaluating their communication skills. *American Annals of the Deaf, 121*, 409–424, August 1976.

Justman, J., & Maskowitz, L.   *The Integration of Deaf Children in a Hearing Class*. New York: New York City Board of Education, Bureau of Educational Research, 1957.

Katz, L., Mathis, S. L. III, & Merrill, E. C., Jr.   *The Deaf Child in the Public Schools: A Handbook for Parents of Deaf Children*. Danville, Illinois: The Interstate Printers and Publishers, 1974.

Kazmierski, P. R.   *The Effects of Cloze Procedure Upon the Literal Understanding of Text Materials by Postsecondary Deaf Students*. Unpublished doctoral dissertation, Syracuse University, 1973.

Kennedy, P., & Bruininks, R. H.   Social status of hearing impaired children in regular classrooms. *Exceptional Children, 40*, 336–342, 1974.

Kirk, S. A.   *Educating Exceptional Children* (2nd ed.). Boston: Houghton-Mifflin, 1972.

Kolstoe, O. P.   *Mental Retardation: An Educational Viewpoint*. New York: Holt, Rinehart & Winston, 1972a.

Kolstoe, O. P.   Programs for the mildly retarded: A reply to critics. *Exceptional Children, 39*(1), 51–56, 1972b.

Lane, H. S.   Academic achievement. In B. Bolton, Ed., *Psychology of Deafness for Rehabilitation Counselors*. Baltimore, Maryland: University Park Press, 1976.

Lane, H. S., & Schneider, J. L.   A performance test for school age deaf children. *American Annals of the Deaf, 86*, 441, 1941.

Leiter, R. *The Leiter International Performance Scale.* Chicago: Stoelting, 1948.

Lenneberg, E. H., & Lenneberg, E., Eds. *Foundations of Language Development* (vol. 2). New York: Academic Press, 1975.

Levine, E. S. *The Psychology of Deafness.* New York: Columbia University Press, 1960.

Lilly. M. S. Forum: A training based model for special education. *Exceptional Children, 37*(10), 745–749, 1971.

Loban, W., Ryan, M., & Squire, J. R. *Teaching Language and Literature.* New York: Harcourt, Brace, & World, Inc., 1961.

Luterman, D. M. *A Comparison of Language Skills of Hearing Impaired Children in a Visual Oral Method and Auditory Method.* Unpublished manuscript. Boston: Emerson College, 1974. (Available from D. M. Luterman, Emerson College, Boston, Massachusetts)

Massachusetts Department of Education. *Proposed Regulations for the Implementation of Chapter 766 of the Acts of 1972: The Comprehensive Special Education Law* (for public hearing). Boston: Massachusetts Department of Education, 1974.

McHughes, D. F. A view of deaf people in terms of Super's theory of vocational development. *Journal of Rehabilitation of the Deaf, 9*(1), 1–11, 1975.

Meadow, K. *The Effect of Early Manual Communication and Family Climate on the Deaf Child's Development.* Unpublished doctoral dissertation, University of California, Berkeley, 1966.

Melaragno, R. J. *Tutoring With Students: A Handbook for Establishing Tutorial Programs in Schools.* Englewood Cliffs, New Jersey: Educational Technology Publications, 1976.

Mercer, J. R. IQ = The lethal weapon. *Psychology Today,* pp. 44–50, 95–97, September 1972.

Montanelli, D., & Quigley, S. *Deaf Children's Acquisition of Negation.* Urbana, Illinois: University of Illinois, Institute for Research on Exceptional Children, 1974.

Moores, D. F. Psycholinguistics and deafness. *American Annals of the Deaf, 115,* 37–48, 1970.

Moores, D. F. *Educating the Deaf: Psychology, Principles and Practices.* Boston: Houghton Mifflin Company, 1978.

Moores, D. F., & Quigley, S. Cloze procedures in assessment of language skills of deaf children. *Proceedings of the International Conference on Oral Education of the Deaf,* The A. G. Bell Association for the Deaf, 1363–1395, 1967.

Myklebust, H. R. *Auditory Disorders in Children.* New York: Grune, 1954.

National Association of State Directors of Special Education. *An Analysis of P.L. 94–142.* Washington, D.C.: Author, undated (a).

National Association of State Directors of Special Education. *Section 504/P.L. 94–142: A Comparison of Selected Provisions of the Proposed Regulations.* Washington, D.C.: Author, undated (b).

Nix, G. W., Ed. *Mainstream Education for Hearing Impaired Children and Youth.* New York: Grune and Stratton, 1976.

Northcott, W. H., Ed. *The Hearing Impaired Child in a Regular Classroom.* Washington, D.C.: The A.G. Bell Association for the Deaf, 1973.

Northcott, W. H. The oral interpreter—a necessary support specialist for the hearing impaired. *The Volta Review, 79,* 136–144, 1977.

Oléron, P. *Recherches sur le developpment mental des sourds-muets.* Paris: Centre National de la Recherche Scientifique, 1957.

Osguthorpe, R. T. *The Tutor/Notetaker: A Guide for Providing Academic Support to Deaf College Students Through Peer Tutoring and Notetaking* (paper series No. OM-1). Rochester, New York: National Technical Institute for the Deaf, Department of Research and Development, 1975.

Osguthorpe, R. T. *The Hearing Peer as a Provider of Educational Support to Deaf College Students.* Paper presented at the annual meeting of the American Education Research Association, San Francisco, April 1976.

Osguthorpe, R. T., & Harrison, G. V. Training parents in a personalized system of reading instruction. *Improved Human Performance Quarterly,* 5, 62–68, 1976.

Osguthorpe, R. T., Whitehead, B. D., & Bishop, M. E. Training and managing paraprofessionals as tutors and notetakers for mainstreamed students. *American Annals of the Deaf,* 123, 563–571, 1978.

Pettinghill, D. *How To Involve Impaired Individuals in All Types of Meetings.* Paper presented at "The Silent Minority" Conference in Columbia, Maryland, April 1977.

Power, D. *Deaf Children's Acquisition of the Passive Voice.* Unpublished doctoral dissertation, University of Illinois, 1971.

Pufall, P., & Furth, H. G. Double alternation behavior as a function of age and language. *Child Development,* 37, 653–662, 1966.

Quigley, S. P., Smith, N., & Wilbur, R. *Comprehension of Relativised Sentences by Deaf Children.* Urbana, Illinois: University of Illinois, Institute for Research on Exceptional Children, 1973.

Quigley, S. P., & Thomure, R. E. *Some Effects of Hearing Impairment Upon School Performance.* Urbana, Illinois: University of Illinois, Institute of Research on Exceptional Children, 1968.

Quigley, S. P., Wilbur, R., & Montanelli, D. *Development of Question Formation in the Written Language of Deaf Students.* Urbana, Illinois: University of Illinois, Institute of Research on Exceptional Children, 1974.

Raven, J. *Progressive Matrices.* New York: Psychological Corporation, 1948.

Reynolds, M. C. A framework for considering some issues on special education. *Exceptional Children,* 28, 367–370, 1962.

Reynolds, M. C., & Birch, J. W. *Teaching Exceptional Children in All America's Schools: A First Course for Teachers and Principals.* Reston, Virginia: Council for Exceptional Children, 1977.

Rosenstein, J. Cognitive abilities of deaf children. *Journal of Speech and Hearing,* 3, 108–119, 1960.

Ross, B. M. Probability concepts in deaf and hearing children. *Child Development,* 37, 917–928, 1966.

Ross, M. Assessment of the hearing impaired prior to mainstreaming. In G. W. Nix, Ed., *Mainstream Education for Hearing Impaired Children and Youth.* New York: Grune & Stratton, 1976.

Rudser, F. S., Witter, A. B., & Gillies, K. G. *The NTID Interpreting Services Position Paper: State of the Art.* Rochester, New York: National Technical Institute for the Deaf, Office of Support Services, 1978.

Sabatino, D. A. Resource rooms: The renaissance in special education. *Journal of Special Education* 6(4), 335–347, 1972a.

Sabatino, D. A.   Revolution: Viva resource rooms! *Journal of Special Education,* 6(4), 389–395, 1972b.

Santa, C. M., & Burstyn, J. N.   *A Comparative Study of the Readability of Several Successive Editions of Two Popular College Textbooks.* Rutgers, New Jersey: Rutgers University, 1977

Schein, J. D., & Delk, M. T.   *The Deaf Population of the United States.* Silver Spring, Maryland: National Association of the Deaf, 1974.

Schlesinger, H. S., & Meadow, K. P.   *Sound and Sign: Childhood Deafness and Mental Health.* Berkeley, California: University of California Press, 1972.

Spache, G.   *Spache Diagnostic Reading Scales.* Monterey, California: California Test Bureau, 1962.

Spradley, T. S., & Spradley, J. P.   *Deaf Like Me.* New York: Random House, Inc., 1978.

Stark, R. E., Ed.   *Sensory Capabilities of Hearing Impaired Children.* Baltimore, Maryland: University Park Press, 1974.

Stewart, L.   A truly silent minority. *New York Times,* March 16, 1972.

Torres, S.   *A Primer on Individualized Education Programs for Handicapped Children.* Reston, Virginia: Council for Exceptional Children, 1977.

Vernon, M., & Brown, D. W.   A guide to psychological tests and testing procedures in the evaluation of deaf and hard of hearing children. *Journal of Speech and Hearing Disorders, 29,* 414–423, 1964.

Vlahos, P. N.   Developing legal rights for handicapped citizens. *The Volta Review* 79(5), 270–273, 1977.

Wagner, P.   Analysis of a retarded-tutoring-retarded program for institutionalized residents. *Dissertation Abstracts International, 34* (5-A), 2426, 1973.

Walker, J., Ed.   *Functions of the Placement Committee in Special Education.* Washington, D.C.: National Association of State Directors of Special Education, 1976.

Wechsler, D.   *Wechsler Intelligence Scale for Children.* New York: Psychological Corporation, 1949.

Wechsler, D.   *Wechsler Adult Intelligence Scale.* New York: Psychological Corporation, 1955.

Weigl, E., & Metze, E.   *Experimentelle untersuchungen zum problem des nicht sprachgebundenen begrifflichen Denkens. Schweizerische Zeitscrift fur Psychologie,* 27, 1–17, 1968.

Weintraub, F. J., Abeson, A., Ballard, J., & LaVor, M. L., Eds.   *Public Policy and the Education of Exceptional Children.* Reston, Virginia: Council for Exceptional Children, 1976.

Welsh, W. A., & Wilson, F. L.   *Another Approach to the Analysis of Attrition at NTID* (Technical Report #8). Rochester, New York: National Technical Institute for the Deaf, Division of Management Services, 1977.

White, K. R.   *A Summary Report of an Evaluation of NTID's 1977 Summer Vestibule Program* (technical report). Rochester, New York: National Technical Institute for the Deaf, Department of Research & Development, 1978a.

White, K. R.   *Enhancing Personal/social Competencies of the Deaf: Which Competencies Should Be Emphasized?* Department of Research and Development, National Technical Institute for the Deaf, unpublished manuscript, 1978b. (Available from K. R. White, Rochester, New York, 14623)

White, K. R.   *Predicting Academic Success Among Postsecondary Deaf Students.* Department of Research and Development, National Technical Institute for the Deaf, unpublished manuscript, 1978c. (Available from K. R. White, Rochester, New York 14623)

Wilbur, R., & Quigley, S. P.   *Deviant Processing of Relative Clauses by Deaf Children.* Paper presented at National Convention of the American Speech and Hearing Association, San Francisco, 1972.

Williams, B. R., & Sussman, A. E.   Social and psychological problems of deaf people. In A. E. Sussman & L. G. Stewart, Eds., *Counseling with Deaf People.* New York: Deafness Research & Training Center, 1971.

Wrightstone, J., Aranow, M., & Moskowitz, S.   Developing reading test norms for deaf children. *American Annals of the Deaf, 108,* 311–316, 1963.

Yater, V. V.   *Mainstreaming of Children with Hearing Loss: Practical Guidelines and Implications.* Springfield, Illinois: Charles C Thomas, 1977.

Youniss, J.   Concept transfer as a function of shifts, age, and deafness. *Child Development, 35,* 695–700, 1964.

Youniss, J., Feil, R. N., & Furth, H. G.   Discrimination of verbal material as a function of intrapair similarity in deaf and hearing subjects. *Journal of Educational Psychology, 56,* 184–190, 1965.   □

Index

A

Abstract concepts: difficult in verbal form, 125; use of audiovisual materials, 130

Academic: disadvantages by age of adolescence, 122; excellence possible, 10; expectations, 37, 38; modifications to requirements, by law, 39; gap, 39

Academic variables: ability to learn, 83; intelligence tests, 83; previous achievement, 85

Age at onset of hearing loss, influence on: ability to cope with deafness, 13; hearing loss, 6; language development, 121

Ameslan, American sign language: different from English signs, 45; teacher in Ameslan or interpreter necessary, 45; used by interpreters, 136

Amplification of sound: in classroom, 107; psychological support, special telephone equipment, 12; sound discrimination difficulty, 6; amplification systems, 108

Assessment and evaluation: academic achievement, 85; collecting data, 80; confidentiality, 29; intelligence, 84; personality, 87; provisions by law, 27; school variables, 89; standardized tests, 123; student variables, 80; underlying principles, 77; use of, 94; variables, 76

Audiogram, plot of sound frequency hearing ability, illustration of, 5

Audiological assessment, 80, 100, 104

Auditory: access, in classroom, 106; residual hearing, 42; nerve, 3; training as a support service, 120

C

Child development, role of family and community, rights to education, 18

Classes: size, for mainstreaming consideration, 47; special class in public school, 100; special and separate, only by law, 25

Classroom: discussions, pace, 111; handouts, 111; physical characteristics, 105; size, 92; variables, 90

Cochlea (inner ear), 3

Communication: Ameslan (ASL), 45; arguments for and against sign language and fingerspelling, 40; in classroom, 108, 110; body language, 111; classroom discussion, 111; classroom handouts, 111; effects of language deprivation, 109; development, implications of hearing impairment on, 40; evidence for bridging "gap," 39; expectations, part of conceptual framework, 39; formulating young attitudes, accepting older foundation of, 41; methods considered for placement, 45; mode for prelingually deaf, effects of peer pressure, effects of adult role models, 40; necessary to personal/social development, 8; oral, 40; peer awareness, 115; use of repetition and rephrasing, 111; skills adequate for regular class placement, 65; skills for tutoring, 153; skills, receptive and expressive, 37; as a student variable, 80; with hearing peers, 46; fingerspelling and sign language, 45

Communication profile, NTID, measuring skills, 82

Communication variables in placement decision: audiological assessment, 81; expressive, 82; language base, 83; receptive, 81

Community: historic concepts toward handicapped people, 18; role of, in development of hearing-impaired children, 18

Competencies, personal/social: illustration of, 8; in need of improvement, 8, 88; self-value, 101; success need, 102

Conceptual framework for placement decisions: available programs, academic expectations, 39; for determining educational goals, 35; illustration with educational components, 36

Conductive hearing loss, 3, 4

Configuration (or shape) of hearing loss, 4

Consultant process of education, 61; definition of, 63; student characteristics for, 70

Coping with deafness: a subjective description of, 13; dependent on many variables, 13; native intelligence, a variable in, 13

Courses, content and delivery, modification of, for reducing educational "gap," 39

Cranial nerve, VIII, route of sound to

M

N

O

P

V

W

Cover Design:
C. Thomas Sollenberger, Jr.